Anti-Colonial Texts from ~~~
Student Movements 1929–1983

Anti-Colonial Texts from Central American Student Movements 1929–1983

Edited by Heather Vrana

EDINBURGH
University Press

Edinburgh University Press is one of the leading university presses in the UK. We publish academic books and journals in our selected subject areas across the humanities and social sciences, combining cutting-edge scholarship with high editorial and production values to produce academic works of lasting importance. For more information visit our website: edinburghuniversitypress.com

Edinburgh University Press Ltd
The Tun – Holyrood Road
12(2f) Jackson's Entry
Edinburgh EH8 8PJ

Typeset in 10.5/13 Sabon by
Servis Filmsetting Ltd, Stockport, Cheshire,
and printed and bound in Great Britain by
CPI Group (UK) Ltd, Croydon CR0 4YY

A CIP record for this book is available from the British Library

ISBN 978 1 4744 0368 9 (hardback)
ISBN 978 1 4744 0370 2 (webready PDF)
ISBN 978 1 4744 0369 6 (paperback)
ISBN 978 1 4744 0371 9 (epub)

Published with the support of the Edinburgh University Scholarly Publishing Initiatives Fund.

Contents

Series Editor's Preface

Key Texts in Anti-Colonial Thought re-publishes selections of anti-colonial texts and locates them in their colonial/neo-colonial contexts. Leading scholars in Postcolonial Studies introduce a wide variety of hitherto hard-to-access anti-colonial writings. Each volume opens with a substantial introduction contextualising the selected texts, setting out the specific forms of colonial governance, economic exploitation, and cultural imperialism they wrote against, as well as the communities of resistance, the solidarities and the distinctive political cultures that sustained them. In addition, the volumes provide extensive explanatory notes, annotated guides to further reading, and concluding discussions of the texts' relevance today. The series aims to counter the dependency of Postcolonial Studies on a narrow range of theorists and literary texts, and to provoke reflection on the connections between anti-colonial thought and contemporary resistance to global inequalities.

David Johnson

Acknowledgements

To edit a source reader is to become indebted to many people. First, I must thank David Johnson. As a new friend and editor, David has been kind, generous, funny, persuasive, and provocative, by turns. His subtle encouragement has shaped this volume and my thinking in many ways that I am still coming to appreciate. At Edinburgh University Press, Adela Rauchova, Jackie Jones, and Rebecca Mackenzie have been so very helpful and enthusiastic in their support of the project.

In Guatemala, I am forever thankful for the generosity of Thelma Porres Morfín and the excellent team of archivists at the Centro de Investigaciones Regionales de Mesoamérica (CIRMA). Likewise in Nicaragua, Margarita Vannini and Lissette P. Ruiz at the Instituto de Historia de Nicaragua y Centroamérica (IHNCA) gave generously of their time and expertise, providing a most welcoming intellectual community in Managua. Yale University's library staff, especially in Microfilm collections and Interlibrary Loan, were key to the success of this volume. Many thanks to the North American Congress on Latin America (NACLA) for decades of important advocacy and for the use of many texts. The university presses of the Universidad Nacional Autónoma de Honduras, Universidad de El Salvador, Universidad de Costa Rica, Universidad de San Carlos, and Universidad Autónoma Nacional de Nicaragua also continue to provide inimitable intellectual resources. My thanks to David Díaz Arias for the *La Tribuna* article. Thanks, too, to the families of Manuel Mora Valverde and to Daisy Zamora, who kindly permitted the inclusion of their texts in the volume. Kevin Coleman enthusiastically granted permission for the use of the photograph that appears on the cover.

Along the way, the generosity of Vikki Bell, Kevin Coleman, David Díaz Arias, Anne Eller, Jeff Gould, Peter Guardino, David Kazanjian, Ellen Moodie, Claudio Pérez Cruz, Alexandra Puerto, Christy Thornton, and J. T. Way shaped this project in ways for which I am very grateful. Many of these kind scholars I met through the Tepoztlán Institute for the Transnational History of the Americas, which has become my intellectual home.

Without the hard work of Rachel Nolan, Allessandra Paglia, Jorge Cuéllar, Claudia Rueda, and Vikram Tamboli, this project would have been impossible.

As ever, thank you to my mother and father, Mary and Jon Vrana, and to my sister, Anna Vrana. Thanks to kidd, whom I blame for this. This book has taken shape in New Haven, Seward, London, Managua, Antigua, Guatemala City, Bloomington, New York City, and Brighton. In each of these places, the friendship of Alex Abbotts, Siobhan Carter-David, E. Cram, Taylor Dean, Brie Gettleson, Julie Gibbings, Laura Grover, David Kazanjian, Lauren Lederman, Álvaro León, Devi Mays, Fabian Menges, Cassi Meyerhoffer, Chris Sloan, Chris Sullivan, and Mike Tallon has enlivened the solitary process of curating this text.

Notes on Translations

All of the texts below (except those by Daisy Zamora) were originally published in Spanish and carefully translated by a team of translators: Rachel Nolan, Jorge Cuéllar, Allessandra Paglia, Vikram Tamboli, and Claudia Rueda. These translators gave generously of their time and attention – tremendous scholars, they are also excellent translators. When necessary, I have edited the translations and added explanatory footnotes. Occasionally, when a text was especially difficult to translate and required a more involved process of editing, I have noted dual authorship. The poems by Daisy Zamora were translated by Margaret Randall and Elinor Randall, and published in *Clean Slate: New and Selected Poems*, Willimantic, CT: Curbstone Press, 1993. Translators are noted below each text.

Notes on Sources

This project presented a curatorial challenge. Only a fraction of the nearly two hundred texts that I initially considered for the volume are included here. Ultimately, the principle of selection was based on two criteria: authorship and exemplary or unique expression of anti-colonial thought. Most of the texts below were written by students. Occasionally, texts written by faculty or administrators were included when they represented an important moment or conversation at the university about students or students' roles in society. Sources that reflected exemplary or unique perspectives were often chosen over manifestos that were, generally, the most common type of student-authored anti-colonial text. After all, a book of only manifestos would soon become a tedious read. The sources reflect a variety of genres, including manifesto, memoir, legislative decree, interview, and poetry. In order to capture a range of understandings and deployments of anti-colonial theory, I also selected texts that pursued anti-colonial perspectives in unique ways. Given the scope of the series, documents that outlined global solidarities and affinities between Central American student movements were especially important.

The texts included in this volume came from many different archives, libraries, and microfilm collections. Below they are listed by chapter in the original Spanish with archival information in the order in which they appear in the book.

Chapter 1. GUATEMALA: 'En plena tiranía', *El Estudiante*, Año I, No. 13, 14 March 1920; Manuel Galich (1940), *Del pánico al ataque*, Guatemala: Tipografía Nacional, 149–55. Centro de Investigaciones Regionales de Mesoamérica (CIRMA); Asociación de Estudiantes Universitarios (AEU), 'Manifiesto', 26 January 1946. Collection of Arturo Taracena, Doc. No. 1709. CIRMA. EL SALVADOR: 'Discurso pronunciado por el doctor Miguel Rafael Urquia, en el acto solemne de la apertura de clases universitarias del corriente año lectivo, el 1o de Marzo de 1933', *La Universidad*, 30 September 1933; 'Discurso pronunciado por el Br Reinaldo Galindo Pohl, a nombre de la Asociación General de Estudiantes Universitarios (A.G.E.U.S.)', *La Universidad*, 1944. NICARAGUA: Universidad Central de Nicaragua (1941), *Universidad Central de Nicaragua: memoria de su fundación, 15 de septiembre de 1941*, Managua: Talleres Nacionales; David Sánchez Sánchez, 'El estudiantado como fuerza política', *El Universitario*, 27 December 1945. Instituto de Historia de Nicaragua y Centroamérica (IHNCA); Juan F. Gutiérrez, 'Hagamos patria', *El Universitario*, 1st week of March 1946. IHNCA. COSTA RICA: '"En Costa Rica nos enorgullecemos de nuestra libertad de pensamiento, y todos los costarricenses estamos acostumbrados a discutir y criticar los actos de los hombres públicos," dicen los miembros de la liga anti-imperialista de estudiantes de derecho', *La Tribuna*, 29 April 1931; Manuel Mora Valverde (1940), *Imperialismo: nuestra soberanía frente al Departamento del Estado*, San José: Partido Comunista de Costa Rica. HONDURAS: Jorge Fidel Durón, 'Función de la universidad', *Revista de la universidad*, 12 December 1949; Jorge St. Siegens, 'Cooperativismo en Honduras', *Revista de la universidad*, 11 August 1950.

Chapter 2. GUATEMALA: Comité de Estudiantes Universitarios Anticomunistas Guatemaltecos en Exilio (CEUAGE), 'De pie frente a la dictadura roja en Guatemala', *Boletín de CEUAGE*, Vol. 1, No. 1, June 1953. Hemeroteca Nacional (HN); Comité de Estudiantes Anticomunistas Universitarios (1954), *Plan de Tegucigalpa*, Tegucigalpa: CEUA. Archivo Vertical, No. D-1489. CIRMA; 'AEU contra discriminación', *Informador Estudiantil*, January–February 1956. General Document Collection, No. 4152. CIRMA; Editorial, *El Estudiante*, Época II, No. 3, 19 September 1957. Collection of Arturo Taracena, No. 229. CIRMA; Asociación de Estudiantes 'El Derecho', 'La Asociación de Estudiantes el Derecho impugnando el decreto 1215 del congreso de la república, declara a Carlos Castillo Armas, traidor de la patria', 17 January 1958. Collection of Arturo Taracena, No. 106. CIRMA. EL SALVADOR: AGEUS, 'Manifiesto', *Opinión Estudiantil*, 16 October 1956. IHNCA; AGEUS, 'Solidaridad con los exiliados de Nicaragua', *Opinión Estudiantil*, 16 October 1956. IHNCA; 'Comunicación', *Opinión Estudiantil*, 16 October 1956. IHNCA. NICARAGUA: 'Aquí están los asesinos y sus víctimas', *El Universitario*, 1960. IHNCA; 'COSEC recibe cablegrama de SOMOZA', *El Universitario*, 1960. IHNCA. HONDURAS: UNAH (1957), 'Asamblea Nacional Constituyente de 1957', *Estudio Histórico-Jurídico sobre la autonomía* *de la Universidad Nacional Autónoma de Honduras*, Tegucigalpa: UNAH. 'Ley Orgánica de la Universidad de Honduras', Decreto Legislativo No. 170, 30 April 1958.

Chapter 3. NICARAGUA: 'Cuba y Latinoamérica sí! Yankis no!', *El Universitario*, September 1960. IHNCA; Centro Universitario de la Universidad Nacional (CUUN) (1971), *Imperialismo*, Managua: Editorial José Martí. Doc. No. 71. Instituto de Historia de Nicaragua (IHN). Guatemala: Jaime F. Pineda S., 'La participación del estudiante universitario en la vida nacional', *Tribuna Económica (Órgano de la Asociación de Estudiantes de Ciencias Económicas)*, Año III, No. 25, 31 May 1962. Figueroa Ibarra Collection, No. 197. CIRMA; 'Comunicado de la Rectoría dc la Universidad de San Carlos sobre el préstamo que el gobierno de la república ha contratado con el BID con destino a instituciones privadas de enseñanza superior . . .', 7 June 1974. CIRMA; 'Fondo Monetario Internacional, tentáculo del capitalismo', *7 Días en la USAC*, 3–9 March 1980. Figueroa Ibarra Collection, No. 172. CIRMA; 'Carta de un ladrón a sus vecinos'. Inforpress Centroamericana Archive, No. 478. CIRMA. COSTA RICA: FEUCR, 'Que la historia señale nuestra posición', *El Universitario*, May 1970. North American Congress on Latin America (NACLA); 'Porque participé en los actos del 24', *El Universitario*, May 1970. NACLA; Editorial, *El Universitario*, November 1970. NACLA. HONDURAS: 'La FEUH y la AGEUS se pronuncian', *Boletín del Instituto de Investigaciones Económicas y Sociales*, No. 24–5 (January and February 1974). NACLA; 'Los asesinos de la CIA', *Presencia Universitaria*, January 1976. NACLA. EL SALVADOR: Consejo Superior Universitaria (1964), *Libertad y cultura en torno al debate universitario*, San Salvador: Universidad Nacional; Asociación General de Estudiantes Universitarios Salvadoreños, 'En torno al problema agrario', *El Universitario*, 15 November 1979. NACLA; Asociación General de Estudiantes Universitarios Salvadoreños (1981), *Salud en El Salvador, otra razón para el combate popular*, San Salvador: Universidad de El Salvador, Instituto de la Historia de Centroamérica (IHCA).

Chapter 4. NICARAGUA: Carlos Fonseca (2006), 'Mensaje a los estudiantes revolucionarios', *Obra fundamental*, Managua: Aldilá Editor. IHNCA. GUATEMALA: Editorial, *No nos tientes*, 1966. Satirical Publications Collection, No. 44. CIRMA; Juventud Patriótica del Trabajo (JPT), 'A quién servirá la guerra en Belice?' *Juventud*, July–August 1977. Archivo Inforpress Centroamericana, No. 913; CIRMA; Asociación de Estudiantes Universitarias (1977), 'El Movimiento Estudiantil Guatemalteco en la lucha por el respeto a los derechos humanos y democráticos y por contener la escalada de terror fascista en Guatemala', *Jornadas de agosto*, Guatemala: USAC Facultad de Ciencias Económicas. Collection of Robert Trudeau, No. 498; CIRMA; Oliverio Castañeda de León (1978), 'Discurso en la toma de posesión del Secretariado General de AEU, May 22, 1978', in Rebeca Alonzo Martínez (ed.), *Oliverio vive!*, Guatemala: Ediciones CEUR. EL SALVADOR: 'Pronunciamiento del Consejo Superior Universitario de la Universidad de El Salvador sobre la situación nacional', *El Universitario*, 18 December 1979. NACLA; 'Comunicado', *Opinión estudiantil*, July 1980. NACLA; 'Guatemala: En la dura lucha por su libertad . . .', *Opinión estudiantil*, July 1980. NACLA; José María Cuellar (1979), '1932' and 'Guerras en mi país', *Poemas*, San Salvador: Editorial Universitaria de El Salvador; 'Poesía de una heroica mujer de nuestro pueblo', *Opinión estudiantil*, June 1981. NACLA. HONDURAS: 'Honduras–Nicaragua: se constituye comité de solidaridad', *Presencia Universitaria*, January 1976. NACLA; Armando Valladares (1978), 'Alcances y significado de nuestra autonomía universitaria', in *Universidad y autonomía: un encuentro del presente*, Tegucigalpa: Editorial Universitaria UNAH.

Chapter 5. COSTA RICA: R. Morua, 'Los estudiantes decimos: "Queremos construir nuestro mañana"', *El Universitario*, May 1970. NACLA. HONDURAS: Federación de Estudiantes Universitarios de Honduras (FEUH), 'Declaración Pública', *Presencia Universitaria*, January 1976. NACLA; Enrique Astorga Lira, 'Modelos marginales de reforma agraria en América latina: el caso de Honduras', *Alcaraván*, No. 3, April 1980; Editorial, *El tornillo sin fin: el órgano viril de los estudiantes universitarias de Honduras*, 1981. NACLA. GUATEMALA: Boletín No. 2 de la Huelga de Dolores, 1980. Robert Trudeau Collection, No. 482. CIRMA; Saúl Osorio Paz, 'Carta abierta del Rector Saúl Osorio Paz al Consejo Superior Universitario', 1980. Robert Trudeau Collection, No. 486. CIRMA. EL SALVADOR: 'Los estudiantes salvadoreños ante la intervención imperialista en El Salvador', *Opinión Estudiantil*, July 1981. NACLA; AGEUS, 'Augustín Farabundo Martí, ejemplo de la lucha antiimperialista y de la guerra popular de liberación', *Opinión Estudiantil*, February 1982. IHNCA. NICARAGUA: Daisy Zamora and Margarita Randall, trans. 'Commander Two', 'Report of the Demonstration in Front of the US Embassy Protesting the Pino Grande Manœuvres', and 'Song of Hope', in Zamora and Randall (2002), *Clean Slate*, 44–5, 118–19, 42–3. Permission for the inclusion of these poems was generously granted by the author and Northwestern University Press as rights holder; Jaime Wheelock Román (1983), 'La

universidad por la independencia económica: la universidad beligerante'
in *Hacia la independencia nacional por la revolución: la universidad
beligerante*, Managua: UNAN. IHNCA.

For the students – past, present, and future – of course

Introduction

We make a call to the Youth to lend support to the principles of the Cuban Cause, because the Cuban Cause is the Latin American cause, because yes, no one can deny, the Cuban Revolution is the loyal interpreter of the struggles and the banners of Bolívar, Juárez, Martí, and Sandino and we are fully convinced that Cuba broke the chains with the same strength and intensity that our Latin American brothers will soon. We declare and advise that in response to any direct or indirect attacks by Imperialism, the Latin American Youth will stand and fight with the Cuban people to deliver the First and Final Independence – definitively, NATIONAL LIBERATION ... Yes, this is the epoch where the cry and the struggle is: Cuba Yes! Yankees No! Latin America Yes! Yankees No! It is time now that the Latin American youth, indestructible and monolithic fist, like the Youth worldwide, prepares to join in solidarity and to occupy the place that history chooses for us, [such] that neither prison, misery, nor death can make us retreat from our inevitable goals, nor can they hold us back from paying homage to *Truth, Justice, and Friendship.*

'Cuba and Latin America, Yes! Yankees, No!', *El Universitario* (1960)

University students are not **abstract** beings removed from real life, absorbed with themselves, their only desire knowledge for knowledge's sake. On the contrary, students arrive at the University with a whole range of multiple problems and express in their most divergent worries and aspirations the problems of the social organism. Their concrete attitude towards national and student problems reflects the contradictions of their real lives, past, present, and future ... The belligerence of Latin American students very much resembles that of students in colonised and dependent countries in Africa and the Middle East, who continue fighting for their independence with much success ... We have arrived, then, to the point where now we are no longer satisfied by explaining the world, but we seek to transform it to meet our present and future needs and above all to maintain the material and spiritual integrity of man.

Jaime F. Pineda S., 'The Participation of University Students in National Life', *Tribuna Económica* (1962)

While the student uprisings of Prague, Paris, Berkeley, New York, and Mexico City in the summer of 1968 dominate most peoples' conception of twentieth-century student movements, the first quotation above, from the Nicaraguan student paper *El Universitario*, disrupts some of the most persistent assumptions about the decade. These students were *not* the product of the global conjuncture of the late 1960s, but rather were inheritors of the struggles of Simón Bolívar, Benito Juárez, José Martí, and Augusto César Sandino. Nor were these students speaking from global metropoles, although both texts position Central American youths at the vanguard of contemporary worldwide youth anti-colonial struggles. Together, these texts are far from the account of the so-called Global 1968 offered up by most, which tends to portray student protesters as isolated in two ways: in the proverbial 1960s, spontaneous in their time; and in the colonial centre or metropole. This volume argues to the contrary. The texts gathered here show how students in Guatemala, El Salvador, Honduras, Costa Rica, and Nicaragua had long been at the forefront of revolutionary anti-colonial nationalist movements. They reorient anti-colonial movement scholarship toward a region peripheral even within anti-colonial and postcolonial studies.

An Anti-colonial History of Central American Student Movements

The first social movements of students *as students* arose in Central America as early as the 1920s. At that time, university students organised a rigorous campaign for the Guatemalan Unionist Party, which sought to revive the project of a pan-Central American federation and to combine economic, military, and political resources against North America. Then again, in the 1930s, a small number of university students participated in Sandino's struggle against the US Marines' occupation of Nicaragua. Subsequent student movements in the 1950s and 1960s built upon the anti-colonial legacies of these earlier movements. Take, for instance, the name of the Sandinista National Liberation Front (Frente Sandinista de Liberación Nacional [FSLN]), which was formed by a handful of young men who met while organising at secondary school and university. The group's name was homage both to the Algerian National Liberation Front and to the Nicaraguan anti-colonial hero. The umbrella organisation of guerrilla groups in El Salvador, in turn, was named the Farabundo Martí National Liberation Front, a celebration of both the Nicaraguan and Algerian combatants against colonialism and another revolutionary martyr, Farabundo Martí, who had attended the University of El Salvador before dropping out to give his life to global anti-colonial struggles. Yet this book is not dominated by a single figure or movement. While the texts chosen for this collection highlight the contributions of a few well-known figures, the majority are individuals who have often been overlooked, even by scholars within Latin America. These young people were clearly in communication with one another, as many of the letters and statements of solidarity below make clear, but they were also connected to larger global networks of anti-colonial thinkers and combatants.

Anti-imperialism was a central theme among many Latin American intellectuals in the first decades of the twentieth century, and while there has been robust scholarly discussion about the pitfalls of eliding the colonial and the imperial, the texts below do so as a matter of principle. In *Colonial Discourse and Post-Colonial Theory*, Laura Chrisman and Patrick Williams argue that colonisation ought to be understood both as direct control of other people's land and as a particular phase in the history of capitalism and imperialism. They go on to define imperialism as the globalisation of capitalist forces and relations of production alongside the destruction of pre- or non-capitalist forms of social organisation. To the contrary, Central American students offered interpretations of Spanish colonisation and North American occupation that complicated any notion of a clear distinction between colonial, imperial, and decolonial moments. Further, students challenged the idea that Central America had ever uniformly advanced to later stages of capitalism by referring to forms of land tenure in rural regions as 'feudal'. In this respect, the texts below are not postcolonial in so far as the authors insist that the colonial moment had not yet passed and, too, in the sense that the politics that they engaged had not yet superseded capitalist modes of engagement. Many of the texts below are at once anti-feudal, anti-capitalist, anti-colonial, and anti-neocolonial. Related, many of the anti-colonial texts below, you will find, wage wars of cultural nationalism – especially in the realm of knowledge-creation and technology – that only further imbricated the movements in global capitalism. When we read these texts dialectically, we can see that not only are they produced by, but also they are productive of, particular forms of knowledge, ideologies, institutions, and practices in global capitalism.

I have selected the texts below as 'key texts in anti-colonial thought' for a few reasons: one, they come from individuals or organisations that were known to be part of political struggles that understand themselves to be anti-colonial; two, they reference other global anti-colonial struggles as analogous or kindred; three, the texts make claims explicitly within the discourse of anti-colonialism; and four, they challenge extant understandings of anti-colonial, postcolonial, or decolonial thought in provocative manners. The reader will, no doubt, find even more ways to read these texts back on to theorisations of the colonial in all its pre-fixed forms, but as I see it, the texts below contribute to the following on-going conversations and debates within the fields of postcolonial, decolonial, and anti-colonial studies and theory: the problematics of nationalism and nativism; the myth of spontaneous resistance and the question of when and why people rise up; the multitudinous forms of colony and empire, including military intervention, political puppetry, economic extraction, land ownership, cultural appropriation and domination; the colonisation of knowledge and technological formation; and the role of university students, professors, and intellectuals in a revolutionary movement or society. Below, I briefly discuss how the texts below speak to these debates, but first I will introduce the region and its universities.

The Region

The colonisation of Central America – present-day Guatemala, El Salvador, Nicaragua, Costa Rica, and Honduras – by Spaniards began in 1524. Before that, indigenous people of dozens of distinct linguistic and ethnic groups lived in cities and rural villages throughout the region's diverse climates, which include tropical and subtropical moist and dry forests, coniferous forests, grasslands, savannahs, deserts, and mangroves. The wars for independence from Spain were not generally fought with the ideological zeal of similar struggles in Mexico or Venezuela; instead, creole elites renegotiated older power structures in new terms, principally through the Liberal and Conservative parties. From 1823 to about 1840, the territories of present-day Nicaragua, El Salvador, Honduras, Costa Rica, Guatemala, and parts of Chiapas formed an unstable republic called the Federal Republic of Central America; the confederates were the supporters of this united government. First threatened with Mexican annexation, then with discord from within, the united provinces were short-lived. But the dream of a unified Central America endured and inspired subsequent experiments in regional state-making through the late nineteenth and early twentieth centuries. Across the nineteenth century, exports in coffee and cotton expanded while these two so-called 'traditional parties' traded the seat of power. In Guatemala, Liberal dictators like Justo Rufino Barrios (1835–85), Manuel Estrada Cabrera (1857–1924), and Jorge Ubico

(1878–1946) jealously guarded their authority while they expanded the power of the military and, more importantly, courted US investment in infrastructure. In Nicaragua, this conflict between the traditional parties resulted in numerous civil wars and lesser spats.

Around this time, the US launched a long series of interventions. The 1920s and 1930s brought both a florescence of leftist organising and strong-armed reaction. Sandino (1895–1934) led a guerrilla army against US intervention from 1927 until the US troops' withdrawal in 1933. He was killed on the orders of National Guard Director Anastasio Somoza García in 1934. Somoza's power continued to grow and, in 1936, he staged a coup and installed himself as president, a position he would hold until 1947 and again from 1950 to 1956. Thus began the Somoza family dynasty, which would rule until 1979. In turn, Guatemala experienced a democratic revolution after the overthrow of dictator Jorge Ubico in 1944, but this was summarily ended just ten years later by US Central Intelligence Agency (CIA) manœuvres. Before long, the nation descended into civil war. Across the region, military presidents turned to the political style of populism to cultivate support. In 1948, Costa Rica experienced a very short forty-four-day war whose resolution utterly changed the shape of Costa Rican society: the military was dissolved and the political system learned to absorb dissent rather than crush it.

The Cold War raged and young people, workers, peasants, and even clergy suffered repression at the hands of the government and military for considering Marxist solutions to endemic social problems. In Honduras, the regime of military rule was unrelenting. By 1970, civil war extended into its second decade in Guatemala. Guerrilla armies in Guatemala, Nicaragua, and El Salvador showed resilience and resolve in the face of the military governments' massive transnational arms and intelligence apparatuses. These civil wars destabilised the region into the 1990s. In sum, unlike most places that are examined under the rubrics of postcolonial or decolonial studies, there was no single decolonial moment or period of decolonisation; rather there were decades of anti-colonial struggle. Of course, there is much more nuance to these histories. The chapter introductions below explain in much greater detail the key events, groups, and personages of each period and place.

The Universities

Most of the texts below focus on the region's public universities. Founded as Catholic universities between 1676 and 1843, they were secularised by anti-clerical Liberal politicians in the mid- and late nineteenth century. By the twentieth century, the public universities occupied a distinct place in Central American society. Students and faculty were situated uneasily between their constitutional duty to lead the nation and their often-changing relationship to the state. For instance, under dictatorial presidents like Tiburcio Carías Andino (1876–1969), Maximiliano Martínez Hernández (1882–1966), Jorge Ubico (1878–1946), and Augusto Somoza García (1896–1956), the universities were scarcely more than factories of professionals. However, by the mid-twentieth century, most students and even some faculty at these institutions interpreted their constitutional remit as a call to weigh in on national-level political questions, including the legitimacy of the government. These contentious changes are discussed often in the texts below.

Importantly, very few Central Americans had access to the university. According to historian Augusto Cazali Ávila, in 1943, Guatemala's National University counted just 711 students. By 1950, that number had risen to 2,373 students. According to the 1950 census, only 6,048 individuals in the entire nation had attended any university-level schooling in their lifetime; of this number, only 17 were indigenous. The rest were recorded as ladino, a complex racial and ethnic category generally understood to denote mixed indigenous and Spanish background. For decades, anthropologists and historians have defined 'ladino' by the shorthand 'not indigenous', though new research by Jorge Ramón González Ponciano is beginning to demonstrate more nuanced understandings of this term. Elsewhere in Central America, and Latin America more broadly, the term 'mestizo' is usually used to indicate individuals of mixed Spanish and indigenous ancestry. The Guatemalan *Boletín Estadístico Universitaria* also noted that in 1950 just 845 of 6,048 individuals of the entire university-educated population were women. In the national census of the same year, 2,148,560 Guatemalan citizens reported that they had no formal schooling whatsoever. An institute focused on improving regional education, the Instituto de Investigaciones y Mejoramiento Educativo (IIME), published reports in 1964 and 1965 that counted only 1,107 university students in Honduras in 1954 and just 1,674 by 1960. The total university enrolment in Nicaragua in 1951 was 897 students, though this had increased to 948 students by 1954 and made a dramatic leap to 1,718 students by 1961. In El Salvador, the national university had an enrolment of 1,704 students in 1953 and 2,257 in 1960. The University of Costa Rica, which would quickly become an academic leader in the region, still had a small university enrolment of 2,029 students in 1954. Meanwhile, John

W. Sherman writes that Mexico's National Autonomous University (UNAM) recorded enrolments of 23,000 in 1949, growing to nearly 80,000 by 1968.

Even as Central American universities sought to 'popularise', they remained mostly off limits to the majority of the population that could not afford to take time away from work to attend classes or who did not fulfil the prerequisites for attendance. Guatemalan national census data confirm that university attendance remained elusive for all but the elite. Just 14,060 out of 3,174,900 Guatemalans (0.44%) had attended any university-level classes by 1964. Only forty indigenous men had pursued some university-level study but more than 1 million indigenous people had not attended schooling at any level. Meanwhile, illiteracy was about 63.3% nationwide and even higher in rural areas. According to Daniel C. Levy, by 1975, total university enrolments in Guatemala were 27,675; Honduras, 12,096; Nicaragua, 18,282; Costa Rica, 32,928; and El Salvador, 28,281 students. Ten years later, enrolments had risen overall: in Guatemala, at the University of San Carlos (USAC) alone, there were 48,283 enrolled students; across all universities in Honduras, 36,620; Nicaragua, 29,001; Costa Rica, 63,771; and El Salvador, 70,499. The opening of major private universities, beginning in 1960 with the Universidad Centroamericana (UCA) in Managua, Nicaragua, had a profound effect on students and student political culture. Some, like UCA in Nicaragua and the UCA 'José Simeón Cañas' in El Salvador, became known for political commitments – and sacrifices – driven by Liberation Theology. In other places, like Honduras, Costa Rica, and Guatemala, the national public university remained the sole centre for university student movements, and although enrolments generally increased, government repression of the universities discouraged many would-be students.

Nationalism and Nativism

These anti-colonial texts can help us to think through the problematic of nationalism and nativism in decolonial and postcolonial studies. In *Rescuing History from the Nation*, Prasenjit Duara calls into question how the very discipline of history acts as a way of instantiating the nation-state. More recently, Frederick Cooper has highlighted how anti-colonial politics in mid-twentieth-century Africa sometimes resulted in quite unexpectedly nationalist projects as political leaders negotiated with the French government within the terms of citizenship. In Central America, the complicated relationship between public universities and the nation-state enabled a similar negotiation. Public universities were, in a sense, institutions that were part of the national government: they received a portion of their funding from the national budget and, until autonomy was won, the president and his advisors had the ability to hire and terminate faculty and administrators. The importance of university autonomy is explored in many texts in the chapters below. But in each case, autonomy implied the ability for the university to manage its own affairs (while still receiving government funding) and territorial sovereignty of the university campus or classroom buildings. Students and faculty were often also state-makers as intellectual elites and they believed, especially after their universities became autonomous, that they had the responsibility to seek solutions to national problems like underdevelopment, illiteracy, natural resource exploitation, and cultural development.

Anti-colonial students were nationalists, but nationalism could extend to include something like a pan-Central American nationalism, too. Indeed, as I demonstrate elsewhere, student nationalism – a belief in the principles of liberalism and the responsibility of students to lead the nation – was one of the most constant features of student life in the twentieth century. Often, students debated about whom to include within the nation. In Guatemala especially, the large rural indigenous population seemed so distant as to be something of a distinct republic. Most students agreed that they must be incorporated in order to secure democracy, but how? The recent memory of eager US invasions when disunity destabilised markets must have also contributed to students' sense of urgency, but they found some citizens easier to include than others. For instance, there is little mention of Afro-Central Americans, though they were certainly present in Guatemala, Nicaragua, and Costa Rica.

Across the region, student nationalism shaped the meaning of the middle class as it positioned students as purveyors of knowledge and provided a vocabulary and a shared history for *universitarios*.[1] Perhaps it is for this reason that Central American students were most closely in dialogue with one another, rather than Latinos in the US or other anti-colonial students worldwide. Yes, Central American students revered revolutionary Cuba and participated in international student congresses like the International Student Conference (ISC) that swept the globe

[1] A term for university students, faculty, staff, and alumni, denoting a strong emotional and personal tie to the university and the moral responsibility to lead and protect the people.

after World War II, and some of the texts below do mention anti-colonial struggles in Africa and Asia. However, these movements did not have the effect on Central American anti-colonial students or the Central American diaspora that African anti-colonial movements had on the African diaspora; nor did Central American students take into account diasporic experiences in their anti-colonial theorising.

Some revolutionary nationalisms focused on the formation of national skills and cultural forms. Some *universitarios* sought to develop the study of traditional dances, novels, poems, and music in order to combat what they saw as a form of cultural dependency on Europe and North America. Where civil war had eroded the legitimacy of the government, by the 1970s and 1980s, student nationalism had become a nationalism without a viable state. And still, nationalism itself endured. You will see the frequent use of the term *pueblo* in the texts below. I do not translate this word into English because in translation it loses some of its depth. *Pueblo* signifies place, community, a nation, a people, a people's history, and individuals. It was a way for students to cultivate in a single word a sense of common interests. But how do leftist revolutionaries negotiate citizenship once they have seized state power? Taking up questions asked by Dipesh Chakrabarty and Partha Chatterjee, what does radical citizenship look like and what does it require of individuals?

Spontaneous Resistance to (Neo-)colonial Rule

Most colonial and postcolonial studies seek to break with the myth of spontaneous resistance by asking when and why people rise up. In which historical conjunctures? The texts below also seek to understand these questions and so offer up their own recursive anti-colonial theories of militancy and revolt. From Ernesto Che Guevara's *foco* theory to anti-communist millenarianism, Central American anti-colonial students tried to animate the *pueblo* using a variety of tactics. It would be worthwhile to think about them and how they articulated with global power. A related question continues to vex scholars of student and youth movements, but seems largely set aside by postcolonial and anti-colonial scholars: why are young people so often at the centre of social movements? Some scholars have suggested that perhaps it is an inherent recklessness in young people or lack of investment in the status quo; perhaps it is their clear and unsullied conscience; perhaps it is their schooling and critical thinking. The texts below refuse to offer any single answer, but they uniformly insist that youth must take responsibility for the nation's future by reckoning with its past.

Most of the texts below that employ historical rhetoric offer up a version of regional history that sees Central America fighting for independence from Spain only to become a colony of Britain, and then North America, through loans and the extraction of natural resources, including labour. Of course, the list of instances of direct US invasion or intervention in Central America since independence from Spain is exhaustive: in Nicaragua, in addition to William Walker's filibuster in 1856, US Marines invaded in 1894, 1896, 1898, 1899, and 1910; and in 1907, William Howard Taft made Nicaragua a protectorate in practice, which was magnified and formalised during the extended 1912–33 occupation. In Honduras, US Marines intervened in 1903, 1907, 1911, 1912, 1919, and 1924–5. In Guatemala, US military forces participated in or precipitated armed conflicts in 1920 and 1954, and from 1966 to 1967, at least. US troops intervened in Costa Rica in 1921 during a border dispute with Panama. In El Salvador, the US Navy sent supplies to combat forces led by Farabundo Martí in 1932. And for decades during the civil wars in Guatemala, El Salvador, and Nicaragua, the US military sent advisors and supplies. Bases built near the border in Honduras facilitated these manœuvres.

But students also pointed to more subtle operations. The US ensured the endurance of despots and secured favourable tax arrangements for businesses owned by friends and family members. Then there were regimes of land ownership where North American companies like the Aluminum Company of America (ALCOA) could dispossess communities on speculation that significant bauxite deposits lay beneath them. And students and some faculty critiqued the dominance of North American and European cultural forms like films and literature, drawing on Frankfurt School critiques of mass culture.

Anti-colonialism and Knowledge-Creation

Their critiques of technology and knowledge-formation were even more strident. For many Central American *universitarios* – a term used to denote students, but also faculty and staff of universities, and sometimes alumni who remained involved in campus life – knowledge-creation was crucial territory in the anti-colonial struggle. They argued that the lack of scientific knowledge made them reliant upon foreign technicians and that curriculum and textbooks designed by foreign academics were irrelevant, at best, or even dangerous, when applied in the Central American context. Given this, decolonisation required the development of national knowledge forms and technical skills, especially in engineering, chemistry, physics, agronomy, medicine, biology, and veterinary sciences. Understood as a sort of pedagogy of development theory, this call for reform, which targeted curriculum and teaching methods, can help us to think more broadly about decolonial political forms. In this way, the texts may return our focus to the questions, debates, and praxes of dependency and development theories as an anti-colonial mode. Elsewhere in the world in these years, anti-colonial nationalist movements achieved independence only to discover that the multi-faceted reach of imperialism endured. Central American anti-colonial students knew this endurance well and sought to combat it slowly and persistently with knowledge, as well as with arms.

Of course, we must be critical of the relationship between urban – and urbane – students and people they purported to represent. The texts below reveal tireless interrogation of the relationship between the university and the community, including the role of the organic intellectual and the university's implication in the state as a public institution oftentimes staffed with cronies of the ruling party. As I wrote above, Central American anti-colonial students used the term *pueblo* to attempt to theorise the 'legitimation of collective action' (to borrow from Chrisman and Williams), even as the idea of the unified *pueblo* was probably a product of the populism of the 1930s and 1940s that had mixed outcomes for the people it ostensibly included. Yet, as Chrisman and Williams anticipate, when the authors of the anti-colonial texts below speak about the *campesino* (the rural indigenous peasant) and the worker, they also develop and circulate theories that appropriate objects of knowledge. But rather than discount these theories, we can read them critically as a signal of students' understanding that this was fecund political work. This is, not incidentally, how most leftist students had come to see matters by the 1970s. But the texts below can offer a foothold into an important conversation about the rhetorics of individual and collective action. The students themselves invited such a critique. Students were self-conscious of their constructions of national unity and their imbrication in exploitative systems. Again following Chrisman and Williams, I think we can be critical of how uncritically nationalist these anti-colonial students were and how they promoted and employed Enlightenment cultural and political forms, like novels, poetry, history, historiography, elections, assemblies, constitutional assemblies, universal human equality, individual rights, and self-government. It might be interesting to see how Guatemalan and Nicaraguan students' use of the term *pueblo* can demonstrate the limits of such concepts as Gayatri Chakravorty Spivak's 'strategic essentialism' or Edward Said's 'orientalism' by pointing to the complicated ways in which intellectual elites in a peripheral nation sought to represent their nations vis-à-vis North American imperialism. More generally, focusing on the histories and vocabularies of specific anti-colonial struggles demonstrates the limits of elevating theoretical categories as paradigmatic. Certainly, the texts below suggest their own theoretical vocabularies.

Conclusion

In this introduction I have sought to offer a few suggestions of themes in anti-colonial, postcolonial, and decolonial thought that the key texts below may help us to think through. It is my sincere hope that, after reading, you will begin to think of student movements, class formation, protest, and memory politics in new ways. To this effect, this volume is structured around five thematically and chronologically organised chapters, each containing around fifteen documents of varying lengths, ranging from short pamphlets to long exegeses. Chapter 1, 'Central American Modernities, 1920–1944', focuses on prosperous boom years for Central America. In this period, Guatemala City was known as the 'Paris of the Tropics' and North American investors streamed into the region to assess and develop bananas, cotton, coffee, and other crops for export. Students uneasily balanced celebration of the indigenous past and enthusiasm for North American and European technologies, cultural forms, and commodities with early critiques of North American businesses and export policies that accused extraction practices of 'neocolonialism'.

In Chapter 2, 'Enduring Militarism, 1952–1960', the national histories of the region diverge: some nations overthrew tyrannical dictatorships and briefly enjoyed a period of democracy (Honduras, Guatemala, Costa Rica), while others turned instead toward tyranny (Nicaragua and El Salvador). At the same time as political expression was circumscribed, economies swelled. This growth permitted the expansion of infrastructural projects and some modest social reforms. Ultimately, these reforms helped to improve the image of military dictators who held on to power despite growing unrest among the working and middle classes, including university students. With political expression limited elsewhere, university autonomy and its implication that campus was sovereign territory safeguarded some space for free speech and opposition.

In Chapter 3, 'Dependency, Development, and New Roles for Student Movements, 1960–1981', anti-colonial student authors observe how endemic and deliberate the unevenness of wealth in their societies seemed to be. They point to what they see as a lag in industrial and technical development, suggest its causes, and go on to offer a range of solutions, from foreign aid to public health programmes. The next chapter, 'Revolution and Civil War, 1966–1981', deals with many of the same years, but focuses instead on how anti-colonial students understood and participated in wars in Guatemala, El Salvador, and Nicaragua. Finally, Chapter 5, 'Revolutionary Futures, 1970–1983', contains texts from all five nations, where, despite their distinct political circumstances, students dreamed of revolutionary futures by the end of the 1970s. In Nicaragua, this takes the form of a Sandinista leader outlining students' roles in a revolutionary society; meanwhile, in El Salvador, students intimately involved in a war against imperialism celebrated Martí and expressed their solidarity with Guatemala. Paired with Chapter 4, this chapter makes starkly clear how the dominant periodisation of student movements and anti-colonialism fails to comprehend both the longer histories of student organising in Central America and the different stakes of student organising for Central Americans who faced kidnapping, torture, disappearance, and death for their protest.

So much more than the street protests of May 1968, though certainly in dialogue with them, Central American anti-colonial students and their six decades of struggle – the subject of *Beyond 1968* – advance anti-colonial and postcolonial studies by recasting thematics of the peasantry and the intellectual, nationalism, nativism, forms of empire, and motives for revolt. What you hold in your hands is a diverse archive of foundational documents from more than seven archives and six countries. Taken together, they reorient anti-colonial movement scholarship toward a region peripheral even within anti-colonial and postcolonial studies and demand that we rethink how we see the 1960s. Perhaps this stretches the terms anti-colonial, postcolonial, and decolonial to their limits. Indeed, we should see these texts as offering counter-theories of anti-colonialism. It should be so, since, in Jaime F. Pineda S.'s Marxian echo from my epigraph: 'We have arrived . . . to the point where now we are no longer satisfied by explaining the world, but we seek to transform it . . . .'

Works Cited

Cazali Ávila, Augusto (1976), 'Síntesis histórica de la Universidad de San Carlos de Guatemala', in *Publicación conmemorativa tricentenario, 1676–1976*, Guatemala: Editorial Universitaria.

Chakrabarty, Dipesh (1992), 'Postcoloniality and the Artifice of History: Who Speaks for "Indian" Pasts?', *Representations*, 37 (Winter 1992), pp. 1–26.

Chatterjee, Partha (1986), *Nationalist Thought and the Colonial World: A Derivative Discourse?*, London: Zed Books.

Chatterjee, Partha (1993), *Nation and Its Fragments*, Princeton: Princeton University Press.

Chrisman, Laura and Patrick Williams (1994), *Colonial Discourse and Post-Colonial Theory*, London: Routledge.

Consejo Superior Universitario Centroamericano (1965), *El sistema educativo en Nicaragua*, San José, Costa Rica: Consejo Superior Universitario Centroamericano.

Cooper, Frederick (2014), *Citizenship Between Empire and Nation: Remaking France and French Africa, 1945–1960*, Princeton: Princeton University Press.

'Cuba y Latinoamérica sí! Yankis no!', *El Universitario*, September 1960, trans. Jorge Cuéllar, Instituto de Historia de Nicaragua y Centroamérica (IHNCA).

Duara, Prasenjit (1995), *Rescuing History from the Nation: Questioning Narratives of Modern China*, Chicago: University of Chicago Press.

González Ponciano, Jorge Ramón (2005), 'De la patria del criollo a la patria del shumo: Whiteness and the Criminalization of the Dark Plebeian in Modern Guatemala', PhD dissertation, University of Texas, Austin.

Instituto de Investigaciones y Mejoramiento Educativo (1964), *El estudiante universitario: progreso académico de los estudiantes de la Universidad de San Carlos, informe personal de la IIME*, Guatemala: IIME.

Levy, Daniel C. (2005), *To Export Progress: The Golden Age of University Assistance in the Americas*, Bloomington: Indiana University Press.

Pineda S., Jaime F. (1962), 'La participación del estudiante universitario en la vida nacional', *Tribuna económica (Organo de la Asociación de Estudiantes de Ciencas Económicas)*, Año III, No. 25, 31 May 1962, trans. Rachel Nolan. Figueroa Ibarra Collection, No. 197. Centro de Investigaciones Regionales de Mesoamérica (CIRMA).

Said, Edward (1978), *Orientalism*, New York: Vintage Books.

Sherman, John W. (2010), 'The Mexican "Miracle" and its Collapse', in William H. Beezley and Michael C. Meyer, eds, *The Oxford History of Mexico*, Oxford: Oxford University Press.

Spivak, Gayatri Chakravorty, Sara Danius, and Stefan Jonsson (1993), 'An Interview with Gayatri Chakravorty Spivak', *boundary 2*, 20:2 (Summer 1993), pp. 24–50.

Spivak, Gayatri Chakravorty, Donna Landry, and Gerald M. MacLean (1996), *The Spivak Reader*, London: Routledge.

Vrana, Heather (forthcoming), *This City Belongs to You: A History of Student Activism in Guatemala, 1944–1996*, Oakland: University of California Press.

Further Reading

Below is a selection of texts that contextualise and expand the preceding texts. I have also included a small group of biographical and autobiographical texts that offer an intimate view of Central American anticolonial student movements from diverse perspectives. Many of these texts have extensive bibliographies that will guide further inquiry.

Decolonisation

Le Sueur, James D., ed. (2003), *The Decolonization Reader*, London: Routledge.
An excellent and accessible introduction to the major themes in the study of decolonisation and decolonial movements. Chapters by Aletta J. Norval, Dipesh Chakrabarty, Frederick Cooper, and Dane Kennedy are especially recommended.

General Histories of Twentieth-Century Central America

LaFeber, Walter (1993), *Inevitable Revolutions: The United States in Central America*, 2nd edn, New York: W. W. Norton & Company.
A thorough history that emphasises US foreign and economic policies and their effects on Guatemala, Honduras, El Salvador, Nicaragua, and Costa Rica as individual nations and as a region. This book also has a detailed bibliography.

Pérez-Brignoli, Héctor (1989), *A Brief History of Central America*, trans. Ricardo B. Sawrey and Susana Stettri De Sawrey, Berkeley: University of California Press.
Although first published in Spanish in 1985 (and translated in 1989), *A Brief History* remains the foundational general history of the region. Its chapters on the colonial and early national periods are especially noteworthy; twentieth-century colonialism and imperialism are discussed in relation to these longer histories of engagement with global powers and the world market. The text also includes a very useful chronology and bibliography.

Woodward, Ralph Lee (1999), *Central America: A Nation Divided*, 3rd edn, Oxford: Oxford University Press.
The product of four decades of research, this text includes Panama and Belize in its regional frame and encourages readers to think of the Caribbean coast of Central America in relationship to the rest of the Caribbean. In its third edition, it devotes considerable space to the civil wars and the subsequent boom in scholarship.

Memoir, Autobiography, *Testimonio*, and other Published Primary Sources

Belli, Gioconda (2002), *The Country Under My Skin: A Memoir of Love and War*, New York: Knopf.
A popular memoir of a member of the elite-turned-Sandinista, Belli's account of her conscientisation and struggles as a woman in the revolution includes memorable personal anecdotes of her life underground and thoughtful discussion of the failures and triumphs of the revolution. It is a very gripping text, and excellent for teaching at all levels.

Cullather, Nick (1999), *Secret History: The CIA's Classified Account of its Operations in Guatemala, 1952–1954*, Stanford: Stanford University Press.
In 1992, Cullather worked for the CIA, sorting 180,000 pages of unclassified material for redaction and the creation of a 'secret' internal report for CIA officers and trainees on the covert CIA Operation PBSUCCESS, which overthrew the government of Jacobo Arbenz. *Secret History* is the public version of that study, which includes large segments of redacted text that sometimes speak through their silence. From the training files for PBSUCCESS, one text in particular, entitled 'A Study of Assassination', is noteworthy.

Dalton, Roque (1995), *Miguel Marmol*, Willimantic, CT: Curbstone Books.
This text by Roque Dalton is a *testimonio* of the life of Miguel Marmol, written from several weeks of interviews. Marmol was a Salvadoran *campesino* communist who helped organise the infamous 1932 protests that ended in *La Matanza*. This book affords an invaluable look into the social realities confronted by the rural poor in the early twentieth century. It invites discussion on the *testimonio* as a genre, ethics in oral history, and the role of the intellectual in revolution.

Ramírez, Sergio (2012), *Adiós muchachos: A Memoir of the Sandinista Revolution*, Durham, NC: Duke University Press.
Lively memoir from Sandinista partisan turned critic, *Adiós muchachos* provides a vivid account of one student's experiences as a university recruit of the Sandinistas but also presents a critical postscript on the revolution, emphasising internal disagreements among the party leadership.

Randall, Margaret (1995), *Sandino's Daughters: Testimonies of Nicaraguan Women in Struggle*, New Brunswick, NJ: Rutgers University Press.
This book is a collection of short testimonies that captures, in vivid, often visceral, detail, the struggles of many Sandinista women. It is largely a sympathetic work but is critical of the movement's shortcomings, especially around gender, homosexuality, and race.

Monographs and Articles

Chomsky, Aviva (1996), *West Indian Workers and the United Fruit Company in Costa Rica, 1870–1940*, Baton Rouge: Louisiana State University Press.
In this well-researched social history of the lives of West Indian workers on United Fruit Company (UFCO) banana plantations, Chomsky emphasises the unintended consequences of relations between workers and the company. Focused on black migrant labourers' communities on Costa Rica's Atlantic coast, this book provides an important counterpoint to the vision of Costa Rica evoked by Costa Rican university students.

Euraque, Darío (1996), *Reinterpreting the Banana Republic: Region and State in Honduras, 1870–1972*, Chapel Hill: University of North Carolina Press.
This important revisionist record of modern Honduran history documents the development and influence of liberalism among Honduran elites. Comprised of nine short chapters, the book offers important background to the brief period of state-run reform projects after the 1972 coup by accounting for the formation of society's most powerful sectors: the military, capitalists, and intellectual elites.

Gleijeses, Piero (1991), *Shattered Hope: The Guatemalan Revolution and the United States, 1944–1954*, Princeton: Princeton University Press.
There is no better account of the Ten Years' Spring (1944–54) and its premature conclusion than *Shattered Hope*. In great detail, Gleijeses outlines the many reasons for its failure, balancing internal factors and US intervention.

Gobat, Michel (2005), *Confronting the American Dream: Nicaragua Under US Imperial Rule*, Durham, NC: Duke University Press.
More than US imperialism, it is the Americanisation of Nicaraguan

elites that is the focus of Gobat's study. Seeking to explain why these elites, once the fiercest supporters of US intervention, became anti-American, Gobat demonstrates how they strategically adapted some American ways of life while rejecting others that threatened their interests and power.

Gould, J. (1990), *To Lead as Equals: Rural Protest and Political Consciousness in Chinandega, Nicaragua, 1912–1979*, Chapel Hill: University of North Carolina Press.
To Lead as Equals explains the development of peasant political consciousness, from their initial support for *Somocismo* to unity with the urban middle classes and the painstaking organising of the FSLN.

Gould, J. (2009), 'Solidarity Under Siege: The Latin American Left, 1968', *American Historical Review*, 114:2, 348–75.
In this article, Gould outlines the unique preconditions for Latin American student movements in Uruguay, Mexico, and Brazil in 1968, including authoritarian governments, tremendous economic inequality, and important worker–student and urban–rural solidarities constructed in the early 1960s in response to the two aforementioned conditions. The article also addresses the legacies of the states' violent response to these movements.

Grandin, Greg (2004), *The Last Colonial Massacre: Latin America in the Cold War*, Chicago: University of Chicago Press.
Grandin recasts the familiar Cold War in new terms as a conflict over the meanings of democracy, and by doing so, draws out the personal and local stakes of global geopolitics. Based on research in twelve archives and more than one hundred oral history interviews, Grandin's writing is as accessible as his research is rigorous.

Hale, Charles R. (1994), *Resistance and Contradiction: Miskitu Indians and the Nicaraguan State, 1894–1987*, Stanford: Stanford University Press.
This text is a detailed ethnography of the territorial struggle between the Pacific coast Miskitu Indians and the mestizo Sandinista state, which erupted soon after the triumph of the revolution. Hale carefully explains the conflict by tracing the history of key positions sustained by each group: for instance, the Miskitus' 'Anglo affinity' and the Sandinistas' anti-imperialist, anti-Yankee sentiment, and the Sandinistas' revolutionary nationalism counter to the Miskitus' local indigenous identity.

Hammond, John L. (1998), *Fighting to Learn: Popular Education and the Guerrilla War in El Salvador*, New Brunswick, NJ: Rutgers University Press.
Hammond examines the politics of pedagogy and discusses the varied educational practices put into place by the guerrilla in Christian Base Communities, in the field of combat, and among political prisoners and refugees. Based on qualitative analysis of five years of fieldwork in rural communities at the end of the civil war, this book outlines how popular education, especially literacy, changed the guerrilla struggle during the Salvadoran civil war.

Joseph, Gilbert M., Catherine C. Legrand, and Ricardo D. Salvatore, eds (1998), *Close Encounters of Empire: Writing the Cultural History of US–Latin American Relations*, Durham, NC: Duke University Press.
A collection of essays on nineteenth- and twentieth-century Latin America, this interdisciplinary book brought Latin American history and anthropology into dialogue with postcolonial studies at a crucial moment of growth in both fields. While this dialogue has deepened considerably since the book's publication, the wide-ranging empirical essays remain relevant today.

Paige, Jeffrey M. (1998), *Coffee and Power: Revolution and the Rise of Democracy in Central America*, Cambridge, MA: Harvard University Press.
This book examines how, though they followed divergent paths through the 1980s, Costa Rica, El Salvador, and Nicaragua arrived at similar positions in global economics and geopolitics by the 1990s. Paige pays especially close attention to the political ideologies of enduring dynastic elites.

Zimmerman, Matilde (2001), *Sandinista: Carlos Fonseca and the Nicaraguan Revolution*, Durham, NC: Duke University Press.
This book is the first English-language biography of charismatic revolutionary leader Carlos Fonseca. It emphasises his evolving political philosophy alongside the vicissitudes of friendship and comradeship. It is based on unique access to Fonseca's unpublished papers and interviews with family and friends, as well as archival research.

Chapter 1

Central American Modernities 1920–1944

Introduction

In some respects, the 1930s and early 1940s were boom years for Central America. North American investors streamed into the region to assess and develop export potential in bananas, cotton, coffee, and other crops. The Boston-based UFCO led the development effort in Honduras, Costa Rica, and Guatemala, financing railway and port city construction to facilitate shipping. Perhaps because of this economic influence, European and North American cultures and languages, especially French and English, became status symbols among elites. At the same time, a period of cultural effervescence produced new, distinctly Central American forms in the arts, especially poetry, fiction, theatre, dance, painting, and sculpture. These new forms celebrated the region's indigenous past, though urban artists and intellectuals were decidedly less enthusiastic about the indigenous people who lived among them. The tension between the celebration of an indigenous past and enthusiasm for North American and European technologies, cultures, and commodities is reflected in the documents featured in this chapter. Remember, too, that university attendance remained quite limited in this period. Despite the aspirations to social justice expressed below, students remained intellectual elites amidst a majority of poor rural and urban labourers.

While urban middle classes balanced these ambivalent and often contradictory desires, national power-holders were less conflicted. Dictatorships in Honduras (Tiburcio Carías Andino), El Salvador (Maximiliano Hernández Martínez), Nicaragua (Anastasio Somoza García), and Guatemala (Jorge Ubico) concentrated power in the hands of a single individual and his cronies. Within these governments, US economic and political influence was so extensive that the military might that had characterised US–Central American relations in previous decades was all but unnecessary. Then the prices of bananas and coffee plummeted. The legitimacy of the dictators and their reliance upon the US was in doubt. The dictatorial status quo ended in El Salvador and Guatemala in 1944 when university students from both countries led successful revolutions. In Honduras, Carías managed to weather similar pressures until 1948 when, in his seventies after sixteen years of rule and at the urging of the US, he permitted free elections. In Nicaragua, Somoza also agreed to hold free elections in 1947, though less than a month into the term of his successor, he orchestrated a coup and appointed a member of his extended family to the presidency. This pattern would endure and, formally or informally, the Somoza dynasty would rule until 1979.

The coffee-producing elite dominated Costa Rica through the 1940 election of Dr Rafael Angel Calderón Guardia. Then, to his supporters' surprise, Calderón instituted a number of social reforms and aligned with the Communist Party and the Catholic Church to form the Social Christian Unity Party (PUSC). After the four-year term of his successor, Teodoro Picado, Calderón again ran for president but failed to win re-election in 1948. He accused the opposition party of electoral fraud. A bitter war broke out, pitting Calderón, Picado, the communist Popular Vanguard Party, and Somoza's Nicaraguan National Guard against the US government, anti-communists, anti-welfare state conservatives, and some social democratic intellectuals, including José Figueres Ferrer. The war ended after forty-four days and thousands of causalities with a victory for Figueres's side. Figueres served as interim president and managed to pass significant social reforms in a brief eighteen-month period even as he censured dissent. A Constituent Assembly drafted a new constitution that abolished the military, nationalised banks, expanded education and social security programmes, and promoted cooperativism. Political and economic stability has defined the country against its neighbours since the 1948 civil war.

This chapter contains texts written during these critical years, when the anti-colonial sentiment of students involved in university-based and national movements for social change reflected the contradictory positions negotiated by students as intellectual elites in marginal countries. Many of the themes that emerge here continue to be key for students across the next several decades, including European colonisation, critiques of US and British imperialism, duplicitous political parties, the exploitation of natural resources, and students' sacrifices in struggles against tyranny. Other texts reflect students' split gaze, at once outward toward Europe for cultural innovation in art, music, and literature, and at the same time, inward toward their nations' indigenous populations. Their visions of progress required electrical streetlights, widened roads, pedestrian *paseos*, and some disavowal of their past, as detailed in a speech given at the beginning of the school term in 1933 by Salvadoran intellectual Dr Miguel Rafael Urquia. Taken together, these texts reveal how early articulations of anti-colonial thought informed students' protests against dictatorship. They also evince Central American students' ambivalent place in the world in the 1930s as they wrote with an aspirational gaze toward Europe, scepticism of indigeneity, and the belief that North American extraction businesses were a form of colonialism. Articles from the Honduran *Revista de la Universidad* and the Nicaraguan *El Universitario* poignantly capture this ambivalence.

GUATEMALA

'In Complete Tyranny'

(1920)

Liberal dictator Manuel Estrada Cabrera (1857–1924) ruled from 1898 to 1920. During his presidency, the power, influence, and wealth of UFCO and other foreign-owned businesses swelled. Cabrera sought to create an enticing environment for foreign investors, and he secured this by exploiting indigenous labour and persecuting workers who dared to strike. Grandiose and megalomaniacal, Cabrera renamed the national university after himself and erected other temples and monuments in his honour. Here, in 'In Complete Tyranny', anonymous university students critique the steep cost of the parties and festivals that Cabrera demanded of the largely impoverished citizenry. Cabrera was overthrown just weeks after this document was published. Students were key to this endeavour. They formed the first student political organisation called the Association of University Students (AEU) in 1920. *El Estudiante* was the AEU's official newspaper.

From the pages of History there leaps out a truth that tends to become a social law, that in villages crushed by more or less odious tyrannies, the Master employs a vulgar manœuvre with the ostensible intention of making the People forget their many pains and repress the shouts of their protest; this device is the almost continual festival, sometimes celebrated on pointless occasions, or else without occasion at all.

[Abilio Manuel] Guerra Junqueiro,[2] the famous Portuguese rebel, put it in a sublime manner in his angry extended poem entitled 'Finis Patria'. Opíparus, an imaginary character who in the work is one of the many puppets who surround the tyrants, in exactly the same way that the current Guatemalan ministry dances its dance for Estrada Cabrera, advises the Monarch the following in a robust verse that reads:

'Festivals, sir! Cheerful, crazy, many, and various!
There is no food? . . . Spectacle. Lacking bread? . . . Light displays.
People are walking around naked and there is no way to shut them up?
Banners to the air, musicians to the street!
Hunger, pain, night howl, for the ages?
Dawns, bugles, long live the kings, flags!
Happiness! enjoyment! ease! No mourning!
Bombs! Gunpowder salutes from minute to minute!
And to every shout of misery or death rattle,
the bronzes of the "Te Deum" and the drumhead.'

Despots believe in their aberration of dominion without responsibilities, that the villages are like children whose weeping is forgotten or who can be suppressed with toys or cylinders[3] of music; that through bacchanals and tapestries painted with ridiculous legends, through bombastic speeches and performances to the sound of jangling fanfare, the social element will change its well-motivated gesture of anger for a simple-minded smile. Oh, stupid faith!

Circumscribing ourselves to the historical memory of Caesarean Rome, under the bloody thumb of Gaius Nero (epoch with deep analogies to the present in Guatemala), the recourse to drowning the people's pain in unbridled orgies, public spectacles, shows, and popular pseudo-gaiety seems natural and to our observation this is of irrefutable truth. In the leap between Nero's age and Cabrera's age there is only one significant difference: in the period of Nero's nepotistic dominion over the starving people, to distract their pains of abstinence, they distributed foodstuffs in Caesar's gardens amid fanfare and festivities, while under the pretext of festivities, [the tyrant] snatches away their bread from the People of Guatemala, pained by oppression and hunger.

An example taken at random.

Estrada Cabrera's birthday, an event to be celebrated in the most

---

[2] Abilio Manuel Guerra Junqueiro (1850–1923) was a major Portuguese poet, whose poems bravely attacked the Portuguese government and inspired revolution in 1910.

[3] Refers to phonographic cylinders, the most popular commercial music reproduction technology between the 1880s and 1920s.

intimate home, put the people in a difficult stupor by dint of forced req-
uisitions of money for festivals. And that day, on which all Guatemalans
with chests full of pleasure and the smile of satisfaction waited to see
if our *cacique*[4] had behaved in at least a dignified way toward the
Fatherland, showed dismal signs: it was the precursor of a long period
of need in all homes.

Continual festivals impoverish the Nation; through them the Executive
lavishly squandered the contributions collected from the people at the
cost of a thousand labours and privations.

We note this plague of wanton festivals, product of the *Cabrerista*
gangrene, so that future legislators will get rid of it as [their] first service
to the scourged, long-suffering People.

Translated by Rachel Nolan

Manuel Galich, 'The Manifesto of 1942', in *Del pánico al ataque*

(1949)

This well-known memoir, *Del pánico al ataque*, details both the quotidian
and exceptional experiences of law student Manuel Galich and his friends
as they united in opposition to dictator Jorge Ubico. In 1942, Manuel
Galich and some friends from the *Facultad*[5] of Law at USAC began to circulate anti-Ubico screeds in student newspapers and leaflets. They lamented
what they called 'the death of the intellect' in Guatemala, as few professors
dared to oppose Ubico's regime. The young men's hopefulness and spirit
are counterposed by the enormity of the task that lay before them. In just a
handful of years, these young men – many of them teenagers – would find
themselves sitting in the very seats of power that they had opposed. In his
memoir, published after the revolution, Galich recounts how they ran from
the chambers of Congress to class, balancing homework with law-making.
Galich himself later served as Minister of Education from 1945 to 1947
and as Minister of Foreign Relations from 1951 to 1953. Throughout the

---

[4] A *cacique* is a Spanish-colonial term used to describe a local political leader, previously an indigenous leader or elder.

[5] *Facultades* are disciplinary units, like history, biology, and literature, within universities. *Facultad* could be translated as college or department, or even faculty, but for
the sake of clarity and because there are also occasionally schools or colleges within or
alongside *facultades*, I have left this word in Spanish throughout the volume.

memoir, Galich transcribes and annotates significant manifestos and tracts published by the group. In the section entitled 'Manifesto of 1942', Galich describes a secret meeting of the *escuilaches*, as they came to call themselves, and a manifesto that they drafted to explain their *raison d'être*.

Friday, 15 May 1942, the *'escuilaches'* furtively entered the Third Court of the First Instance, at nine o'clock at night. Beneath the arcades of the old house where [former President José María] Reyna Barrios died, without more light than the bluish penumbra of the moon, each one of us felt the seriousness of the venture we were about to undertake. There was the grave face of Bocaletti, the dedicated expression of Julio Méndez, the impassivity of Marco Tulio Ordóñez and of Manuel María Avila Ayala, the enthusiasm of Heriberto Robles, the avidity of [José Manuel] Fortuny, the disgust of [Julio Antonio] Reyes Cardona, the gravity of Hiram Ordóñez, and in all, the consciousness that we were moving towards a transcendental, solemn act and a difficult commitment.
[. . .]
The document reads: 'We have wanted to call this meeting of *'escuilaches'* because, as discussed at various times, it is urgent that we set certain objectives to pursue. Until today, our ties have been purely those of affection; certainly, we have made a conquest of moral order that is ever-rarer for humanity, as we see every day: solidarity, already tested; forgetting selfishness; lack of acquaintance with jealousy; condemnation of disloyalty; disgust towards servility; aversion to injustices, and in the end anything that contradicts our devotion to integrity, to decorum, to character, to generosity, to the union of affection and aspiration. These are the sentiments that feed and sustain our individual efforts, making *escuilachism* a yearning for improvement, for human perfection: it gives the character of a conscious, spontaneous effort towards an ideal of a more honest, healthy, and if you will permit it in the most ample sense in which we wish to use the word, more Christian, life.

We have the right, then, to feel satisfied by the position that we have adopted; for what this nucleus of friends has done; and we must also not feel obligated but rather [wish to] persevere so that this good beginning may reach a good end. Still, *escuilachism*, for the qualities of those who we have integrated and by the virtues we have tried to cultivate, now becomes a civic attitude, a concern for the problems and future of Guatemala. And with this we become more complete, more responsible, more valiant. A good *'escuilach'* cannot contemplate the ostentatious farces of servility without disgust; a good *'escuilach'* cannot hear the lash of the whip without trembling with indignation; a good *'escuilach'* does not cease to feel profoundly wounded by the current state of intellectual stagnation, of lethargy, of abjection, of spiritual degradation to which a system of all-knowing military men is subjecting the country, of circus tamers taking up riding crops; a good '*escuilach*' cannot stop grinning with courage at the same time as he ridicules the enrichment of a few, while he plays the drum and cymbals of organisational rectitude; a good '*escuilach*' cannot have in his hands the nation's daily newspaper without feeling anger and sadness that the intellectuals, those who guide public opinion, those who should be bastions of civil liberties, are now nothing more than dogs who lick the swineocracy; a good '*escuilach*', in short, does not have the right to deny that we are plunged into a cistern of anguish that carries us to a miserable destiny, and that those who have managed to seize public power consider us to be slaves, forming part of the fief, contemptible galley slaves, almost without human condition; and that in this medieval state, the use of weapons like the violation of all laws, [as well as] torture, espionage, [and] farce, will not move us forward but perpetuate the disaster that corrodes Central America for more than a century, because only in this way may the pleasure taken in the seats of government be perpetuated. And because of all this, '*escuilachism*' should acknowledge that indifference is not just immoral but punishable because it conceals the attitude of betrayal of our aspirations, our youth, our Fatherland; and even more gravely, our children.

Now, the foregoing does not mean that immediate action is demanded from us: a conspiracy, for example, as classified in the penal laws, or the laziness of unleashing a useless yell, or the naïveté of propaganda among accusers and frightened gazelles. No. In that case, we would be the first enemies of our own cause. On the other hand, we understand that the problem is not about men: namely, to throw one despot or another off his throne. It is a systemic problem, consisting in rising above all despotisms and all the aftermath of its shames. Further: supposing we launched a quixotic action to undo injustices, that our attack on windmills was lucky and we destroyed those windmills – would we have saved ourselves and saved the country? No. We would be the first to be betrayed, we would have to deal with the shame of the continuation of the regime we fight, with other puppets, yes, but with the same curtains of painted paper and the same shameless adulating phraseology. Here I may leave judgement to history, even to recent history, which verifies what I have just said. We would not be more than the bait on the fishhook of certain fishermen who promise abundant fish when the choppy river gives them a propitious opportunity.'

'Through the History of Guatemala' – read the manifesto in another part – 'the intellectual element has frequently been in the service of a dictatorship, of an autocracy; and at other times it has imprudently divided into differences of caste, religious conviction, personal interests; others, at least until now, have been persecuted, hounded, alone before the power of despotisms.' And by underscoring the barbarous character of military dictatorships endured by Guatemala during its brief history and the subordination of intellectuals, the manifesto continued in its untidy but winnowed-down style: 'One says, then, that we are between the sword and the wall. If we remain indifferent, we are immoral and traitors; and if we sacrifice, we sin by being naïve and clumsy. In effect, this is the painful personal conviction of many of our compatriots: they are obligated to admit, not without bemoaning, their foolish condition; to direct all the rage and shame of being Guatemalan into love for Guatemala, to dream of a dignified destiny for Guatemala and to cross one's arms, resigned to being condemned to pasture for centuries for a haughty and almost illiterate caste, which not only neglects it but also hates, deprecates, and humiliates it. One is obliged to resign oneself to live and die, without recognising their human condition, now that a declaration by a Pope is not worth the same as the Papal Bull of Paul III was to our indigenous people.[6] One is obliged to recognise that [in order] to live an honourable life in the real sense of the word, one should flee Guatemala, forget the fatherland, reject one's own blood and origin, and be a renegade, an outcast; hide one's cradle and disparage one's own [kin], to beg among foreigners. And one sees that this choice is also not honourable and if one must seek out foreign bread, they cannot ignore those who prevent them from eating their own bread, though each may be as bad as the other. Still, this pessimism should cede [the] path to faith; and faith at once gives us arms and strength to fight and patience to wait. We do not ask for resignation, nor [do we] wait for a Messiah to save us. Everything is within us: struggle and triumph. We are not between the sword and the wall; we may be neither immoral nor traitors without being imprudent nor naïve; we may feed our ideals and live with hope; we are not condemned to be lackeys of a militiaman; and one day we will give the fatherland the status among the nations of the world that it deserves.'

'We have the weapons that our ancestors either did not have or did not know how to brandish or did not want to know how to use in order to expel others who [have] supported the empire of sabres and boots.

---

[6] Refers to the Papal Bull of Paul III (1537) that forbade the enslavement of indigenous people.

Three weapons used well could transform this group of boys – who nobody would hesitate, in hearing them, to call crazy – into a formidable force, capable of opposing and replacing those of the bayonets. These three weapons are: our youth, our intelligence, and our unity.'

The manifesto made an extensive historical survey, from independence to 1920, to demonstrate how intellectuals had been 'frequently at the service of a dictatorship' and to 'infer a useful lesson: the lack of cohesion, lack of civic values, and lack of preparation to swiftly initiate the work of reconstruction and to impede the counter-coup of those who thought themselves eternal and absolute holders of power, and are the causes that have maintained our class – that of well-intentioned men who love freedom and have the chance to acquire culture and the technical education that is indispensible for enlivening the country – in the position of courtiers, propagandists for our own enemies and the enemies of the fatherland.'

'What then', – it went on to ask – 'does our country deserve, if we wish to achieve our just aspirations? Not to incur mistakes. Not to tremble before the whip or the gun: stay unified, *structure our new ideology along the lines that Guatemala requires*[7] in light of its particular circumstances; and finally, and this is the most important, to prepare and train ourselves to one day lead and open the fatherland to a completely new era, free of connection to its terrible past.'

It urged this group of youths to enter into a period of preparation for the resolution of national problems. It placed hope in scientific capability and moral value on hope as a sufficient galvanising force to go to battle against tyranny. And it proposed a training plan of ten years, with the intention of then assuming leadership of a great popular movement that would destroy the old institutions from the root and set about [making] a radical transformation, channelling Guatemalan life into political, economic, and social currents that at that moment we saw only remotely though already intuited. Further, it made a call to those present with respect to their responsibility to the generation in the beginning of its development. 'If a fair number of men who possess this firmness' – prophesied the manifesto – 'unify in opposition at the first propitious opportunity, against the pretensions of those who only pursue personal gain, the triumph cannot but be with the former. Think how the youth of Guatemala never has had teachers, ideologues, leaders who speak from the heart the truth about the destiny of the fatherland, as [Domingo Faustino] Sarmiento and [Juan Bautista] Alberdi spoke to

---

[7] Italics are as they appeared in the original.

South American youth or [José] Martí and [Eugenio María de] Hostos to the Antilleans or, finally, [José] Ingenieros to those of [South] America.[8] We have never known an apostle who, after reflection, did not turn out to be a charlatan: our youth is taught to love [Francisco] Morazán and [Justo Rufino] Barrios, as in other places they love Martí or Sarmiento or [Andrés] Bello. And what teachings have these masters of sacking and assassination left us? They are too bloody to mention.' 'We thought about all this and would come to understand the eagerness of Guatemalan youths to find someone who says the word they desire to hear, the word of courage, truth, real science, legitimate patriotism, supported in deeds and not in lies, in things that do not attract intrigue. Our problems are many and [we are] still untested: we also are many and pure of spirit.'

The manifesto announced what history was soon to become. It hoped for that generation to lead affairs of State within ten years. The group did not know that within two years, this generation would almost punctually carry out the proposals of the manifesto, and also feel in their own flesh the frauds and destructions that were foretold. It was a generation made responsible, prematurely.

Translated by Rachel Nolan

AEU, Manifesto

(1946)

As in the overthrow of Cabrera, the AEU was a key actor in the overthrow of President Jorge Ubico. After the revolution, the National University was renamed the University of San Carlos and was granted autonomy in its affairs. Here, the AEU's leadership reacts to rumours that the group had come under the influence of external political forces: namely, national political parties. The responsibilities and rights of the AEU enumerated here correspond to the demands made by Galich and the *escuilaches*, above, and the speeches by Salvadoran professor Dr Miguel Rafael Urquia and student Reinaldo Galindo Pohl, below. Although this text is not explicitly anti-

---

[8] Sarmiento (1811–88), Alberdi (1810–84), and Ingenieros (1877–1925) were influential philosophers, statesmen, and writers who are celebrated as founding fathers of Argentine democracy. Martí (1853–95) died fighting for Cuban independence from Spain. Hostos (1839–1903), in turn, was a celebrated Puerto Rican jurist, educator, and philosopher who advocated for Puerto Rican independence from European and North American powers.

colonial, it outlines the intentions of a group that would become a leader in Guatemalan students' anti-colonial struggles.

The Association of University Students considers it of the utmost importance to once again make its postulates and its true objective known to the national consciousness, whereby it makes the following declarations:

1st. – The Association of University Students is established for cultural ends and for collaboration between its members.
2nd. – It will preserve and defend the Autonomy of the University of San Carlos.
3rd. – It will develop the ethical and civic principles of the university population.
4th. – It will preserve university respect and tradition.
5th. – It will maintain unscathed the decorum and dignity of the student.

Cultural activities throughout the University form the essential elements that its members should create so that culture, not the exclusive patrimony of a privileged group, spreads to all sectors of the country. And collaboration between *universitarios* will unite their efforts to elevate the cultural level of the community.

Since the Autonomous University is one of our most important achievements, it is logical that we should maintain it and avoid the meddling of party politics in university life.

The Student Body has great responsibilities before the fatherland, which should be translated into the highest ethical and civic attitudes. Absolute non-partisanship and defence of the dearest yearnings of the citizenry.

Given the dual capacities of those who belong to student associations, as citizens and students, there is no doubt that they should have only one limit with respect to outside ideas: the apolitical condition of the [university] associations.

But if this respect becomes lacking and partisan manœuvres of any sort upset the harmony of the union, fatal consequence will not be far behind, and *universitario* decorum and dignity would be nothing more than dead precepts in our bylaws.

Recently within the student body there have been movements which, once made public, have served journalistic sensationalism and certain influences from outside the university have called into question that which we consider fundamental to uphold: student harmony above all party interests.

In accordance with that expressed above, WE DECLARE steadfastly that our only flag is dignity and under no circumstances will we permit meddling of a political character in our midst.

Guatemala, 26 January 1946

ROLAN CASTILLO
President of the Congress

MARIO ALVARADO RUBIO
Secretary of the Congress

ANTONIO COLON ARGUETA
President of the AEU

FRANCISCO LUNA RUIZ
General Secretary of the AEU

RAFAEL S. ROSALES S.
General Treasurer of the AEU

Delegates to the Congress from various associations:

Alfredo España T. and A. Girón Padilla, from Medicine; Mario González Orellana and Manuel Villacorta E., from Economics; Julio A. Amézquita, from Law; M. R. Toledo and Gilberto Zea Avelar, from Humanities; Enrique Arias Ripoll and Héctor Duarte Villela, from Dentistry.

Members of the AEU: Francisco J. Silva F.; Mario Villanueva; J. Luis Solórzano; Vincente Secaira; A. Cruz R., Assistant Treasurer; and Oscar Saravia, Assistant Secretary.

Presidents of the Various Associations: Guillermo López V., from Economics; E. Lehnhoff D., from Medicine; Guillermo Reiche H., from Pharmacology; Francisco Poggio L., from Law; Angel Martínez, from Engineering; M. F. Villamar, from Dentistry; and Manuel Chavarría Flores, from Humanities.

Translated by Rachel Nolan

EL SALVADOR

Address, Dr Miguel Rafael Urquia

(1933)

Law professor Dr Miguel Rafael Urquia delivered a revealing speech to students, government and university officials, and faculty colleagues on the first day of classes in March 1933. Speaking against invisible and unnamed detractors, he insisted that the university was key to national defence, the progress of the professions, and specialised knowledge. Yet he also suggested that the university had become merely an arm of the state. To combat this deleterious situation through university reform was urgent and he worked to reach students and other members of the community by republishing his speech in a September edition of the Salvadoran student newspaper, *El Estudiante*. Urquia argued that the university ought to create culture, not merely grant credentials to graduates. He was one of El Salvador's most pre-eminent law scholars for decades, and in the late 1950s he became a United Nations Ambassador for El Salvador. This speech, like the AEU text above, outlines specific responsibilities for the university vis-à-vis the government and civil society.

Mr Undersecretary of Public Education,
Mr President of the University,
Ladies,
Young Ladies,
Young Students
Sirs:

The University of El Salvador inaugurates, with this solemn act, the tasks of a new school year; and with most gracious thanks to the Honourable University Council, I have the honour of making this speech.

There exist and are increasingly deepened in the spirit of certain people – not always [those] limited in intellect, preparation, and influence – such rancorous and at the same time violent attitudes against the University, that the defence of this Centre, in whose preservation, dignity, and development are bound the very prestige of the State and the true value of the nation, seems urgent to uphold.

Such a task I seek to carry out before you.

The campaign against the University, open and obvious, cunning and hidden, as you know, is not uniquely our evil. Since they began emerg-

ing in the Middle Ages, universities have had the misfortune of enduring slander and injustice. However, I find a precision in these words
in a foreign newspaper: 'The University is an imponderable asset that
should, in all civilised nations, have the reverence and devotion of the
rulers and the ruled. The University is the field in which the genius of the
race is grown. The University is the card by which the *pueblos* identify
themselves in the concert of nations.'

And so, you will say to me, why do so many forces conspire to
estrange us, seeking out obstacles to their free development, which
is constantly in the throes of suffocation and death? It is not easy to
answer this question, and it is not in my plans to attempt to [do so] at
this time. It is enough for me to underline the fact that the University has
many enemies and it must be defended.

Above all, what mission does the University carry out?

In El Salvador, as in many other places, at least these days, the
University is merely an institution of the State, a quasi-bureaucratic
organisation that imparts the necessary learning for the exercise of some
intellectual professions like: law, medicine, pharmacy, etc. Sometimes,
it also tries to shoulder the task of 'making culture': it leads a series of
conferences, it hosts a prominent person, and opens the doors of its
auditorium in a maternal embrace, to a literary Athenaeum .... Its
mission, then, in practice, shows us it is notoriously meagre.

Yet, it must not be rejected because it is a deficient institution, it can
be improved, as no sane men would leave arable land infertile if they
could improve their conditions and achieve an appetising harvest.

This requires a change of goals and a change in the direction that, up
until now, the University has followed. Its primary mission should be a
different one and the means by which it is achieved must be different.

Therein lies the dual aim of the [present] urgent university reform.

The fertile and prodigious spirit of José Ortega y Gasset, lecturing
before the 'F.U.E.' of Madrid[9] with his wonderful prose, has highlighted
the shortcomings of the university regime and has especially lamented
that the University does not often exercise its true function: to spread
culture, that is, the system that has in each epoch clear and firm ideas

---

[9] José Ortega y Gasset (1883–1955) was a prolific Spanish philosopher whose thinking
on phenomenology, existentialism, and historicism has been broadly influential. Ortega
y Gasset studied and later taught at the Central University of Madrid throughout his
career. The Federación Universitaria Escolar (FUE) was a student group founded there in
1926 after student protests against the dictatorship of Miguel Primo de Rivera. Some of
its members went on to join various leftist factions in the 1930s.

about the universe, [and] positive convictions about man and things. Exceedingly interesting is the paradox that such a fine thinker of a Spain in the process of rebirth points out: the professional specialist – engineer, doctor, lawyer – is now wiser than ever in their field, but is also more uncouth than ever, because the University did not bestow [upon him] a minimum of convictions and ideals.

For Ortega y Gasset, the primary and central function of the University is to make the average man a learned man – to place him at the height of the times – by teaching the great cultural disciplines: the physical vision of the world (Physics); the fundamental themes of organic life (Biology); the historical process of human life (History); the structure and function of society (Sociology); the realm of the universe (Philosophy). And it is all the more urgent that the University fulfils this mission, 'as we now pass through a terrible period of cultural ignorance. Perhaps the average man has never been so behind his own time, what it demands of him. Therefore never before has there been such an abundance of counterfeit and fraudulent beings. Hardly anyone is in their right mind, following their true destiny. Man survives using subterfuge to lie to himself, pretending to live in a simple and arbitrary world, despite the vital consciousness that makes him proclaim loudly that the real world, the one that corresponds to the fullness of the present, it is enormously complex, precise, and demanding. But he is afraid – the average man is now very weak, despite his gestures of thuggishness – he is afraid to open up to the real world, that will require much of him, and he prefers falsifying his life, while it is hermetically sealed in a caterpillar-like cocoon within his simplistic and fictitious world.'

That is to say that the University is obliged to shape people with broad preparation, able to face the problems of their time and their people on an equal footing, rather than the one-sided characters [that it has] up until today.

It is the same concept that, passing through El Salvador and in this very place, the admirable Aztec Vasconcelos[10] hinted at, declaring the urgency of continental universities in establishing chairs of social and political sciences, led by the study of philosophy, in which the best

---

[10] José Vasconcelos (1882–1959) was a philosopher and an innovator in the philosophy of education. After the Mexican Revolution, he served as Rector of the National Autonomous University of Mexico and twice as Minister of Education. He was influential among Central American academics in Guatemala and El Salvador, especially, for his analyses of race and *mestizaje*, the controversial – sometimes celebrated, other times reviled – mixture of Spanish and indigenous races.

minds of the race should go about forming guidelines that already appear scattered in periodicals, but must be set in a doctrine adapted to Hispano-American goals.

I have noted that our University is nearly alone [as it] takes care to prepare us for the practice of our professions. In none of the *Facultades* does the professor of philosophy exist, and you well know that secondary education is less than suitable in this regard. The law student by the nature of their studies barely, lazily skims through some books on history, sociology, or politics.

Therefore the need for reform of the university curriculum that organises the dissemination of culture in the various *facultades* in a practical manner is urgent. Of course, such a [curriculum] reform must be nothing but the [most] critical detail in the total revision of those plans, conducted with serenity, nobility, and enthusiasm.

This work is much less difficult than one might imagine, because it is already done for the most part. There are thoughtful projections of university statutes and regulations – in whose formulation collaborated exquisite minds and gentlemanly hearts – that assign to the University a three-part aim:

1. Carry out in its highest bodies the task of national education and culture;
2. Disseminate the scientific and literary knowledge of the professions;
3. Fight illiteracy and disseminate civic education in El Salvador.

However, bred in the flattering view of a different regime, the autonomous university, these projects are not ideologically consistent with the kind of limits that the University faces today.

Undoubtedly, the regime of autonomy, which can only be achieved by the efforts of the youth and the understanding of the finest Salvadoran temperament, is the only foundation capable of promoting and sustaining any reform that [may be] glimpsed through new unrest.

Universities are the most propitious terrain for the development of *self-government*.[11] Their economics, technology and administration in the hands of a Council, subordinated only to the General University Assembly, provides the best guarantee of success and opens unexpected horizons for the advancement of the *pueblo*.

It is good that [the universities] are State institutions, because by this means [the State] carries out, alongside its cultural function, the task of preventative policing by preparing and authorising the exercise of

---

[11] English in the original.

certain activities, thus avoiding the dangers of empiricism;[12] this does not, however, mean that institutions of this nature, in which the broadest liberal spirit should survive, are not boxed in by the narrow limits of centralisation.

This is not the time to examine the reasons for the partial suspension of university autonomy. Whatever they may have been, it is undeniable that, while it remains, all efforts at innovation will be futile and sterile; and therefore, there is a need for joint action not just by professors and students, but by all academics and intellectuals worthy of El Salvador, to draw the Government's attention to the principle that [autonomy] should be restored to this Institute, without delay, in the full exercise of the rights reached by virtue of Executive Order on 23 May 1927.
[. . .]

Disregarding the importance of the University; seeing it as a burden of the State; constantly attacking and discrediting it, making it the target of all grievances, is nothing more than externalising the terrible ignorance marked by Ortega y Gasset as the highest sphere of university labour. It is to defend unconsciously, as the very illustration of ignorance, the institution it aims to take down.

But all is not lost. Fortunately, there is always a group of bright men, whose work and whose example are enduringly reflected in History; and it is the duty of the University to discover those men, and to exalt and glorify them.

Enemy of all praise with the appearance of flattery, there is no reason to lie to the Salvadoran people, who, in my estimation, currently constitute our moral and intellectual 'elite'. Nor do I want to silence an illustrious name – the more exalted, the more humble – for me the greatest asset of the country's culture: Francisco Gavidia.[13] Rather, I wish

---

[12] At a time when extended courses of study required for the *bachillerato* degree remained out of reach for most while the demand for basic education soared, a group of teachers called '*empíricos*' taught the majority of primary education courses in Mexico and Central America. *Empíricos* were often hardly more educated than their pupils and carried out the difficult work of teaching unprepared students with scant resources; however, the learning they imparted usually lacked innovation and their efforts were often judged harshly by wealthy, urban, privately educated scholars.

[13] Francisco Gavidia (1863–1955) was one of Central America's most famous authors in the early twentieth century, alongside Ruben Darío, whom he mentored and befriended. Once a student of law at the University of El Salvador (UES), Gavidia abandoned his studies to write more than a dozen books of poetry, history, short stories, and studies of around nine languages, including Greek, Latin, and K'iche'. In 1933, the government of El Salvador bestowed upon him a medal of honour, which is the reason for Urquia's brief reference at the conclusion of his speech.

to remind the University at this time that Professor Gavidia deserves a tribute, from a true apotheosis, and [the University] is the only body responsible for carrying out this just act, for the glory and honour of the Republic.

To Francisco Gavidia, worthy Honorary Fellow of this Centre [of Study] and, embodied in the Professor, to that which is higher and more noble in the intelligentsia, in the press, in professional and student unions in El Salvador, I direct the passion of my words, shoring up a campaign of defence and aggrandisement for the university, to win the right to say, in the words of Unamuno of his Spain, that the University is more our daughter than our mother . . . !

Translated by Allessandra Paglia

Address, Br Reinaldo Galindo Pohl

(1944)

The General Association of Salvadoran University Students (Asociación General de Estudiantes Universitarios Salvadoreños [AGEUS]) was founded in 1927 as part of a number of social reforms instituted by President Romero Bosque. Like the AEU in Guatemala, it sought to unite students across academic discipline and was inspired by the 1918 Córdoba Reforms. Here, AGEUS leader, Reynaldo Galindo Pohl, whose name was misspelled in the original publication in the university newspaper *La Universidad*, addresses governmental officials and fellow classmates in a speech just months after the overthrow of President Maximiliano Hernández. The excitement and sense of purpose and duty are so clear in the young man's words. Perhaps this speech was meant to inspire its audience, especially his fellow students, to great achievements. He refers to the pre-revolutionary university as a place where professionals were forged without conscience, in a 'stagnant cloister'. He calls for a democratic state that would not merely represent the desires of an elite class, but also help the poor. Note the references to the Four Freedoms and the Atlantic Charter, two key texts for post-World War II democracies, both authored by US President Franklin D. Roosevelt. In 1948, Galindo Pohl participated in the overthrow of Hernández's successor, Salvador Castaneda Castro, and helped to draft the 1950 Constitution. He later served in several national and international government positions from the 1960s to the mid-1990s. This speech is usefully compared to that of Dr Urquia and Galich's memoir of the Guatemalan revolution: what does each individual expect of students and of the university?

His Excellency Mr President of the Republic:
Ministers and Undersecretaries of State:
Diplomatic Corps:
Sirs:
Classmates:

The shadows of our forebearers rest easily. The work of the founding fathers has been nourished. El Salvador, honouring its name, as it did a century ago, has begun the race for its second national independence. As it did a century ago, the cry of freedom rose up in this city – and today, not only as a romantic gesture, but as the clarion call of a successful conquest – in this city that deserves glory and worship for its successes, not to boast, but to stimulate, emulate, and guide the generations to come. The town's worth is in its history. A mysterious fate is ours, that of being the custodians of redemptive ideas. Subtle enigma, that of entrusting the greatest American idealism to the smallest American country, as if the magnitude of the spirit is enough to make up for the smallness of the temple and does not need the broad lands of the Leviathans' might.

The moments full of idealism, full of patriotic devotion, which have just passed, let us recognise this, we will never live them again. This enormous achievement that required total unification of the Salvadoran people is ruptured [and] divisions will once again arise. But it does not matter: great are the *pueblos* that in suffering find the anvil that tempers character, great are the *pueblos* that never succumb to corruption or flattery, not even with the blow felt on living flesh do they lose the spirit to gracefully lift themselves up.

In the exploits of 5 May, worthy of troubadours, the University was given a leading role; better said, it knew how to fulfil its duty. That is why there has never been a university action that justly brought so much satisfaction to students and academics. Never has the University's contribution been so valuable, decisive, and risky as it is today. They were sixteen unforgettable days of campaigning, full of incidents, unchangeable for many long years of life. Just remember the solemn acts of 24 and 25 April, when forty student delegates were sworn into the School of Medicine, by the Constitution of 1886, by the memory of the *próceres*,[14] and that each offered more, maintaining the strike, extending it, and not returning to the University until our country had regained its denied freedoms. Those youthful voices, serious and deliberate, were the echo of destiny. Today we return because we are sure that the opprobrium

---

[14] *Próceres* were the national heroes or founding fathers of Central American nations.

has been washed away, that these classrooms will once again open, stirred by the winds of renewal, and that our people will raise their heads, decorated with the Phrygian cap of freedom.

After the struggle, these youths justly propose to crystallise their aspirations, repressed for many years. The University will no longer be the stagnant cloister and forge of professionals that have no objective other than finding a satisfactory position for themselves. It will stop being the centre of abstract digressions, in order to extend with a practical and human sense its guidance on the arduous problems of the present. Discussions will come, interpretations of the law will come, not to entertain ourselves with old books, but instead to note the delay that codified bodies always take in relation to social evolution. No longer will they be historical interpretations, reaching back to resolve the problems of the twentieth century in the way the [traditional Liberal and Conservative] Parties or the Justinian Institutions wanted to, as if in two thousand years the world would not have changed. The text of the law should be interpreted according to the needs and mentality of the actual era, the way Bellot-Besupre, President of the Supreme Tribunal of France, suggested to interpret the Napoleonic Code. Interesting problems that the University will have as it converts doctrine into practice.

We are men of order, of principles and not *caudillos*;[15] we are not opportunists that after the dangerous hour has passed go to collect the finest harvest; we go backed by ideals, not benefits; we do not have ties to vested interests, nor are we defenders of privilege nor bastions of injustice. Our aspiration is to bring this land in tune with the evolution seen in other free lands, to prepare ourselves to ease the difficulty of these transformations, and enter upright, united, in the new post-war world where hopefully lack of understanding does not dismiss utopian ideas. This is possible because democracy is not just a word that sounds like the echo of a bell that rings repeatedly, but [is] transient like the internal fruition of those who feel free by law but a slave to their needs. To the wise one or to the idealist, democracy of the eighteenth century will suffice, just as the East that looks to mysticism for psychological compensation of their misery, or to philosophy that conflicts with freedom of the spirit and reason. But conquests in social life are for the majority and not for the few. Real democracy is full of accomplishments that satisfy popular desires for material well-being. This does

---

[15] Political leaders or strongmen, especially military presidents, who exercised power through fear and personal loyalty.

not break with ideal or tradition – fertile fields of action, and anchors that have sustained the state during political storms – but rather to the gains made since the French Revolution are added work toward the true redemption of the poor and their incorporation into the joys of culture. The democratic state does not want to be representative of a dominant sector or caste, but instead the supreme harmoniser of popular interests, the maintainer of liberties, the maker of culture and of social justice. Democracy, with its new projections, is not an out-dated system as totalitarianism accuses it of being, but rather a system that is in agreement with eternal longings that, translated into several languages and expressed in different shades, maintain men of all times in their quest to pursue a better life. Their support is found in the Atlantic Charter and the Four Freedoms,[16] the same flag that flies around armies of the United Nations, leaving behind a trail of blood, which is an offering to progress, in its victorious march through the venerated French lands.

Every Salvadoran has the capacity and ability to donate their [unique] contribution to national reconstruction. Comparing what happened and what is to come, we say that nothing has been done yet. We still have to conquer the world. To destroy, one needs audacity, intelligence, and fate. But to construct is the real work of the giants. We Salvadorans must create a new life. It is labour without compensation, as great as the modesty that drives them, pure as any selfless enterprise. Our rights should not be the gift of a good ruler, but rather the defence and foundation of our national conscience. Otherwise we will continue to have sporadic periods of freedom, and once the progressive leader disappears, the institutions [of democracy] will not be sufficiently embedded to resist the megalomaniac attacks of the treacherous and ambitious. In these moments freedom is not built on firm foundations. It would be senseless to think otherwise when dealing with a population so high in illiteracy and with a drastically high percentage of individuals lacking civic culture. The majesty of the moment does not make us proud of qualities we do not possess; the complacency of victory does not allow us to forget that the danger of a reaction exists. So we are democracy, which is culture, remaining in unstable equilibrium; democracy, which

---

[16] The Four Freedoms (freedom of speech and expression, freedom to worship God in one's own way, freedom from want, and freedom from fear) were outlined in a State of the Union address by US President Franklin Delano Roosevelt on 9 January 1941; together they justified US intervention in wars against fascism in Europe – or anywhere in the world. The Atlantic Charter was a joint declaration issued by Roosevelt and British Prime Minister Winston Churchill on 14 August 1941; it outlined their war aims on the eve of the Second World War, as well as their post-war plans.

is the claiming of workers' rights through legal actions, [and which] can decline in the hands of those who exploit passions and needs born of social problems that out of cowardice we never wanted to face.

We should have the freedom to take on what this new time gives us. Let us not be ridiculous pygmies fighting the inexorable mutation of matters. Let us also not be passionate fiends, racing toward overly sentimental impulses, flightier than [our] natural evolution. It is a difficult balance of maintaining the right individual and collective conscience between the always influential inertia of yesterday, and the tumultuous magnetism, especially for a youth that is rebellious by definition, of that dawn of peace and perfection, a distant goal where unrealised hopes of a thousand generations have been dumped, the prayer of the faithful, and the strength and the fiery words of the redeemers and the men of action. Let us be as broad as the sky that holds the soil of America. In the robustness of the wild blossom we find the example of what a well-developed and well-conditioned spirit can give to this continent, which is the hope of humanity, and not only hope, but also a flourishing harvest, by taking on responsibility with the United States of America for the destiny of the world, along the path of goodness. We should be open to receiving the way of living that will be born in the post-war era, which will be forged with the patient aid of all *pueblos*, for duties are born instantaneously and completed only in legends, the way Minerva was born made of the head of Jupiter.

Ah gentlemen, our thoughts, our desires! How we have dreamed of this land! There is a sea of tasks and a volcano of concerns. The contribution of the student body to national liberation was not the result of one enthusiastic moment; it was the proper use of one occasion staked out for years in the shadows. Whatever the future brings, you can never erase the great leap that El Salvador made, with the passive revolution of 5 May.[17] It does not matter if we are pained or embarrassed. From darkness light was made; from chaos, order. The sadness of the winter is necessary to the radiant light of spring. The greatness of the good would be imponderable without the evil of cruelty. Without moral degradation, virtue would be meaningless. Opposition continues, a necessary conflict in individual and collective life, whose essence is the very essence of the inscrutable mystery of the Universe.

---

[17] On 5 May 1944, a National Reconstruction Committee was formed, carefully including a representative from each of the most powerful urban social sectors: the student body, the military, medicine, law, and workers. The group demanded Martínez's immediate resignation.

The word of the youth will always be the word of the Catiline Orations.[18] There are no compromises when national interests are at stake. No ambitions, the fleeting life of worldly pleasures, the only ambition is to fulfil one's duty. Bodies die, but the spirit is eternal; the spirit is the purity of dreams, the strength in youth, the brave centaur that exists in the souls of brave men.

The greatest strength that a man can have in an endeavour is to be always prepared to die. And he who is, is invincible, for supreme punishment and supreme revenge find the bulwark of an earlier renunciation in the impenetrable enclosure of moral strength. And so, fellow students, ever onward! Ever onward, until death brings us peace or complacency denies us life!

Reinaldo Galindo Pohl
San Salvador, 6 June 1944

Translated by Allessandra Paglia

NICARAGUA

Excerpts, Central University of Nicaragua, *Report of its Foundation*

(1941)

The following is an official and commemorative account of the acts of foundation of the Central University of Nicaragua during the regime of Anastasio Somoza García. The event bestowed pomp and circumstance on its participants, who included dozens of intellectuals from throughout Latin America, government ministers, and, of course, Somoza. This text, like others in this chapter, makes an argument for the role of the university in national culture, but unlike the others, it is written for an audience still living under a dictator. In the text below, a brief account of the importance of the university is followed by an address from Somoza. There is no anti-colonial sentiment expressed in this official text, to be sure, but it depicts in the clearest terms the type of university that subsequent students risked their lives to reject.

---

[18] The Catiline Orations were speeches given by Cicero of Rome to the Roman Senate, denouncing an anti-government plot led by Lucius Sergius Catilina. Cicero railed against bribes and corruption, sedition and disloyalty.

Central University of Nicaragua
[Founded] 15 September 1941
From the Office of the President 7 May 1942

Importance of the Central University of Nicaragua

Among other features of the current Nicaraguan Government, at the foreground lies the promotion of national culture to the fullest extent permitted by the economic capabilities of the country.

In the past, education was entrusted almost exclusively to private initiatives and yet when it counted on protection from the State and conducted its work efficiently, the Administration understood the expediency of supporting Official Establishments of education, in order to fulfil the growing cultural needs and desires of the country.

The foundation of Normal Schools for Ladies and Gentlemen deserves special mention, where a large student population, representative of all sectors of the country, find enough culture and vocational training for the most optimistic of estimates of the future of national Teachers and the creation of the Military School, genuine pride of Nicaragua and exemplar in Central America.

The National Institutions of Secondary Education have received the assiduous attention of Public Authority and some, like the one in Granada, revived from their total disintegration.

Thus, Nicaragua, a small Nation located geographically at the very centre of the Americas, which is at the forefront of continental solidarity, and feels in its soul the pain that humanity is experiencing, does not forget the spiritual values that appear to have gotten lost in the smoke from the conflict in which nearly everyone is embroiled and in which projectile missiles, packed with the materialistic ambition of man, destroy hearts and make the earth shake; and one most evocative day in the history of its Fatherland, when it celebrates its independence, it stands proudly in an act of great national importance, to inaugurate the Central University that represents the backbone of the nation's cultural organisation.

In international politics, the defence of self-determination of the people and of the spiritual unity of America is integral.

In domestic politics, Nicaragua extends its respect for all inclinations and the assimilation of values that contribute to the welfare of the Fatherland: Peace and Democracy.

In Economics, grand public works, budgetary austerity, and protection of national resources, even in the midst of universal economic imbalance.

In Public Education, innovation of teaching, focused attention on Schools, new fields for scientific and artistic endeavours (the creation of the School of Engineering and Fine Arts) and as its apex, the Central University.

And we have a Nation, a President, and a Government.

And a *pueblo*, there are no undisciplined people when an intelligent mind and firm hand guide them.

The Central University of Nicaragua was born during eventful moments, but [times] with indisputable opportunities. Whatever the current universal conflagration, the vital energy of the people will carry them to better times when weapons will be lowered, and the strengths of the spirit and the mind will blossom. We must be prepared for these moments. Young America has a serious responsibility: it is the repository of traditional European culture that is shattering and it must return this to the world so that it can serve as the core of future forms of social coexistence. Spanish-speaking peoples have lovingly preserved relics from the Motherland, and when peace arrives, they will raise them like trophies of glory, uniting the characteristics of the race: Courage, nobility, and Christian love.

Nicaragua fulfils its duty. The University will cultivate the values of today that have been forgotten, it will spread true culture throughout the nation, it will form the men that tomorrow will be the pride of the Fatherland and elevate culture to a level that will earn the admiration of all.

Blessed are the people who have, after having known pain in their own flesh, like our own, had the power to discover a leader for their destiny that knew to give them inner peace and prepare them for days ahead filled with prosperity and greatness.

[. . .]

Mr President's Address (transcript)

Most excellent Distinguished Delegates and Diplomatic Envoys:
Sirs:

In my duties as Ruler, never before have I felt such deep emotion, because in creating the Central University of Nicaragua, I think I have reached the highest aspiration of Government and met the greatest cultural need that our Country feels today.

In my administrative efforts I hope to translate this aspiration into actions, the way the Nicaraguan public demands it, the way the modern world understands it, and the way democratic ideology demands it: I always have in view three aims to which my energies are directed, to disseminate public education to every corner of this nation; to purify the lives of the Nicaraguan people by introducing Sanitation systems to all parts of the nation; and lastly to establish an effective network of roads that not only facilitate exchange within Nicaragua, but extend to neighbouring countries.

Therefore, in founding this University I reciprocate in the best and most fruitful manner the confidence placed in me by the Nicaraguan people; because this Centre of High Culture responds not only to the enormous needs of today's society, but also to the future of Nicaraguan society; it is the radiant conduit that connects us with the spirit of our America.

The increasingly intimate relationships between Latin American Nations demands that our youth is trained with a global and American perspective that elevates human solidarity to an undisputed and indisputable creed; it is with this criterion that my Government has founded the Central University with a steady gaze on Nicaragua and Columbus's continent that is part of our Fatherland.

As a ray of light, as an Institution of High Culture that, 'as a unique entity, spreads the culture of the great disciplines of Science, Literature and Art, forming a unified pedagogical effort that not only ensures the fulfilment of the lofty goals that are pursued, but also coordinates cooperation between similar Centres that already exist in the country', and as such is inaugurated the Central University of Nicaragua.

The last words spoken by Mister President were drowned out by applause from the audience that broke into demonstrations of warm-hearted enthusiasm, at the same time that the Orchestra sounded the reveille.

This is how the Central University of Nicaragua was inaugurated, under the glory of September fifteenth nineteen forty-one; and the act continued with a succession of speeches from the Minister of Public Education, the Dean of the University, the Deans of Law, Engineering, and Medicine, the Most Excellent Special Delegates from the Mexican and Central American Governments, the Delegates from the University Centres of León and Granada, and finally, a Representative of the students of the University . . . .

Translated by Allessandra Paglia

David Sánchez Sánchez, 'The Student Body as a Political Force'

(1945)

Student resistance to Somoza's regime began as early as 1937, although it remained mostly underground until 1944, when several protests ignited popular resistance in June and July. On 27 June, university students organised a march in support of Guatemalan students who continued to fight to depose Juan Federico Ponce Vaides, dictator Ubico's hand-picked heir to the presidency. More than 2,000 people gathered in the streets of Managua, staging demonstrations at key locations, according to historian Knut Walter. The National Guard retaliated with force, arresting around five hundred protestors. Many were quickly released, but some remained in police custody. Family members, students, professionals, and *campesinos* petitioned Somoza for the release of all prisoners. Somoza closed the university. In response, several governmental ministers resigned. The protests expanded, and some workers and shopkeepers went on strike, demanding Somoza's resignation; counter-protestors rose up in support of the President and the National Guard struggled to keep order. Ultimately, on 7 July, Somoza agreed not to seek re-election. This was little more than political theatre. Somoza continued to exercise executive power until his assassination in 1956. Written after these partial successes in 1945, however, the text below, written by David Sánchez Sánchez and published in the popular paper *El Universitario*, provides a valuable view of the ways that student revolt was imagined before the ideological polarisation of the Cold War. He discusses at some length the 1918 student movement at the University of Córdoba in Argentina, which is often understood to be the first Latin American student movement. The successful protests of the Córdoba students resulted in a set of reforms: university autonomy; territorial sovereignty of campus and university buildings; co-governance with alumni and professors on university committees; university extension programming; open admission for all qualified applicants; an advisory role for the university over national social, economic, and political problems; new forms of teaching that focused on research rather than memorisation; and an increase in full-time faculty and other means to build the university community. It is striking how the author positions students as an almost transcendent force for good in contrast to corrupt politicians (as if students never became politicians and politicians were never students). Yet this formulation, like the demands of the Córdoba students, would recur throughout the region in the coming decades, inspiring students to see themselves as a moral compass for the nation and the region. Ultimately, this article is a bold assertion of regional revolutionary student consciousness.

The Latin American student revolutionary movement, initiated 10 March 1918, in the eccentric and dignified Republic of the Plata [River], and later carried out in Bolivia, Peru, Chile, Ecuador, Paraguay, and Cuba, has not ceased in Guatemala, and it continues in Nicaragua.

[Presidents] Siles in Bolivia, Leguía in Peru, Ibáñez in Chile, Ayora in Ecuador, Guggiari in Paraguay, Machado in Cuba, and Ubico in Guatemala have felt, not across their backs, but in their burly tyrannical breasts, the fatal blow of a new revolutionary element, a new force, virile and impetuous, heroic, selfless and intelligent: the students. The students are a new revolutionary force, potent and conscious; a new force that does not follow *caudillos*, [but] flies the flag; it does not follow movements, it creates them; and conscientiously and powerfully wins freedoms for the people that other forces, other parties, other leaders do not seek, for they only seek resolutions based on the distribution of treasuries and purses.

The students are a selfless force, idealistic, quixotic; they are not moved by their stomachs, but rather by the beauty gathered in their textbooks: freedom, justice, rights.

It is the representative force of the yearnings of the people, and not of the ambitions of individuals. For this reason they have triumphed.

For many of our politicians, the goal is [to acquire] the means to win the treasury; for the students, conquering the treasury would be, if it were pursued, the means by which to carry out the goal.

For this reason, this tender and beautiful [student] body of Nicaragua should not corrupt itself; it should continue to remain always pure, immaculate; and as such, it should not pursue the destruction of systems; it should scorn personal hatred and elevate itself to the level of public interest; it should not be an element of 'revolt', that is to say, an element that aids in the changing of names on payroll only; they should be an element of 'revolution', and radical revolution, a total change of face, and the installation of systems that fulfil the legitimate yearnings of the people, so that they remain victorious.

The national movement, the civic ideological revolution, born of the university movement of 27 June 1944, which has achieved the nearly complete restoration of all public liberties, demonstrates that students are a force with deep roots in the public conscience; it is poignant proof, which now forms an overpowering force, capable of demolishing tyranny and implementing democracies that benefit all and not just a group of gutless opportunists.

A force that has changed the direction of the Executives and guided them towards more human endeavours is already a respectable force; it is a combat force with which all political forces of the nation must contend in the future.

The Nicaraguan student movement has won a prominent place in these fights and it must influence, perhaps decisively, the election of the new men that must come.

We continue this fight. Persistent manliness, incessant rebelliousness must change the face of the entire nation.

David Sánchez Sánchez
Managua, 21 December 1945

Translated by Allessandra Paglia

Juan F. Gutiérrez, 'Let's Build the Fatherland'

(1946)

Open opposition to President Somoza carried great risk of reprisal, but some students and professors continued to speak out after the initial protests of 1944. The article below, written by Juan F. Gutiérrez and published in *El Universitario* like the Sánchez Sánchez text above, provides a vivid if partial portrait of rising resistance to Somoza's rule. In the downcast and dehumanised masses forced to process like cattle in a military parade, Gutiérrez saw potential for a new nation. Urban university students, perhaps previously ignorant of the suffering of their rural counterparts, could no longer ignore the toll of *Somocismo* in the countryside. Before freedom could be restored, though, Somoza had to be overthrown and the people unified 'by the conviction of their civic rights and responsibilities'. Many leaders of the opposition were forced to flee to Costa Rica or Guatemala; however, resistance continued to grow among some students, urban workers, and rural peasants. Others, especially some labour unions, conditionally supported Somoza because he promised to resolve some of their grievances in state-run unions.

The largest demonstration recorded in the history of Nicaragua is undoubtedly the Pro-government [protest] on the 24th. There was no peasant, from border to border, and even beyond the border, that was not brought to Managua for the great demonstration. These poor people were herded like cattle, in every rolling mechanism that [Andrés] Murillo[19] was able to find, so that later on he could place them in an improvised pen on the Quinta Nina and in other strategic locales around the capital.

The young Nero marched at the head on a shining steed. With the city's crowd booing and jeering he responded with greetings and smiles. Meanwhile Murillo, Luis Manuel, José María, sweet-talked him: 'See General, this is how the people want it.'

Later came the mob of charity cases: pushing and shoving one another to get close to the dictator, who more or less wanted to ingratiate themselves to him to get their piece; they were like vultures over prey, trying to grab the very last scraps.

Behind these came the *pueblo*, a mute and downcast people; thousands upon thousands paraded before the eyes of the capital city residents that bit their lips with rage upon seeing the way these people were treated, each side street had rope stretched across to prevent the herd from scattering. Their condition as free men was degraded down to the very last rung.

[. . .]

Well, we the university students should thank Murillo for having shown us our fellow citizens, for having brought these people from the most remote mountains before our eyes so that we could take note of the extent of the work our country needs from us, so that we could understand how these Nicaraguans, more than anyone, need this dictatorship to end, that they like none other are suffering the absolute poverty, despotism, and corruption of this regime.

First of all, the first obstacle we have to overcome is SOMOZA. While Somoza has not fallen, we cannot nor should we have illusions of free elections, the very demonstration that took place Sunday was nothing other than a demonstration of what he could do with the power of weapons and the power of money.

Second, we should fight together for the candidate that we deem most fit, and drag behind us all of the people we saw parading down the streets on Sunday, but drag them not by *Somocista*-like force but instead by the conviction of their civic rights and responsibilities.

Once the landscape of the government has changed, to fight with all of our strength for these poor, illiterate people to be illuminated with the light of education and so in future political events they can march with

---

[19] Andrés Murillo was mayor of Managua, officially the 'Minister of the National District', between 1945 and 1947.

their heads held high, conscious of their actions and not humiliated and dejected as in that march on Sunday.

We must BUILD A FATHERLAND: this frightening picture we have witnessed should make us fight without losing heart to reform our community.

We must not allow our poor countrymen to continue serving as a stepping stool for upstart dictatorships and professional politicians.

Juan F. Gutiérrez
Managua, 27–2–1946

Translated by Allessandra Paglia

COSTA RICA

'"In Costa Rica we are Proud of our Freedom of Thought . . ."'

(1931)

Unlike its neighbours in the isthmus, Costa Rica's government had been stable with regular elections held every four years since 1902 (with the brief exception of the rule of Federico Tinoco and the 1948 civil war). While other Central American presidents outlawed communist parties or required unions to submit to governmental control, most Costa Rican presidents handled dissent by incorporating opposition leadership into the government and instituting social reforms, and in so doing crafted a brand of reformist Liberalism that accommodated a limited range of political perspectives, a political process with far-reaching consequences. This expectation of free speech, much less the duty to criticise a government gone astray, was unthinkable in Somoza's Nicaragua, yet Costa Rican students from the League of Anti-Imperialist Law Students boasted 'we are proud of our freedom of thought' in this article published in the national newspaper, *La Tribuna*.

'We believe that we are within our rights, seeing as we are children of the twentieth century, and not of the Medieval Ages'

The Interior Minister has for days now committed violations against the Constitution.

The undersigned members of the Costa Rican Anti-Imperialist League of Law Students, conscious of our duties to ourselves and to our country, appear on this occasion before the Costa Rican people to energetically reproach the passive attitude towards the serious problems with some alarming features that are emerging today. We refer here to those attacks on the Constitution along with some of our most esteemed institutions, which the Interior Minister has perpetrated for several days, attacks that have reached an extreme that we believe is sufficient to awaken the outrage of all Costa Ricans.

The Minister began by ordering the dismantling of a radiographic station in Heredia, protecting himself by using the ridiculous pretext of merely serving the President of the Republic. We believe that if the President was personally insulted in some way by that station, then the path to reparation, *according to our laws*, is not the one being adopted by Lic. Guardián. In Costa Rica, we are proud of our freedom of thought and all Costa Ricans are accustomed to discussing and critiquing the acts of politicians. We believe that we are within our rights, seeing as we are children of the twentieth century, and not of the Medieval Ages. On the other hand, we know that no attacks against the President were made in that station, and on the contrary, there were some made against the electric companies where the minister was, just months ago, a lawyer, a position which he renounced in order to accept the ministry.

We have reason to doubt the impartiality of this gentleman, and mainly, knowing what we know about a conversation between the boss of the national radios (with orders from him [Guardián]) and the interested parties of the aforementioned station of Heredia, wherein these men were promised that their station would not be dismantled only if and when they WILL CEASE their attacks on the electrical companies. Thus, we can ask the minister, has he continued in his previous job or has he renounced it?

And he was not content with this, but instead went deeper, establishing in an unspeakable manner the reviled 'censorship' of literature with more or less radical ideas that enters the nation. Was it really true that Mr Guardián was prepared to leave us without the right to think freely? So the minister, with a limited devious standard, continues believing that ideas are fought with force and not with better ideas? Does he not understand that proceeding in this way will not only violate citizens' rights, but also stain national esteem? These methods of tyranny do not belong to the level of civilisation that fortunately we have achieved.

But there is more. In order to put into practice this recent measure, the minister has to commit another crime: to violate the post from where it is suspected the literature that disgusts him originates. We understand that he has already dared to attempt this. We urge those concerned to take this matter to the Tribunals, where it is safe to say that the judges will know how to punish he who believes himself authorised to break laws due only to the fact of having become minister, unexpectedly.

Another problem: the minister sent Mr Francisco Conejo a note a few days ago prohibiting him from continuing to use radio transmitters for his speeches, because Mr Conejo referred to the unemployment issue and those educational reform projects initiated by Secretary [Justo A.] Facio. The offence is of the gravest importance, and yet once again we ask ourselves: Where does the Interior Minister think this will end? But there is another, still graver, issue: we are told that in the Ministry of Foreign Relations there are two memos from the US Department of State in which our government is ordered to proceed quickly against the upsurge of radical ideas. We know that the last memo is very recent and that it originated from a complaint presented by two North Americans to their Minister. So is our government blindly obeying orders given by the United States? Have we reached such a state of vileness?

In view of all of these things, we call forth to all conscious citizens (intellectuals, students, and workers), that they take stock of this matter; that it will shake them from their criminal apathy, and everyone, as one, [will] prepare to defend the institutions in danger. More, we believe: the Minister that has proceeded in this way must fall; he, most of all, should have understood that he was placed where he is in order to respect and enforce the rights of citizens and not to step all over them. If we are deliberate, he will fall, if not from the will of the President, then from the will of the people.

Costa Rican Anti-Imperialist League of Law Students
Manuel Mora, Jaime Cerdas, Luis Carballo

Translated by Jorge Cuéllar

Excerpts, Manuel Mora Valverde, *Imperialism: Our Sovereignty before the State Department*

(1940)

Manuel Mora Valverde, one of the authors of the statement above, came of age listening to his father José Rafael Mora Zúñiga discuss Marxism–Leninism at reading groups and political meetings. His life reflects the 'polarisation of politics' carefully outlined by Costa Rican historian Iván Molina and Kirk Bowman. Mora Valverde began attending these meetings himself around the age of fifteen, when he was in secondary school at Liceo de Costa Rica. Out of these meetings grew the Costa Rican Communist Party, founded in 1931 when Valverde was just twenty-two years old. Along with other Communist Party members, Valverde was quickly able to organise unrest among UFCO banana workers for a series of small strikes and a major strike in 1934. Although Valverde was offered a scholarship by the Ministry of Education to study mathematics in France, he chose instead to enrol as a law student at the University of Costa Rica. Quickly, Valverde's political career accelerated: he was elected as a deputy to Congress at age twenty-five. Valverde became one of Costa Rica's foremost jurists and was key in shaping the country's Labour Code and Social Security and Guarantees system. The essays below were collected and republished by the Communist Party in a tract entitled *Imperialism* in 1940, when Valverde was just thirty-one. The book is pocket-sized with a red cover, which features an illustration of a menacing silhouette of the Statue of Liberty, looming over rows and rows of faceless workers who are bowed over, toiling.

'A Nation Commits Great Folly When It Waits for Altruistic Favours from Others'

The threat of Yankee imperialism to the sovereignty of our country continues. The President of the Republic and other various distinguished individuals in our intellectual life – with whom the journalist Ramón Caldera[20] effectively collaborates – have articulated, in an emphatic manner, why we should continue to make all the territorial concessions that the United States requests under the pretext of the urgency to defend the continent against a possible German invasion. Yet, neither the President nor the aforementioned persons have been able to seriously

---

[20] Caldera was a Nicaraguan journalist who was very popular in Costa Rica and a good friend of thrice-president Ricardo Jiménez Oreamuno.

debate, even, anything outside of their commonly held positions. They seem more inclined to insult and slander than to debate. They, who are more obliged than anyone to restrain their passion and not act flippantly, have no problem forgetting a person's past in order to pile on unjust claims against them. For this reason, for the serious crime of opposing that our country becomes a Yankee protectorate, we are seen as members of a 'fifth column' and lumped with Hitler and even Stalin for helping to bring about an invasion of our nation.

The Dies Committee of the United States[21] – composed of a few ultra-reactionary senators advised by even worse sorts, all unconditional servants of the great Yankee monopolies – have put in motion a horrifying policy that makes a game of the previously mentioned accusations. The Dies committee says that the communists of Costa Rica and Colombia are working to bring down the current governments of those countries with the purpose of substituting them for others, hostile to the United States. Such version has as its objective the preparation of continental opinion in order to enable crimes and repression that the State Department undoubtedly launches in these countries against all those who oppose their plans to pillage. We should not forget that this Dies Committee is the same one that financed the candidacy of [Juan Andreu] Almazán in Mexico[22] and that is now trying to foment a bloody revolution in the great Aztec country, not with the objective of defending democracy, which is more than guaranteed with the presidency of General [Lázaro] Cárdenas, but rather to protect for the petroleum companies the fruits of their theft.

But let us leave these considerations aside and go deeper into the issue. Our thesis can be formulated by way of a question: Is there, actually, a risk that Latin America would be invaded by the Germans? Germany is committed to a war that will absorb it for various years, after which it will be exhausted; Germany has strong adversaries in Europe and Asia that it needs to defeat before it decides to cross the Atlantic to attempt an invasion of our continent. If the invasion of England, with the English

---

[21] Also known as the House Un-American Activities Committee (HUAC), this was a special investigative committee of the US House of Representatives formed in 1938 by Martin Dies, Jr, of Texas to investigate potential fascist or Communist sympathisers. It quickly became a weapon of domestic ideological warfare in the Cold War.

[22] Almazán fought with Emiliano Zapata's forces in the Mexican Revolution, but in 1940 he ran for president as a conservative with the support of businessmen and landowners in an election that was widely reported in Mexico and the United States. The results were so contested that yet another civil war threatened. Almazán purportedly led groups of protestors in the chant, 'Death to Ávila Camacho,' his opponent.

Channel between them, is so difficult for Germany, how can there be such extreme suspicion of the invasion of America, which does not have the English Channel separating [it] but rather the Atlantic Ocean? Where is the German fleet that could serve Hitler for such invasion? These are our reasons. Based on these reasons, we have come to be convinced that we are facing one of two situations: the United States is preparing itself for an offensive and not defensive war; or, pure and simple, it wants to take advantage of the global confusion to better consolidate its dominion over our continent through greater military and economic penetration. If our continent becomes threatened by a Nazi invasion, we agree that it should defend itself. But not if it is defended from Germany in order to leave it enchained to the tycoons of Wall Street; not to take it out of the flames to let it land on the embers. Now, if the United States wants to drag us into war that only interests them for some economic reason, we cannot agree to cooperate with them in such a crime; and if the question is what seems to be our transformation into a protectorate, our position is one of open struggle, regardless of the costs, against such an ambition. This is our proposition. Voices like that of George Washington were raised a long time ago to prevent a betrayal of the people's confidence through the 'altruistic' favours that foreign nations want to lend: 'It is necessary to never forget that one nation commits a great folly when it expects altruistic favours from others.' As can be seen, we are not relying on caprice but rather logical analysis. And what argument has risen in opposition to our reasoning? None. If it is said that we have to make concessions in order to defend the Continent, then it is necessary to demonstrate the possibility that the Continent will be attacked. And even more: one has to demonstrate that it is absolutely necessary that a nation such as ours surrender its sovereignty so that its defence can take place. But the only reason that has been given by the people who have brought us to this is: that imperialism is a spectre that only we see; that imperialism does not exist any more. At the root of this is ignorance of an economic phenomenon that has been studied even by authors on the right. Imperialism has not been forbidden to exist – such as affirms the omniscient Mr [Roberto] Brenes Mesén[23] – because the United States has signed some papers speaking of American fraternity and preaching respect for the rights of weaker nations. Papers are papers; and treaties, according to the famous phrase, are *'chiffon de papier'*.[24] The [world]

---

[23] Roberto Brenes Mesén (1874–1947) was an influential liberal journalist, poet, essayist, and educator who spent many decades of his career at universities across the US.

[24] Scrap paper. French in the original.

powers overlook treaties when they find it convenient to do so. Has the all-knowing Mr Roberto [Brenes Mesén] not noticed this? What guarantee can a piece of paper signed by some Yankee diplomats be for us? Meanwhile, in the United States where there are massive monopolies in need of markets and raw materials, [US President Calvin] Coolidge's phrase must be fulfilled: 'behind every Yankee dollar, there is a Yankee bayonet.' Governments move much quicker than large economic interests. The large monopolies, when they need to, push these respective governments towards 'the big stick' or they overthrow these governments if they neglect to obey them. The large Yankee monopolies need our continent to be a protectorate of the United States so that when the war ends, all competition, which up until now had been a product of European imperialism such as that of Great Britain, is definitively eliminated. Whoever doubts this should read the last bulletin of the National Bank of the City of New York. Thus, so long as there are big monopolies like these in North America, imperialism will continue being a reality despite Roberto Brenes Mesén and all men of his viewpoint, who live by composing verses to the stars, and ignoring or feigning ignorance of what occurs on the surface of the planet.

If there are still some who doubt what has been said, I find it relevant to call attention to what has befallen President [Franklin D.] Roosevelt: he has been forced by imperialism to shift his domestic and foreign policies. The Roosevelt who we are seeing today act with his gaze on re-election is not the Roosevelt who we have known before. This Roosevelt certainly thought very differently from, in terms of imperialism, certain Costa Rican citizens who are turning out to be more Papist than the Pope himself. Let us listen, to conclude this article, to what Roosevelt said on 28 December 1933 in a famous speech delivered at the 'Woodrow Wilson Foundation': 'I do not hesitate to say that if I had taken part in the political campaign of any other American republic, I would have been tempted to accuse the United States of imperialist tendencies with aims of selfish expansionism. As a citizen of any other republic, I would have found it very difficult to believe in the altruism of the richest American republic. In particular, it would have seemed difficult to approve of the occupation, even as a temporary measure, of territory in Latin American republics.'

'Imperialism Consists Above All of Economic Activity'

In my previous article I wanted to give a general overview of our conception of the European conflict and its possible repercussions in our continent. Now I believe it is necessary to clarify some of the erroneous conceptions that remain in our midst and impede the understanding of our proposal. I will speak first about the term 'imperialism'.

[...]

Imperialism is not a demagogic theory; it is a scientific theory. The theory of imperialism does not rest on passionate caprices, but on statistics that reflect economic reality. Mr Brenes Mesén could find the first proof of this by flipping through any Encyclopaedia; and second, by studying Political Economy. There is no serious economist who does not study – though each one does so from their own point of view – the economic process that has been classified as imperialism. And of what does this process consist? In the following: the concentration of capital, in industry as well as in agriculture, is a law of the capitalist system. Every day, wealth is concentrated in fewer hands, impoverishing the weakest producers. This is how monopolies in the great capitalist countries have been formed. 'Cartels', 'consortiums or syndicates', 'trusts', and finally 'konzerns' appeared, organisations in which diverse companies from different branches of industry and commerce are grouped, under the direction of large monopolist banks. There are admirable and eloquent statistics about these enormous concentrations of capital in the more advanced countries, not prepared by people of the left but rather by [social] scientists of the liberal school and by the engineers of the League of Nations. There are disagreements in the explanation of the phenomenon, but not in its existence. Mr Brenes said that the new Frankenstein scared the world from 1898 to 1913.[25] This is an imprecise assertion. The real process of capitalist evolution that culminated in imperialism is this: 1860–1870, a free market remains and monopolies begin to form; 1873, crisis in Europe, important development in the 'cartels' is observed. After this comes a period of prosperity that ends in a cyclical crisis (1900–1903). In this moment the cartels become the foundation of all European economic life and it is then that capitalism becomes imperialism. Why? The phenomenon can be explained in a few words: the large industrial nations outperform national markets and have enormous merchandise surpluses that they need to sell in foreign markets; more, colossal development of industries demands an ever-greater quantity of raw material, which the capitalists have to seek out and find wherever it may be; and lastly, from the link between banking

---

[25] This is a reference to a comment made by Brenes Mesén; purportedly, he said 'Frankenstein's new monster has died,' referring to the death of North American imperialism after two pan-American conferences. Mora Valverde disagrees, of course.

capital and industry, the exportation of finance capital arises; and all of this together results in fierce competition between the huge capitalists of the different countries. They fight for markets, for colonies, for opportune environments for their investments. And the capitalists do not act alone in this; they act with the support of their respective governments, who create militaries for what they call 'the defence of the national interests abroad'. This is imperialism. The backward continents are split up amongst the powerful capitalists; the weak nations, subjugated. It is a struggle to the death between these powers to secure their share of the wealth of the world.

In 1902, the English economist J. A. Hobson published a book in London that he called 'imperialism' [sic], in which he studied the same economic phenomenon that I have just sketched. In it he notes that imperialism 'entails the use of the machinery of government for particular, particularly capitalist, interests to attain economic gains outside of the country'. The North American economist W. S. Culberston [sic] says that imperialism is 'the economic expression of civilization beyond the oceans'. The English writer Lilliam C. Knowles [sic], in a book titled *Economic Development of the British Overseas Empire*, studied the imperialist phenomenon and reached the same conclusions as the above.[26] I make these citations so that it is clear that imperialism is not how Mr Roberto [Brenes Mesén] describes it, a fantasy, created recently; but rather it is an economic phenomenon [that is part] of capitalist society studied by men of science without links to Marxism for a long time, since the time when [Victor] Haya de la Torre, who Mr Roberto [Brenes Mesén] cites, was probably a child.[27]

I find interesting to cite here some well-known phrases that the famous English millionaire Cecil Rhodes spoke in 1895 to his friend, the journalist [William Thomas] Stead, to further clarify what I have said. They are: 'Yesterday I was in London's East End (working-class neighbourhood) and I attended an assembly of the unemployed. Upon

---

[26] When Knowles died in 1926, having published just the first volume of her study, her husband completed the remaining two volumes, which provide comparative histories of India, Malaya, Nigeria, Kenya, Uganda, Canada, South Africa, and Australia.

[27] Victor Haya de la Torre was a student leader in Peru in the 1910s and was instrumental to bringing the reforms of the 1918 Córdoba student movement to the National University of San Marcos. Haya de la Torre went on to found a workers' night school, motivated by many of the factors raised by others throughout this chapter. He is most famous for founding the American Popular Revolutionary Alliance (APRA) in 1924. APRA, a pan-American, anti-imperialist party, continues today, although its ideology has shifted over time.

hearing, in said reunion, the impassioned speeches whose dominant note was: bread, bread, bread!, and after reflecting on what I had heard on my way home, I became more than ever convinced of the importance of imperialism. I am intimately convinced that my idea represents the solution to social problems, to knowledge: to save the forty million inhabitants of the United Kingdom from a terrible civil war, we, the colonial politicians, should conquer new territories to place in them the excess population, to acquire new spheres for the selling of our goods, produced in the factories and mines. The empire, I have always said, is a question of the gut. If you do not want civil war, you must become an imperialist.'[28] And this English millionaire Cecil Rhodes, went on to be the principal booster of the imperialist war of England against the Boers. I think that it is now very clear why the large capitalists, obliged by their own economic development, find it necessary to launch wars of conquest and to intervene in small nations by all means at their disposal.

For us, imperialism does not consist exclusively of military action. It consists above all of economic activity. Yankee imperialism, for example, has been for us a force that transformed our Atlantic zone into a desert and took all the millions it produced here to Boston, leaving nothing for our people. Yankee imperialism has been the power that helped our Pacific coasts, an emporium of riches, to be similarly exploited by the United [Fruit Company] in exchange for a plate of beans. Imperialism is the art by which the Electric Bond and Share [Company] takes two million *colones* a year from the country, free and clear, money that we sorely need to construct roads and to help our farmers produce wealth. Imperialism is the force that prevents Costa Rica from having its own industries, so that our country can continue to be a market for Yankee industry. Imperialism is the force that prevents Costa Rica from producing wheat because this is not agreeable to the large mills of the United States. Imperialism is the force that prevents the development of an industrious spirit in our nation to the disadvantage of our farmers and with the aim that this spirit does not create competition with the Yankee petroleum companies that sell us petrol. Imperialism is the force that has made us sign a commercial treaty that has endangered our English coffee markets and taken from us the freedom to manage our own customs duties in the manner necessary for our nation's economic development.

---

[28] Mora Valverde is essentially reprinting a passage quoted by Vladimir Ilyich Ulyanov (Lenin) in *Imperialism, the Highest Stage of Capitalism*. Mora Valverde does not cite this text, indicating that he read Lenin closely and anticipated that his audience probably did not.

Imperialism is the greatest *ukaz*[29] ever known, [and] says that our nation cannot produce items that are produced in the United States, demanding instead that we dedicate ourselves to the cultivation to rubber, bananas, and other raw materials they need. These raw materials will be extracted from our soil by 'humanitarian' companies such as United [Fruit Company]. Imperialism, finally, is a force that, in its eagerness to consolidate its economic dominion in the world, is going to destroy our sovereignty and seize our seas and our coasts to construct military bases. And [this] in exchange for nothing, because, according to president Calderón Guardia, 'national dignity' demands it.

[. . .]

Our America is part of this plunder. Years ago in our continent, England was a competitor, a dangerous one, to the United States. In 1913, Great Britain had investments in Latin America totalling 4,984 million dollars while the United States had barely 1,242 [million dollars]. In 1929 England had reached 5,891 million [dollars] and the United States, 5,587 [million dollars]. What is it that is happening now? The United States is taking advantage of the war in Europe to supplant all of its competitors and take control of all of the loot. What else is happening? The United States is preparing to militarise us and force us, in an opportune moment, to help them defend their treasures, of which we ourselves are a part, with our blood and with our sovereignty. Are these fantasies? Is this an illusion that makes us see a Frankenstein that does not exist? He who affirms this is wrong. Meanwhile the United States has the economic organisation that it does, [so] it will find itself forced to maintain its dominion over our continent, a disgraceful and shameful dominion and deepened by our own weakness and cowardice.

Translated by Jorge Cuéllar

HONDURAS

Jorge Fidel Durón, 'Function of the University'

(1949)

Unlike most of the texts in this chapter, this brief article from the official newspaper of the National University of Honduras, *Revista de la Universidad*, was written by a faculty member and administrator. Jorge

---

[29] A proclamation with the force of law made by the tsar in Imperial Russia.

Fidel Durón served as Rector of the university from 1949 to 1954, a period when the National University did not enjoy autonomy and the government oversaw the affairs of the faculty. At the end of Durón's term as Rector, three Congressional deputies proposed a decree that would confer autonomy on the university. Durón supported the decree and Congressional approval seemed likely, but then was delayed because Supreme Head of State Julio Lozano Díaz refused to validate the results of the vote. In fact, Lozano had declared himself president in 1954 when the elected President, Juan Manuel Gálvez, whose presidency had ended the sixteen-year dictatorship of Carías, was out of the country for medical treatment. In the context of such turmoil, university autonomy was delayed. Durón only served as Minister of Education until July 1957, but in this short time he expanded public education by founding two secondary education schools for teacher training and developed radio-based literacy programmes. The article below reveals some of Durón's political philosophy of education, which undoubtedly informed his actions as Minister.

With every dawn we mortals are witness to an illuminating spectacle: the birth of a new day of renewed opportunities. Knowledge of the sciences, of letters, and of the arts is what helps us to appreciate the value of these opportunities. And this knowledge is what gives us confidence in the basic idea that, if we want, we can have a healthy *pueblo*, enjoy a prosperous economy, and learn to conserve and defend those indispensable natural resources of our national wealth. How? We must start from the beginning: educating ourselves. Elementary education is as essential as professional education. The first lesson consists of learning, exactly, with certainty, what, in truth, we want to make of ourselves, what we really want to be. And, despite what Mr Miguel de Unamuno[30] identified as 'the unknowable purpose of the universe', to discover and arrive at a goal that takes us away from our present *contented uncertainty*. I confess that is it not easy and, perhaps, what has made it less easy is our past attitude. However, we must try and right now is as good a time as any.

What conditions are we going to demand of the average university student, since [our] mission is both research-oriented and pedagogical, as Agustín Nieto Caballero[31] said well, not content with merely

---

[30] Prolific Spanish existentialist philosopher, essayist, poet, and academic. His most influential work is *Tragic Sense of Life* (first published in English in 1921).

[31] Durón's contemporary, Agustín Nieto Caballero, a Colombian educator and dilettante.

instructing but having the desire to educate? James Killian[32] of the Massachusetts Institute of Technology [MIT] enumerates some of the key elements: he speaks of the need to create a sense of the importance of our daily tasks, to stimulate the spirit of adventure that should prevail in all of our actions, to develop self-confidence, to satisfy the unwavering virtue of inquiry and exploration, to strengthen moral valour, the courageous heart, unbreakable faith and patience, a vision that allows us to see beyond our petty individual ambition. Because, as noted by the Colombian previously mentioned, if these sentiments do not guard and guide the path of the Alma Mater, we do not know if they will do so outside of the classroom in the open field in which men fight in a selfish and ruthless manner in order to make a living. [Ralph Waldo] Emerson has already advised the youth not to renounce its ideals and ambitions for simple comforts and premature securities.

I said it is not easy, but we can try. And because we have to begin at some point and from some position, the University, with the help and cooperation of its conscientious elements, is outlining a programme in order to assume its role in the great crusade to follow through on the sensitive half-century-long task that can no longer permit delay or chicanery. Without getting caught up in recriminations of the past, which are already history and, as such, barely have the importance of a memory and, of course, absolutely no basis for the work of the future, rather like a trampoline for new ventures, it is necessary for us to start writing new pages wherein we take into account only the achievements or successes of the past.

There is another timely thought from Emerson that says: 'Why renounce your right to traverse the star-lit deserts of truth, for the pleasure of premature comforts?' Here there is a true challenge that our university youth can rightly accept for a close encounter with the economic and social reality of our time. This challenge is interesting because it includes a moment when one can participate in the formation of our true nationalism. As we know, this is not new. Many have said and repeated it before. The fact is that, just as Schopenhauer's maxim speaks of 'living dangerously', the renunciation that is suggested by Emerson offers the opportunity for adventure, for exercising the imagination, to look beyond our trivial personal ambitions.

---

[32] James Rhyne Killian, Jr (1904–88), was then president of MIT.

Putting aside narrow and insignificant politics, avoiding the possible obstacle of those who, like the character of Benjamin Franklin, had an axe to grind, it would be tremendously attractive to set in motion a programme that offers our university students substantial participation in the approach that we propose. Henry Ford, the industrial magnate, the ex-governor Earle, politician of Pennsylvania, and others were pioneers of a movement that, gradually, brought the employer and the worker closer, it made workers responsible for the fortune of the industries that employed them. And, though these [innovations] did not eliminate worker–employer conflicts, there were far fewer social struggles in their plants and factories at the time.

Of course, it is understood that for this, a higher level of culture is needed. But the University is in a position to offer it, providing a vocational general education for the study of our fundamental problems. And this [higher] level is reached when the university youth, listening to the words of Emerson, become responsible for the individual and collective role they have to play in the daily life that begins with every dawn. Our modern university student has to understand that with the Alma Mater's obligation to educate and instruct him, to show him how to live and make a living in a democracy, there is a parallel obligation to understand in depth the way in which he lives, his tradition, his history, his needs, and his problems. But this is not enough: Nieto Caballero says that all this will be useless without an unselfish standard of living, without honest principles, without professional morals, without ideals that bring decency into being. Ultimately, this is the principal contribution that the university student should make to our University.

The modern *universitario* has to keep in mind that, along with the obligation of the University to prepare and equip him for life scientifically, so that he can participate in the constructive activities of the everyday life of the world in which he lives, there is his own obligation to employ and apply the acquired insights not only for personal benefit but also, even [making] a personal sacrifice, for the sake of greater dissemination of his science, for the benefit of his *pueblo*, with the highest standards of conduct and dignity it merits. Because knowledge, the sciences, letters and arts, liberal professions should help, moreover, to augment the moral stature of the citizen, his spiritual attitude. It is the responsibility of the student, in his dual role of student and citizen, to model this quality by sowing higher ideals among the masses.

As Jaime Benitez, Director of the University of Puerto Rico, says, 'the biggest problems of humanity are never definitively resolved.' If they were, this would be the most boring of worlds. However, little by little we approach a similar realisation. In the same way the French lecturer André Castel might explain, the French Revolution of 1789 barely served to establish the foundations of liberty, equality, and fraternity, having managed the first step. It was in the 1848 revolution that France achieved political equality. Thus we, with these and other plans, will march toward the desired goal, toward real progress, toward the enrichment of Honduras.

Translated by Jorge Cuéllar and Heather Vrana

Jorge St. Siegens, 'Cooperativism in Honduras'

(1950)

In the administration's official *Revista de la Universidad*, Technical Director of the *Facultad* of Economics Sciences Jorge St. Siegens wrote about the particular challenge facing the Honduran economy: dependency on exports. Rather than argue against imperialism, St. Siegens argued that if Honduras were to become less dependent upon exports, it would enjoy greater sovereignty, its citizens would experience more prosperity, and, in a word, the nation would become more advanced. He called for a national economy built on democratic cooperatives and nationalised banks, and argued that Honduras could emerge from its 'economic backwardness' if its wealth of natural resources were combined with technical and financial capacity, provided from abroad. At the same time, he insisted on Hondurans' capabilities, writing, 'what is also important is the confidence of the Honduran people in their economic capacity and in their intellectual and physical aptitude that, on average, are not any worse than the majority of the people of the globe.' In this and other work, St. Siegens drew on local case studies and cited theorists from Peru, Colombia, Italy, and England, developing a position that would become one of Latin America's greatest intellectual exports: development theory.

The socioeconomic problem in Honduras resides in the fact that the country is very rich; meanwhile the people, in general, are very poor. This is a phenomenon and common feature of many economically backward countries. Every Honduran should be aware of this situation, but they should also understand, equally, that this fatalism, which has dominated the life and activities of the Honduran people since the inception of their existence, is not an absolute truth and should not be eternal.

Almost every nation and every country began its economic, social, and cultural development under the same despair.

There is no reason whatsoever that Honduras and the Honduran people should not attain, in a relatively short time, a standard of living and a socioeconomic level superior to the present one.

Nature has endowed this country with an abundance of natural resources, a rare find in many other countries of the world.

In addition to gold and silver, there are mineral resources that are sought the world over in both internal and foreign markets. There are carbon and steel deposits, bauxite, which is used for the production of aluminium, and, probably, petroleum as well. There are extensive forests with precious wood and fertile soil more than adequate to enable agricultural production that satisfies not only increased internal consumption, but also, at satisfactory prices, the growing demands of foreign markets.

What is still missing and impedes more effective exploitation and valuation of the natural riches in the country is, without a doubt, the capital and the technical knowledge that will necessarily be introduced from abroad in large part. But what is also important is the confidence of the Honduran people in their economic capacity and in their intellectual and physical aptitude, which on average, are not any worse than the majority of the people of the globe. To self-confidence and economic capacity we should add the conscious will of the Honduran people to improve their lives and take advantage of everything this land has to offer.

The key to all national activity in the economic realm is *organisation*.

Without organisation one cannot work economically nor achieve economic success, no matter how plentiful the natural resources.

The national economy of this country, without question, is not yet organised. The task is neither easy nor brief because it involves:

1) A large and intense pursuit of technical–scientific research on the soils, on natural resources, on the distribution of riches, on the colonisation of unpopulated and abandoned territories, on highways, on

the mechanisation of the means of production, on the most adequate methods and productive elements, etc.;

2) A study on the extent and the form of participation and foreign investment; and

3) Serious education and preparation of the human element.

Now, on the part of the State, some organisation has begun in one of the more important branches of the national economy. We have a Central Bank that organises and watches over the banking system in general and a credit and monetary policy in particular. We have, in addition, the National Development Bank, whose activity extends to all those areas of production that need technical and economic assistance on behalf of the State. And the government is preparing and, in part, already employing a full set of measures that, on the whole, serve the organisation of the national economy. There should be no doubt whatsoever that the results of these efforts on behalf of the State will be a success, from economic and social points of view.

But the task of the economic organisation of a country is much too large to be carried out solely by the State and its dependencies. All of the people, the whole of the producers and distributors, both large and small, rich and poor, should contribute, as well, all of their means, intellectual aptitudes, and materials to the fulfilment of this national task.

The basic form for such an effort and organisation on part of the Honduran people could be *cooperativism*.

The cooperative system that bases itself on the factors of *man and his aptitudes*, more than any other system of organisation and economic cooperation, has proven and demonstrated its worth and economic and social importance in all of those countries of the world in which it encountered society's understanding and the State's moral, legal, and material support.

In order to demonstrate more clearly the enhancement that cooperativism could give to the economic, social, and cultural development of the country, it behoves us to present here the principles that govern the organic structure of a genuine cooperative:

1) The cooperative joins people through the voluntary adhesion of different social classes and makes no distinction or discrimination according to race, nationality, and religious or political beliefs. This

principle guarantees the freedom of the individual and promotes fraternity, harmony, and social solidarity.

2) The regime that governs the cooperative is truly democratic. In its assemblies and deliberations, every member has only one vote, which does not take into consideration his social position nor his material situation, or financial contribution or obligations. This principle protects parity among members and does not allow for the predominance of capital or of social privilege.

3) The economic aim of the cooperative is to render services and mutual aid, not profit. The financial surplus generated is distributed amongst all members in accordance with the fair contribution of each in the achievement of the profits. This principle establishes a comprehensive redistribution of wealth.

4) The capital that is provided by members is specified in binding documents and is of a fixed value that is not subject to the fluctuations of the market in capital and value;

5) The cooperative is not aimed at initiating competition with extant trade organisations, nor does it replace or displace other institutions of public utility and convenience;

6) The cooperative system educates its members in the healthy habit of saving, stimulating, at the same time, [investing] the return on these investments in the production process in a healthy and advantageous way, for the benefit of the [cooperative] member himself and of the national economy in general;

7) The cooperative most effectively contributes to the professional, cultural, and social education of the people, putting at the disposal of youth and adults of meagre resources the means that allow them to contribute to the economic and cultural progress of their communities.

Today, Cooperativism presents an unprecedented economic and social force.

Genuine cooperatives are groups that benefit the development of a healthy democracy in all aspects of human activity, establishing a just and comprehensive distribution of wealth and stimulating the efforts of its members toward the resolution of problems that inhibit the improvement of quality of life.

The cooperative can be, in each community where it is established according to the proposed fundamentals of true cooperativism, a social and cultural centre where all members can gather not only to solve the problems of their small society, but also to study and discuss those vital problems of the nation that in turn speak to the possibilities of a better world, stripped of all unhealthy individualism.

Very rightly so, the illustrious Italian cooperativist Viquenó could say: 'Cooperativism is a holy society that has produced incredible assets for the community and that holds in its bosom the solution to present and future problems.'

'Rochale's store'[33] [sic], says the Peruvian engineer Alejandro McLean y Estenós, 'contains in its embryo a great cooperative movement of our time, which is at the same time the embryo of a new economy destined to transform the entire economy.'

The study of statistical data regarding the development of cooperativism clearly shows us that the cooperative movement actually includes all of the [necessary] requirements to make of it the economic and social organisation of the future.

Taking into consideration all of this and comparing it to the present situation of Honduras and other countries who find themselves in the same, or in similar, conditions or difficulties in terms of their economic organisation, we believe there is no better solution for the economic and social organisation of this country than cooperativism.

United in a genuine cooperative, the small Honduran producer who represents the majority of the *pueblo* will contribute successfully and efficaciously to a better organisation of national production and will enjoy technical and economic assistance, of which, individually, one can rarely take advantage.

We know that the National Development Bank is bound by law and by reason to a sane credit policy, giving loans only to those in whom it finds sufficient guarantee. Very rarely will a single individual offer such security; but the cooperative to which he belongs could present a sufficient factor of guarantee.

Through his cooperative, the small producer could utilise the machinery, the instruments, the tools of labour, and the systems acquired by his cooperative with the help of the National Development Bank, making capital investment in production equipment unnecessary, which the small producer uses only on a reduced scale and during a shorter period of time. The cooperative also gives him, through the National Development Bank, technical aid so that he can expand his production in a way that is more fulfilling for him than before.

He shall, thus, better cultivate his plot of land, planting seeds of better

---

[33] This is a misspelling of Rochdale's store, which is discussed at length later in the text.

quality, utilising compost and fertilisers, machines and modern tools, without being required to involve himself to the very limit of his finances in unsustainable debts imposed by merchants and unscrupulous lenders.

Okay, how can we better proceed in order to introduce and promote a cooperative system, which appears to be both convenient and opportune for national economic organisation, in this country?

In a country like Honduras all action of public interest must begin with the State. The incentive of the State should manifest itself in a concrete and methodical form. For such purposes, cooperativism needs legislation that assures its right to act with complete freedom and autonomy in the management of its internal affairs, and above all, economic and technical aid. Economic aid should include preferential loans and credits offered by the National Development Bank and, additionally, a series of tax concessions like those given to any other public institution. Such help is justified, plainly, because the cooperative movement is born, as we have said, from economically weak groups.

The regulations in the Commercial Code, in the seventh chapter about cooperative societies, neglect those elements that are the most important catalysts of cooperative movements. For this reason, there is an absolute need to complete and expand the regulations of the Code of Commerce for a *special law of cooperative societies* or rather for an *organic and expansive regulation* of the proposed provisions of Chapter 7.

The basic problem, upon initiating and disseminating cooperativism in Honduras, is what is referred to as education.

In this respect, it is beneficial to proclaim that cooperative education is not limited to learning by memorising what could be called the mechanics of doctrinal cooperativism. The modern concept of cooperativism seeks to extend its meaning in a broader sense. Cooperative education aspires to create conscious individuals [who are] honest, masters of their own destiny, and who, by continuous and intelligent participation among the membership, strengthen democratic functions and contribute in this way to the perfection of human relations and the moral, social, and cultural transformation of the *pueblo*. In this way [cooperativism] can become a progressive force in the service of the nation in particular and humanity in general.

Since the founding of the first cooperative of weavers in Rochdale (1844), education has been a key to the progress and success of the cooperative movement. The weavers of Rochdale did not have as their only end the economic prosperity of their society; rather they tried to combat the factors that up until then had impeded the weaver classes from receiving an adequate education. A historical occurrence came to pass in 1852 when one of its members proposed that 2½% of its savings would be used to develop a solid educational campaign. The proposal was unanimously approved and since then has been known by the name the 'Golden Rule' of cooperativism. Education and cooperation have come, therefore, to form inseparable parts of the whole that harmoniously makes up the doctrine of cooperativism.

As Fernando Chávez Núñez, the distinguished Colombian cooperativist, says: 'To betray the pioneering thought of Rochdale would be to ignore that the objective that singularly animated them was to achieve, by means of education, the economic and social betterment of those affiliated with their society. They considered education as the noblest and highest aim. They sought to destroy the harmful manifestations of mercantilism that had turned profit-making into the ideal of all individuals; they fought tirelessly to create in man a new psychological aptitude wherein the desire for profit would be substituted by mutual aid, tolerance, equality, and sacrifice; in sum, they revived a moral code already extant in the nature of man, but that mercantilist practices had violated. This code seeks to re-educate man and contribute, as a result, to the perfection of human relationships.'

The solidity and strength of the whole cooperative is, without a doubt, the direct result of the favourable conditions offered by the way in which it operates and by the economic and technical aid of the State; but above all, by the education and instruction that are cultivated by members of the cooperative among themselves.

If these objectives are achieved, cooperativism will find in Honduras great and decisive strength for the prosperity of national culture and economy.

Tegucigalpa, 11 August 1950

Translated by Jorge Cuéllar and Heather Vrana

Works Cited

Bowman, Kirk (2009), 'Democracy on the Brink: The First Figueres Presidency', in Steven Palmer and Iván Molina, eds (2009), *The Costa Rican Reader: History, Culture, Politics*, Durham, NC: Duke University Press, pp. 175–82.

Knowles, L. C. A. and C. M. Knowles (1936), *The Economic Development of the British Overseas Empire*, Vols 1–3, London: Routledge.

Molina, Iván (2009), 'The Polarization of Politics, 1932–1948', in Steven Palmer and Iván Molina, eds (2009), *The Costa Rican Reader: History, Culture, Politics*, Durham, NC: Duke University Press, 163–9.

Walter, Knut (2000), *The Regime of Anastasio Somoza, 1936–1956*, Chapel Hill: University of North Carolina Press.

Chapter 2
Enduring Militarism 1952–1960

Introduction

Despite a brief popular resurgence in the mid-1940s, Central American militaries proved resilient. The 1950s saw new military leaders take executive power. The US State Department and business interests like UFCO seemed willing to resort to any means necessary to ensure the endurance of their political and economic influence in the region. The global Cold War fuelled feverish millenarian anti-communism, whose effects were most obvious in Guatemala, though workers' and student movements in El Salvador, Nicaragua, and Honduras also suffered repression at the hands of anti-communists. Given the limitations of political freedoms throughout the region, university autonomy became an important touchstone for free expression. Its implication of the territorial sovereignty of campus buildings and classrooms safeguarded some space for free speech and opposition. Occasionally, students paid for this free speech with their lives. At the same time as political expression was violently circumscribed, the region experienced consistent economic growth fuelled by export agriculture. This growth permitted the expansion of infrastructural projects and some modest social reforms. Ultimately, these reforms helped to improve the image of military dictators, who sought to hold on to power despite growing unrest among working and middle classes, including university students.

By 1952, the enthusiasm for the revolution that had united many Guatemalans during the presidency of Juan José Arévalo had dissolved into political fractiousness. In part this was owed to the differences between Arévalo and his successor, Jacobo Arbenz. Where Arévalo had focused on education, Arbenz emphasised the economy and land reform. He alarmed domestic and North American business sectors when he included a known member of the Guatemalan Communist Party (PGT),

José Manuel Fortuny, among his most trusted advisors. Arbenz further alienated these groups with his 1952 Agrarian Reform Act, which mandated the expropriation of fallow lands and large land-holdings. It had an especially harmful effect on UFCO, which was reimbursed for $600,000 (the value of the land as appraised by the company for tax purposes) for its expropriated land, though the company later valued these lands at around $15 million. Historians Héctor Pérez-Brignoli and James Dunkerley have pointed out that Arbenz's reform was based on recommendations made by the International Bank for Reconstruction and Development (IBRD), a predecessor of the World Bank, which seemed of little consequence to its detractors. Anti-communists, some motivated by denunciations from Catholic Archbishop Mariano Rossell y Arellano and others by the threat posed by Arbenz's reforms, began to organise in neighbourhood and university groups. The most prominent of these was the Committee of Anti-communist University Students (CEUA), which formed at USAC in 1952. Many of its members were soon exiled to Tegucigalpa, where they formed the Committee of Guatemalan Anti-communist University Students in Exile (CEUAGE). The first two texts below come from these two anti-communist student groups.

On 27 June 1954, a small militia called the Army of the Liberation, commanded by Carlos Castillo Armas, succeeded in toppling the Arbenz government. Historians disagree about the causes of the counter-revolution, but commonly cite external factors like the global Cold War and business interests, alongside internal factors like the very environment of free thought enabled by the revolutionary governments. After a plebiscite in October, Castillo Armas became president. His government was largely run on the principles outlined in the *Plan de Tegucigalpa*, written by the CEUA and excerpted below. The last two Guatemalan texts, an article from *El Estudiante* and the letter from the Association of Law Students, provide a clear picture of the growing opposition to Castillo Armas, revealing how some university students viewed Cold War politics as yet another colonial incursion. Castillo Armas was assassinated in 1957, leading to a brief period of political instability. When credible elections were held, another military man named Manuel Ydígoras Fuentes (1895–1982) was declared the winner. University students were at first quite hopeful about the Ydígoras Fuentes presidency but were quickly disappointed, as the final Guatemalan text makes clear.

In El Salvador, the optimism sparked by the overthrow of Hernández Martínez in May 1944 was even more short-lived. First, not long after the overthrow, former president and brigadier general Andrés I.

Menéndez stepped in to lead a provisional government. Then, police chief Osmín Aguirre Salinas cut short the push for elections, as Paul D. Almeida notes, by re-establishing the dictatorship in October. Not even six months after its collapse, the dictatorship had been reinstated. General Salvador Castaneda Castro was elected president in January 1945 and immediately began a campaign of repression against labour and student organisations that continued until he was deposed in December 1948. Limited reforms, including expanded social security and public health programmes and women's suffrage, were passed during the 1950s under yet another military presidency, this time led by Colonel Oscar Osorio. A mid-century boom in coffee exports permitted some industrial growth and agricultural diversification, which helped to finance these new programmes. Nevertheless, the benefits of this boom failed to transform in a meaningful way the conditions faced by many workers in an environment that remained vehemently anti-union. Control over the country would remain more or less firmly in the hands of the military until October 1979. Intellectual life suffered for this lack of free expression. Yet despite the risk, students of the AGEUS spoke out against the region's military governments. The texts below demonstrate the emergence of a Salvadoran student identity crafted in opposition to the ceaseless ascendance of military presidents.

In Nicaragua, the Somoza family's rule remained steadfast. The National Guard and all other government and military entities were squarely in support of the regime, so Somoza did not fall prey to revolutions from within the ranks, as did his counterparts. The reasons for his ability to maintain power are outlined at length by Victoria González-Rivera and Jeffrey L. Gould, but most importantly here, this stability enabled economic growth, especially in cotton, mineral mining, and agricultural exports, which in turn permitted – and demanded – the development of national infrastructure. Citizens benefited from improved roads, rail lines, and communication networks, but the profits from them most benefited the Somoza family, which owned timber, mining, and textile companies, sugar mills, the national airlines, a large dairy, and other industries. Then in 1956, a somewhat obscure poet named Rigoberto López Pérez assassinated the President. Anti-Somoza students celebrated López Pérez's bravery. So did students in neighbouring El Salvador, as the letter from the AGEUS demonstrates. Yet the dramatic action failed to topple the Somoza dynasty when Somoza's eldest son, Luis Somoza Debayle, assumed power as president and his younger son, Anastasio Somoza Debayle, came to lead the National Guard. Two years later, the National University won autonomy, paradoxically on the grounds that the university should be a place entirely free from politics and focused instead on scholarship. Nicaraguan students used this marginal political freedom as a space from which to express their opposition to the Somozas. Other anti-Somoza sectors had also started to organise. Inspired by the recent success of the Cuban Revolution, some began to think about a guerrilla war against the Somoza regime.

Several short-lived student groups, formed at the National University (UNAN) in the late 1950s, became the basis of what would slowly develop into a victorious revolutionary force. First as students, and later as comrades, Carlos Fonseca, Silvio Mayorga, Tomás Borge, Fernando Gordillo, Jorge Navarro, and Francisco Buitrago travelled between the university city of León and exile in Costa Rica, Venezuela, and Cuba to organise anti-Somoza actions. An early defeat at El Chaparral in June 1959, where combined forces of the Nicaraguan National Guard and Honduran army ambushed the combatants, resulted in six dead, four wounded, and more than a dozen taken prisoner. This tempered but did not extinguish their fervour. In León, students organised a protest against the actions of the National Guard. The National Guard responded by opening fire on the protestors. In her close study of Carlos Fonseca, entitled *Sandinista*, Matilde Zimmerman emphasises how these events have been remembered as a bloodthirsty attack on peaceful students and, more broadly, as a symbol of the regime's war against freedom of thought. This tragic cycle of resistance and reaction would repeat for the next two decades. But the Somozas also employed other tactics to defuse anti-Somoza sentiment at UNAN. For instance, the Somoza family backed the foundation of a new private Jesuit university in Managua in 1960, the Central American University (UCA), built on Somoza-owned land and led by a member of the Somoza family. Again, according to Zimmerman, Fonseca's group published its first communiqués under the name the 'Sandinista National Liberation Front' the following year, invoking the name of Augusto Sandino, celebrated folk hero and leader of the rebellion against US occupation from 1927 to 1934.

Somoza's Honduran counterpart, Tiburcio Carías, had lost his verve for strong-armed rule and agreed to permit elections in October 1948. His hand-picked successor, Dr Juan Manuel Gálvez, won the election. Gálvez, a graduate of the National University's Law School, had worked as an UFCO lawyer before accepting a cabinet position in the Carías government. Given this background, it was unexpected that Gálvez would institute progressive reforms, but he did, including establishing freedom of the press and passing multiple labour reforms like eight-hour workdays, paid holidays, and regulations on child labour. Like Osorio in El Salvador, Gálvez took advantage of favourable global markets in coffee and bananas to generate profits. These profits helped to reduce the national debt and finance infrastructural development. As president, Gálvez was often caught between the needs of the nation and those of transnational business: in 1949, he renegotiated contracts with UFCO for better terms for Honduran workers. At the same time, he aided Guatemalan counter-revolutionary forces, offering safe haven for anti-communists and the Castillo Armas Liberation Army, perhaps under pressure from UFCO. When UFCO banana workers went on strike in 1954, Gálvez conceded to the workers' demands; however, it was widely believed that he did so in order to preserve his international reputation, because UFCO's control over national politics had become something of an open secret.

Carías proved reluctant to relinquish power and in 1954 again declared his desire to run for president. In protest, some members of his National Party split off and formed the National Reformist Movement. Matters devolved quickly. The Liberal candidate, Dr José Ramón Adolfo Villeda Morales, secured a plurality of the vote but Congress was empowered to select the winner. Although they usually chose the candidate who had won the plurality, its members refused to elect Villeda (Carías partisans retained control over Congress). In the midst of this deadlock, Gálvez's Vice-president, Julio Lozano Díaz, launched a coup and instituted another short-lived dictatorship, which was soon toppled by yet another military junta. Facing international pressure, this military junta permitted free and open elections for a Constituent Assembly, which ultimately re-elected Villeda to the presidency. As president, Villeda was a moderate who, like so many of his reformist contemporaries, prioritised a model of growth based on foreign extraction, investment, and export. In 1961, he implemented many of the programme recommendations of US President John F. Kennedy's Alliance for Progress. The documents below outline the legislative process by which the National University finally attained autonomy in 1959 in the midst of the national political turmoil described here. Like their peers in Nicaragua and Guatemala, Honduran university students would use the protection of autonomy to oppose UFCO and the Alliance for Progress, linking them to long histories of colonialism.

The texts below display the range of attitudes among students toward the anti-communist military governments that dominated the region during this period. For some students, anti-communism secured democracy from fascist and communist threat; for others, anti-communism was simply another foreign violation of national sovereignty. Shared across this range of perspectives, however, is the understanding that *students as students* had become a formidable political bloc.

GUATEMALA

Committee of Guatemalan Anti-communist University Students in Exile (CEUAGE), 'Standing up to the Red Dictatorship in Guatemala'

(1953)

Ever vigilant in the fight against communism in the Western hemisphere, US intelligence officers quickly identified the CEUA as a potential asset in the hemispheric war on communism. In September 1953, an intelligence officer from the CIA field office (codename LINCOLN) approached CEUA students in Guatemala City.[1] The CIA agents spent a considerable amount of time devising missions for the eager anti-communist students. However, these covert missions posed a great risk to the students, and before long, the CEUA's membership dwindled. The most militant students had been arrested and many had been exiled. Some exiles went to Mexico City but the majority went to Tegucigalpa, Honduras. There, they formed the CEUAGE. In 1953, the group began to publish a newspaper, the *Bulletin of the Committee of Guatemalan Anti-communist University Students in Exile* (*Boletín de CEUAGE*), in order to connect exiled anti-communists to their peers throughout the hemisphere. The article below is from the first edition of the *Bulletin* and is representative of the group's anti-colonial writings: here, it is the USSR rather than the US that presents a threat.

The Committee of Guatemalan Anti-communist University Students in Exile sets forth before the conscience of America its tough stance against the Soviet domination that rules Guatemala and that extends – through an active and effective campaign of organisation and propaganda – to the rest of the countries of Central America and the Caribbean. We who fought fascist systems of government[2] and took up arms to overthrow

---

[1] For more on this relationship, see Cullather in 'Further Reading'.

[2] Guatemala declared war on Germany and Italy in mid-December 1941. Guatemala had a large population of German landowners of coffee estates, so war against Germany was a delicate matter. The authors may also have been referring to their participation in the overthrow of dictator Jorge Ubico and his successor, Federico Ponce Vaides, in 1944.

them now find ourselves standing before red dictatorships that, like that which currently reigns in our Nation, try to embed [within] the American continent a clearly defined plan directed and developed by the Soviet Union.

We emphatically declare that we oppose all totalitarian philosophy and that we will struggle against whichever system of government is guided by its concepts, because we are against slavery, servitude, and dependency, which submits the great majority of people to the dictatorship of autocrats and to the oppression of assemblies or political parties, or to a social class that has managed to seize power. We believe in democracy, as a new form of human redemption, which is the enemy of all despotism, be it individual or collective, Eastern or Western.

Those of us who fought on 20 October 1944, under the banner of democracy and with the ideal of converting our country into a nation rich and prosperous in the domains of spirituality and economy, in the fields of liberty and culture and social justice, contemplate with growing bitterness the collapse of our hopes before the communist expansion that, skilfully directed, empowered the organisation and direction of the working class, and the mechanisms of rule and control over all the agencies of the State in Guatemala.

In our country the first government of the revolution, presided over by Doctor Juan José Arévalo, opened the borders to international communists and entrusted to them advisory positions in various branches of the administration; they preached class warfare and hatred of the employer by his workers and gave all their support to the organisation of vertical syndicalism; they converted social laws into political instruments in their service and propelled Soviet domination within Guatemalan territory. Internationally, the politics are well defined: Guatemala entered into diplomatic relations with the USSR, entrusting its representation to important communists and suspended relations with countries [led by] ideologies distinct from that supported by the leader; interventionism is apparent in armed actions against the states of El Salvador, Costa Rica, and the Dominican Republic and in threats against the security of the other brother nations. Converted into a centre of communist infiltration in the heart of America, the country poses a threat to continental security.

The second government of the revolution entrusted to Colonel Jacobo Arbenz Guzmán identifies with the politics of its predecessor and is even more radical. The Communist Party works openly to draw to its breast all of the labour organisations and the peasants' unions of the Republic, transforming them into the Guatemalan Workers' Party

(PGT), sponsors an agrarian reform law, and takes under its control the agencies in charge of its implementation. The popular fronts and the Communist Party, which make up the government and congress through a coup d'état, seized the judiciary and achieved total domination of the Nation. The army, too, has fallen under its influence, and espionage within its ranks produces a state of anxiety; the military members who retain their dignity are displaced or subsumed to the reigning totalitarianism. The Soviet plan has triumphed in our country . . .

The two revolutionary governments violate the Constitution of the republic; the Constitution prohibits deportations of Guatemalans, and both regimes expel their political enemies; the Constitution guarantees human rights and both administrations abuse citizens, imprisoning them without cause, mistreating them and torturing them in prisons; constitutional law guarantees the life of all human beings and both governments assassinate with impunity even in public streets, as in the case of the Colonel Francisco Javier Arana[3] – the heart and driving force behind the 20 October movement – or in the regional prisons, as in the case of those who were ringleaders of the Salamá coup;[4] the Constitution guarantees the right of assembly and public demonstration, and both governments repeatedly massacre groups of protestors, leaving behind dead and wounded; the same basic law guarantees property rights, and both regimes confiscate properties of Guatemalans and foreigners under the pretext of applying an expropriation law or an unconstitutional law of agrarian reform, and punish with corporal and financial punishments those who try to defend their assets within the norms that the laws themselves dictate; the Constitution guarantees the honour and security of the *pueblo*, and both administrations have granted absolute impunity for the criminal acts committed by elements who make up popular parties and the functionaries who have served in their regimes; in sum, the very Constitution prohibits the participation of political parties with ties to international organisations and both regimes have permitted and legalised the functioning of the Communist Party in the country, with its training centres and newspapers. Furthermore, they have put the great resources of the State, including those for public education and the national economy, at the service of Marxist leaders.

Guatemala is a signatory of the Charter of San Francisco, and as such

---

[3] Francisco Javier Arana was a member of the revolutionary junta who was assassinated under mysterious and still largely unknown circumstances on 15 March 1945.

[4] An attempt to overthrow Arbenz in 1953, supported openly by the US embassy and UFCO.

[has] incorporated the Code of Human Rights.[5] To punish citizens who support a credo different to that of communism is a violation of this international treaty. Guatemala enters into the Organisation of American States and makes an attempt on the security of the member states, infringing [upon] its solemn commitments; it forms part of the Organisation of Central American States who are signatories to the Charter of San Salvador and it strayed from that charter when it proposed the formation of a Central American anti-communist [*sic*] front; and finally within the organisation of the United Nations it strikes a position of sympathy with the Soviet Union and the countries that are subjugated by the Soviet Union.

In internal as in external affairs, the governments of the revolution have defined themselves as unconditional servants of a foreign power, which constitutes a betrayal of the Fatherland; they have defined themselves against the national interest, which also constitutes a grave betrayal of the country; they have sponsored fractures between the distinct groups within the community, which constitutes an attempt on social order; they have pursued, jailed, maltreated, tortured, and assassinated the Guatemalan citizenry, which represents a violation of the most elementary and sacred rights of man; and in short, they have transformed our democratic institutions into totalitarian institutions in the service of the proletariat and the interests of international communism. Guatemala has thus granted the *pueblo* the right of rebellion and the countries of America the right to judge its conduct in accordance with the norms that rule the organisation and functioning of the United Nations.

In the face of these actions by the State, the anti-communist university students' association has organised a committee that has been fighting with the opposition. Our civic campaign, first, and our political action, next, caused a violent reaction from these governments, the popular fronts, and the Marxist leaders. The epithets of reactionaries, retrogrades, elements at the service of Yankee imperialism, enemies of social needs, and even traitors to the Fatherland have been lavished on us by official press, radio stations that belong to the State, and even by communist newspapers. These are totally false imputations lacking any justification because we have never been nor ever will be against the popular interest, against the vindication of workers, or against the national well-being. But we are and have always been against fraud

---

[5] The Charter of the United Nations, signed in San Francisco, California, on 26 June 1945.

and the insincerity of false apostles, against demagogues of the town plaza turned into heads of state, and against the traitors who have made Guatemala dependent on a foreign power and enslaved its people to Marxist leaders.

Because of our anti-communist posture and our struggle in defence of the sacred destiny of our Fatherland, we have often been persecuted, jailed, mistreated, and deported, but we have maintained unwavering faith throughout our sacrifices that sooner or later they will lead to the benefit of our Nation and those who we have tried to save and whom we will save, whatever the cost, from communist domination. We are standing up against the red dictatorship; we know that nothing will hold them back from eliminating us, we feel the close watch that they keep on our persons; and we know that injury, calumny, personal attacks, or any of the other strategies constantly used by communists will be brandished against us; but this does not frighten us, and we will reach the end with the honour of our youth and the sincerity of our grand convictions.

Translated by Rachel Nolan

Excerpts, Committee of Anti-communist University Students (CEUA), *Plan de Tegucigalpa*

(1954)

The *Plan de Tegucigalpa* is the fullest representation of the philosophy of the CEUA. First printed in the *Bulletin of the CEUAGE* on 24 December 1953, the *Plan* circulated quickly in a revised pamphlet format. The US Library of Congress catalogued its copy before the end of the year. In March 1954, some students travelled to the Tenth Inter-American Conference in Caracas to present it to the American heads of state gathered there. It was very well-received. Their comprehensive plan for government combines general denunciations of President Arbenz with specific domestic and foreign policy recommendations. Under the *Plan*, Guatemala would become a representative democracy led by the Social Doctrine of the Catholic Church. After the success of the counter-revolutionary forces, the *Plan* became the foundation of Castillo Armas's government. Although the counter-revolutionary government is best known for its close ties to the US, this text is determinedly nationalist. Like other CEUA texts, its opposition to the USSR is cast in anti-imperial terms and North American imperialism is not mentioned at all. The version of the *Plan* below begins with an appeal to the Constituent Assembly, which was elected in 1954 to rewrite the Constitution of the Republic. Presumably, this published version was given to delegates in an effort to influence their recommendations. Note how the *Plan* includes very detailed recommendations concerning university autonomy.

INTRODUCTION

Esteemed Constituents:

We put in your hands the PLAN OF TEGUCIGALPA. It is the contribution of those who, beyond the borderlands, during a long exile, never stopped thinking of Guatemala.

THE PLAN OF TEGUCIGALPA, Esteemed Assemblymen, is something more than juridical material aimed at guiding the Fatherland from defeat toward a real democracy: it is the inspiration of love for Guatemala and the fruit, lofty and mature, of sacrifice and of blood. It is the historic text that the National Liberation Movement embodied in the struggle and the inheritance that our martyrs bequeathed to the country. We offered it to the *pueblo* and the *pueblo* accepted, throwing themselves into the struggle to put it into effect. And now the people demand the implementation of this PLAN in which they see, not without reason, the motive, cause, and reason for the Uprising.

The anti-communist groups that make up the National Anti-communist Front – (FAN) – accepted the outlines of the PLAN OF TEGUCIGALPA from the beginning. You, accordingly, by accepting candidacy to this National Constitutional Assembly, stand up in solidarity, by your discipline and patriotism, with each and every one of the aspirations, doctrines, and principles contained in such a momentous Document. Hence in this grave hour, we put it once again into your hands so that you may translate it into the juridical reality of Guatemala.

Our symbols: God, Fatherland, Freedom; and our aspirations: Truth, Justice, and Work, [are] the operating summary of the PLAN OF TEGUCIGALPA, a text that tends neither toward the right nor the left, but rather to establish in the realm of reality a solid future, a Fatherland equal to it, a people as happy as possible, and a spirit that will make Guatemala a great, strong, and respectable Nation.
[. . .]
Think about our Fallen; *think about Guatemala*; *think about your children*; think, if you wish, about yourself.

GOD, FATHERLAND, FREEDOM.

Committee of Anti-communist University Students
-CEUA-

PLAN OF TEGUCIGALPA

Unified by the common goal to eradicate from Guatemala the communism that deforms truth, sullies justice, disfigures beauty, and mocks morals; that asphyxiates freedom, tramples on rights; enchains consciences and mutilates the will; that unhinges social order, undermines the national sentiment, preaches historical matcrialism to the exclusion of the values of the spirit as a determining factor in the life of individuals and peoples, and negates the existence of God and the immortality of the soul, anti-communist civic groups and political parties that are active within and outside the republic have joined under a single flag, whose symbols are 'GOD, FATHERLAND, FREEDOM' and make up the ORGANISED OPPOSITION TO THE SOVIETISATION OF GUATEMALA.

Guatemalan anti-communism, systemically and deliberately characterised as negative, [also] inspires a robust ideology of aspirations and clearly defined ends; the ORGANISED OPPOSITION TO THE SOVIETISATION OF GUATEMALA, entity whose goal is the liberation of the Fatherland, the reconstruction of the nationality, and the rehabilitation of the nation, has signed the 'PLAN OF TEGUCIGALPA', so named because of the place in which it was conceived, and its earlier study and discussion, approved.

The ORGANISED OPPOSITION TO THE SOVIETISATION OF GUATEMALA declares, affirms, and upholds the following fundamental principles, which in some way supersede the other refinements considered essential for the whole development of man and the harmonious unfolding of society, considered and included in the PLAN OF TEGUCIGALPA:

I)   Above and beyond any other earthly consideration are national destinies and interests.

II)   If one has an upright spirit, tenacity of purpose, and a store of energy and experiences, with an eye towards the national interest, dispensing with the merely personal or group or class, or any other interests, the prevailing discontent among the distinct social classes, which intensifies day by day, is remediable.

III) For the achievement of the common good, [which is] the basic purpose of the State, the rule of Law is necessary as a source of peace and progress.

IV) Freedom, in order to be genuine, fecund, and useful, should be exercised within the bounds of truth, justice, and morals. Conversely, degeneration into libertinage and anarchy provokes the rise of dictatorship and even despotism and tyranny.

V) The juridical regime is absolutely sterile if it is not irrigated with the vivifying sap of SOCIAL JUSTICE, as an indispensable and irreplaceable complement to Commutative and Distributive Justice, because if these regulate the relations between individuals and within society, respectively, then social justice governs the obligations of individuals to society, dignifies man, puts into equilibrium the distribution of resources and equalises opportunity, at the same time as it favours and facilitates the exercise of freedoms and guarantees full security to all.

VI) Human dignity – in the widest sense of the word, as a synthesis of various characteristics of the intelligent being – should have the highest protection of the State, an entity whose organic function and justification reside exactly in this dignity, for the very reason that it is the result of the will of its members.

VII) Having instituted rules to preserve for citizens the enjoyment of their rights, which are fundamentally life, liberty, equality, and security of the person, of his honour, and his property, the penalties imposed for transgressions against these rights should be of exemplary severity and easily employed for the effectiveness of order.

VIII) Under the protection of democracy the emergence of a world wherein men, liberated from fear and misery, enjoy freedom of expression of thought, freedom of belief, freedom of reunion, freedom of placement and movement, and the other freedoms recognised in the Universal Declaration of Human Rights proclaimed by the United Nations, is entirely possible.

IX) Of all the political systems, representative democracy is the best for Guatemala within the possibilities of our environment for the greatest possible guarantee of human dignity and the maintenance of the common good, [the] basic aims of the State.

X) Required by human necessity, the right to property deserves the recognition and protection of the State, for the satisfaction of individuals, families, and societies, understanding that legitimate collective interests prevail over those of individuals.

XI) For purposes of public usage, duly verified, private property is subject to expropriation in its totality or in part, by the State or Municipalities, pending payment in cash at a fair price.

XII) Noble attribute of human beings which allows them the fulfilment of their aspirations and individual, family, or collective well-being, labour is a right and a duty in the life of a society, and this should be demanded of citizens, at the same time as [the opportunity] is given to them.

XIII) For the practical realisation of [these] ideals, it is essential that those charged with pursuing them in any walk of life should have solid moral and intellectual education and adapt their actions to the most rigorous norms of probity and purity.

SYMBOLS OF THE ORGANISED OPPOSITION TO THE SOVIETISATION OF GUATEMALA

The world is divided into two great forces: one, democracy, the principles of which guarantee coexistence in terms of social harmony, security of the person and his honour and goods, and possibility of individual advancement; the other, communism, which carries inside itself the germ of social destruction, death of freedoms, annihilation of identity, and negation of ethical values, subordinating them in all cases to the most base and vile animality, the ORGANISED OPPOSITION TO THE SOVIETISATION OF GUATEMALA, conscious that the government of Colonel Jacobo Arbenz Guzmán and that of Dr Juan José Arévalo Bermejo, going against popular will and in spite of the democratic structure set out by the Constitution of the Republic, acted and led [in a manner] subject to the outlines and dictates of international communism. Unfurling the flag of the struggle for national salvation, the *labarum*[6] of our sword, burnished to the colour of purest sentiments, overflowing with sincerity, made up the magnificent trilogy of Christian culture and civilisation, [is] 'GOD, FATHERLAND, FREEDOM' [. . .]

GOD

The be-all and end-all of the purest ideals of human beings and the antithesis of the historical materialism that communism has imposed

---

[6] The labarum or Chi-Ro was the military standard used by Roman Emperor Constantine I.

in our country. Denying God is equivalent to denying life – present and future – supreme law, order, and harmony. Without Him, nothing can master the conscience of man: morals are an illusion; virtue, a beautiful lie; vice, an amiable prescript for those who wish to rehabilitate; and relationships be they domestic, social, political, or of any kind, mere fantasies.

God is Light, Truth, Justice, Love, Holiness, Beauty, Work; in sum, the Supreme good. By searching for Him and finding Him we achieve happiness: earthly and eternal. To reach Him, the path to follow is love: Love of God in all ways and love of the other as if he were oneself. And He who says love, says serve. He says to sacrifice ourselves. Love does not consist of receiving; it consists of giving. The more one gives, the larger one's love. God himself is the example: to Him we owe our life and what sustains it and what makes it beautiful. Even more: He gave us Himself. Service and sacrifice. Our shield we proclaim with the Cross.

FATHERLAND

Immortal word that in the heart of all honourable citizens contains whatever great and good we may do for the nation in which we were born. Divine creation tied to us by Geography and by History, the Fatherland occupies a privileged position in our hearts, acknowledging above it only God. It is our past, present, and future. And we are the link between yesterday and tomorrow; the day between the two dawns.

Small, almost infinitesimal in its territorial dimensions, Guatemala is large, enormous, in its spiritual values; and, fortunately, it is those which count and will count in the biggest battle of the centuries: the disloyal, impious war of the hammer and sickle against God and Country.

In defence of this and of Him, we should distinguish and differentiate between what is a **government of force** and a **government with force**. When the government overpowers rights and liberties, it is a government of force. Such was that of Colonel Jacobo Arbenz Guzmán. And a government with force is when [force] is the medium for efficacy and the defence of rights and liberties. Such is the government that we propose.

The Fatherland is collaboration, protection, and affection. It may be pride in a common history, it may be the dignity of great industries in the future; but, in the present, it is fundamentally collaboration in labour, protection of our basic material and spiritual values, and the affection of a common fraternity. Love of the Fatherland without loving our co-citizenry is as incongruous as loving God and vilifying His creatures. Serving the Fatherland in its noble functions in the public sphere is to leave behind us a clean wake of our character in the unfailing life of the spirit. If the Fatherland is in jeopardy, there are no rights for anyone, only duties and obligations. This is the idea of the Fatherland for a democratic world. But communism – which undermines the concept of the family, primordial cell of the Fatherland – destroys the concept of traditional Fatherland to found, on an ashlar[7] of hatred, a 'Communist State', whose purpose is to combat the idea of God [and] to annihilate His reflections on the world: home, religion, Fatherland.

It is Guatemala's great fortune that this sentinel is watching over the battlements of life and with the Clarion in His right hand and eyes fixed on the horizon, announces that soon will come the day.

The Quetzal[8] will make its call heard after a long History of Silence.

FREEDOM

Exercise of the will and self-determination of man. Although it is inherent to human nature, it may not be exercised when it impinges upon that of others or clashes with social rights, by the same virtue of coexistence in society, paying close attention to when one's rights engage the rights of others; in this there is no contradiction, but rather, on the contrary, full recognition of the right to freedom as inviolable patrimony of each and every man in the universe, as inviolable as is the independence of the Fatherland.

International Communism, enslaver of men and peoples, proposes to dispense with all freedoms – annihilating Freedom – and substituting the absolute will of the red Tsar and his political clique. The evidence [of this] is in half of Europe and half of Asia.

Against the overwhelming doctrinal advance and the practice of subjugating the spirit, the ORGANISED OPPOSITION TO THE SOVIETISATION OF GUATEMALA rises to the defence of Freedom, that which 'all creatures love and desire naturally, even more so do intelligent beings, and of these, even more so those of noble heart'. And recalling Goethe we may recognise that those who are worthy of freedom and life are those who know how to exercise them daily. It is true that when a State tries to oppress the free flight of the mind, if

---

[7] A smoothed and squared stone used in construction.

[8] The quetzal is a rare and extraordinary bird – often called the resplendent quetzal – that is found in southern Mexico and Central America. It was revered by pre-Columbian Mesoamerican civilisations, a veneration that has continued through the myth that its red chest comes from the blood shed by K'iche' Mayan leader Tecún Uman in his final battle with conquistador Pedro de Alvarado.

liberty does not have deep enough roots or force to evade pressure, it will fall each time further and further and end in an autocratic paralysis or, spilling over into an uprising against tyranny, will degenerate into licentiousness poorly contained by correctional laws.

It is important to keep in mind the incontrovertible truth that hymns to freedom are vacuous and insufficient – innumerable and beautiful as they may be – because in Guatemala these will be a weak imitation of [freedom's] essence, because [freedom] lacks selfishness and [in Guatemala] there is no sincere concern for the less favoured classes, since for man to be free in the truest sense of the word, he should come out of the darkness of ignorance with education and escape the jaws of misery with an income and other benefits in accordance with the personal needs of the individual and those who depend on him for subsistence; since both – ignorance and misery – are chains that, binding those who bear them and impeding their free development, are a heavy burden for the community; in light of this it is important to consider with respect to Freedom that the rule of social justice is necessary for the vigour of its existence, [as] balancer of opportunities and the enjoyment of wealth, correcting the distribution of both.

ASPIRATIONS

The essentially democratic political credo of the ORGANISED OPPOSITION TO THE SOVIETISATION OF GUATEMALA is rooted in their aspiration that in Guatemala there be Truth, Justice, and Labour as a basis for social organisation, so that the structure of freedom and Fatherland both have the scope and durability to guarantee better enjoyment of the inherent rights of man and a harmonious development of life within society.

TRUTH in man, JUSTICE in the people, LABOUR in the Republic are the three stripes of the Flag that waves on the flagpole of Reality, and in the breeze of Hope and Purpose.

[. . .]

I

BASES OF THE GUATEMALAN NATIONALITY

The ultimate reality of a country, underneath its distinct elements, is basic and unquestionable, that there exist marked differences between the distinct human races and also in the development and financial possibilities of each country. Likewise, culture and social organisation do not meet the same level of development in all nations; for this reason, political and administrative action should take all of the elements [of the nation] into account in order to form a clear concept of the reality of a people.

[The supreme reality] of Guatemala is constituted by Indians and by ladinos, which have been living until now in separate worlds; and in great measure, worlds completely alien from their common destiny, or reciprocally indifferent and even uncomprehending of their inherent worth.

For centuries, until the present moment reached by the History of Guatemala, there has been a great and foolish desire of the men of government to scorn the indigenous, the traditional, that which is essentially ours – the very soul of the Fatherland – in favour of ideas and systems that are not very workable within the particularities of our environment, forcing Guatemalanness to take mistaken paths which, disfiguring the physiognomy of the people, have impeded them from standing up before the world to declare very loudly: 'This is Guatemala.'

Without intelligent analysis or advantageous outcomes, literature, commerce, military, and whatever else available has been copied; and, lately, the crime of importing inhuman and inflexible political ideology from Communist Russia has been committed, poisoning and breaking the ties of the family.

Isolated, fearful, distrusting, and suspicious of the ladinos [are] the Indigenous and the ladinos of the others, [and] they have formed two distinct societies, one separate from the other, when they should have combined energies into a single society for the common good. To this end, a basic goal is the necessary construction of nationality, thanks to the fully Guatemalan politics put forward by the ORGANISED OPPOSITION TO THE SOVIETISATION OF GUATEMELA, deeply convinced that now is the time for us to stop being empty containers for imported thoughts, for strange manners and exotic ideologies, and for us to remember that we are Guatemalans, and that, with strong national sentiment based in the nation's reality, fusing Indians and ladinos, Guatemala will rise upright and follow its course.

Neither extreme right nor extreme left. In the heart of Guatemala. And in the height of its own ideals.

There lies Justice. These are the sentiments, ideals, and goals of the Opposition. And they will be reality, thanks to our movement.

Protected by this movement, indigenous and ladinos will understand one another and that Guatemala is above any earthly concern, [thus] abandoning misunderstandings and resentments, lack of confidence, and unjust scorn, assessing their shared virtues and fusing them together to integrate the nationality and save the Fatherland. Like the sexes, both halves of the same destiny will unite to create the future, and then the Guatemalan spirit will shine. For the first time in history, the people will be one, strong and indivisible, and Guatemala will be herself.

However, for this to be achieved, we still have a long path to walk, of political and social action [that is] favourable to the indigenous, which will lift them from their precarious standard of living and morally and materially incorporate them into the civic life of the country, but without altering their original ethnic physiognomy, with its own customs, and without perverting their special psychological character.

The simple application of general laws cannot resolve the political–social, cultural, and economic problem of the indigenous, distinct from the mass of the ladino population. No sanitary, dietary, agricultural, educational, etc. improvement in indigenous sectors can be realised with success without previous knowledge of the respective peculiar characteristics and the psychological process that govern them. Thus the solution to this problem will not be a mere economic or legislative matter, but rather [a] sociological and psychological one. Aboriginal life, customs, and thought must be taken into account; otherwise any attempt at 'redemption' or 'incorporation' of the indigenous will fail. To achieve this endeavour it will be necessary to substitute the harmful cultural features for others that are beneficial and useful, taking great care not to substitute all that is indigenous for what is Western, but instead to preserve some things and eradicate others. The ideal, advisable and perfectly possible, thanks to this slow but sure process, is to unite both propensities such that the European and indigenous complement one another and what is useful in each can be improved and perpetuated.

In Guatemala it is necessary – so as not to play with democracy, but rather to make it functional – to create a tutelary system, charged with defending the Indians and helping them to obtain and protect their rights; also, to train indigenous teachers, establish summer camps and rural schools, organise groups of missionaries of learning, to create professorships and seminars on *indigenista* studies at the University and, something momentous, the definitive possession of the land for the Indian.

It is urgent to put into force the resolution of the Eighth Interamerican

Conference, held in Lima in 1938, where it was declared that the indigenous have a preferential right to the protection of governmental authorities to compensate for their deficiency in physical and intellectual development, and that it should be the goal of all governments to 'develop policies aiming to completely integrate them into respective national milieux', making an effort so that this integration takes place within norms 'that allow the aboriginal population to take part in the life of the nation effectively and on equal footing'.

It also advises the adoption of special programmes of instruction, education, and culture for the indigenous masses and that preferably this instruction be imparted by indigenous teachers. Equally, and following local conditions – [as] customs, tensions, distrust, etc. vary from region to region and place to place – encouraging this to be implemented in open partnership with ladinos.

[. . .]

AUTONOMY OF THE UNIVERSITY:

The autonomy of the University of San Carlos should be maintained and the State will contribute to securing and increasing the university patrimony.

The incomes that the University gains from the manufacture and sale of alcohol should be substituted with other sources that are not contaminated with vice, because it is a great contradiction that in large measure our highest cultural institute subsists on death. As long as this misguided situation continues, any campaign against alcoholism will be hurt by a lack of sincerity and will be condemned in advance to failure.

Certainly, a vital function of the university will be to combat by all means possible the plague of alcoholism that destroys the individual and the home, implacable scythe of children before their time, precursor of crime and prostitution, determinant factor in vagrancy, misery, and an unthinkable burden for society.

The University must be concerned, and accordingly act, because from her irradiates culture for the general benefit of all Guatemalans. The professor, newspaper, radio, daily press, theatre, cinema, pamphlet, treatise, book, seminars, public debates, conventions, and other means of instruction must be channels to connect [the university] to the *pueblo*, to show them and return to them, even just in part, what the *pueblo* is owed.

This requires professionals, teachers, and technicians, but these positions in turn require education. In just compensation for this mutual need, the people are charged, through taxes and donations, for the initial growth of university patrimony and its potential offerings, but, at the same time, the University as an institution, *facultades*, and individuals, must take on as a moral imperative all of these means of diffusing culture to elevate the level of the people.

Academic freedom should be the cornerstone on which a structure of teaching *par excellence* is built so that the spirit has the freedom required to extend its wings in high and wide flight. If this is not allowed, scientific speculation stagnates, spiritual restlessness disappears, and the fonts of and longings for knowledge dry up.

Without interference or directions from foreign forces, the University ought to proceed under the most absolute apoliticism, which by no means signifies that it wants nothing to do with the Fatherland, quite on the contrary, all of [the Fatherland's] fundamental problems should be subject to study and research, and depending on the case, [even] solved by the University itself or at the least through its opinion, whether transmitted directly or through the professional associations.

But sectarian politics should remain forever banned from the University, primarily because they do not suit its mission, and also because any detour of this sort puts its autonomy at risk.

The appointment of university professors should be through the system of opposition,[9] unless the University agrees on another system. And that of university authorities should be through the students' vote, and that of the professional associations, through their respective representatives and by those who make up the professoriate. The proportions of one to the others and the term lengths of each authority will be set by the institutional law of the University.

To complete this task, [the University] should include the *Facultades* of Agronomy, Physical Science and Biology, Law, Economics, Pharmacy, Engineering, Medicine, Music, Dentistry, Pedagogy, Theology, Philosophy and Arts, etc. The authority to confer titles and corresponding degrees should be the essential task of the University, to the exclusion of the State, and the government is expressly prohibited from extending permits or licences to exercise given professions.

The University should remain open to all, irrespective of sex, colour, nationality, citizenship, political or religious creed, economic or social position, etc., if they meet the prerequisites for entry which shall be limited to intellectual training, moral qualities, and as concerns

---

[9] A system of competitive examination for academic appointments that has been in place since at least the 1880s.

contagious diseases, the state of health, with the goal that the university should be open to all classes of peoples and so that democracy does not suffer.

Tegucigalpa, 24 December 1953

Translated by Rachel Nolan

'AEU Versus Discrimination'

(1956)

This very brief text recounts a letter written by AEU President José T. Uclés to Autherine Lucy, the young African American woman who had been accepted, then rejected, by the University of Alabama in the US. Lucy was ultimately accepted after the National Association for the Advancement of Colored People (NAACP) attained a court order barring her rejection, but she remained forbidden to enter university dining halls or dormitories. Lucy's first weeks of class sparked protests, riots, property damage, and physical violence from white students who opposed school desegregation. Many Latin Americans on the left during the 1950s and 1960s were very critical of segregation in the US, which claimed to be the guardian of freedom and democracy across the globe, but could not manage to provide freedom for all of its citizens. This was a profound hypocrisy. A statement of solidarity with Lucy from a Latin American student group is fairly commonplace, but it is noteworthy that Uclés offers Lucy the opportunity to study at USAC. Of course, this is something that he could not actually assure, but within his offer was a powerful accusation: Guatemala was more free and forward-thinking than the US. The newspaper where this article was published, *Informador Estudiantil*, was a widely read paper published by the AEU. Note how the group understood itself to be an important member of an international student movement in 1956.

As the student body knows, in the United States racial discrimination has not been fully overcome in spite of the great attempts that many citizens of that country – to be fair and recognise them – make in order to oust said discrimination, which is as artificial as it is harmful.

The disturbances at the University of Alabama, in which fair-haired students blocked the entrance of students of colour, reached such a degree that those who merely wished to obtain an academic degree in the University feared for their lives.

Such is the case of Autherine Lucy, 26-year-old black university student who provoked a series of protests against her for the above-mentioned reason.

It is undeniable that the good name and prestige enjoyed by the University of Alabama has [been] dimmed considerably because of these barbaric excesses, and without a doubt this explains why the President of the University received a petition signed by 800 students in which they demanded the punishment of those who took part in the marches against Autherine Lucy. Also, the National Union of Students and a group of university students at the Faculty of Law requested the admission of the coloured girl to all lectures, guaranteeing her personal safety by all possible means, since the girl had been suspended until order was established [in order] to avoid attempts on her life.

Through its president, the AEU sent two urgent messages about this issue, one directed to the United States National Student Association,[10] expressing solidarity with the struggle this organisation continues on behalf of racial equality; and the second message was personally directed to Miss Autherine J. Lucy and read verbatim: 'Comrade: In the name of the Association of University Students of Guatemala, allow me to cordially salute you and send you a message of solidarity from the students of Guatemala after the outrage to which you fell victim.

At the same time that we congratulate you for your valiant struggle in defence of your rights, we permit ourselves to put at your estimable disposal the classrooms of San Carlos, which are open without discrimination of any kind. Saluting you once again and hoping that you continue the struggle for your rights, I sign in the name of my organisation as your humble servant. "GO AND TEACH ALL." From the AEU (signed) José T. Uclés.'

Translated by Rachel Nolan

Excerpts, Editorial, *El Estudiante*

(1957)

In the mid-1950s, the popular student newspaper *El Estudiante* changed its tone. Articles increasingly focused on the contentious relationship between students (especially in the AEU) and the government. The front page of

---

[10] The National Student Association was the largest federation of university and college students in the US, in operation from 1947 to 1978.

every edition featured a small single-frame comic strip entitled 'Hondazos de Juan Tecú', where a diminutive indigenous boy ridiculed some aspect of the government with puns or sarcastic one-liners. Another column called 'Corre la Bola . . .', which can be loosely translated as 'word has it', listed national and international political events that were almost too unprincipled to be believed. The editorial excerpted below is representative of the tense relationship between the editorial board and the government in the months after Castillo Armas's assassination, when the prospects of a national presidential election were uncertain. Like the CEUA above, its authors see Guatemala and Guatemalans as caught in the crosshairs of a contest of Cold War imperialisms. Of course, these authors differ from the CEUA in so far as they understand the Liberationists as sell-outs and offer a line-by-line critique of the group's rationale for overthrowing Arbenz and the political actions undertaken thereafter. In this interpretation, the Liberationists sold the nation to US business interests whereas Arévalo and Arbenz represented the desires of the Guatemalan people. From about this time onward, the AEU became increasingly – publicly – anti-government.

The wide use of the word 'Communist' with which the liberation movement attempts to justify all of their abuses seems to be continuing to terrorise the citizenry. Nevertheless, for a long time now it has been public knowledge that communism was nothing more than a pretext to attack peaceful Guatemala. The world laughs good-naturedly when the 'international communism' of Guatemala is mentioned. The whole world now knows that the people of Guatemala are in jail because they are communist, and they are communist because they are in jail. No more. But the fact remains that Guatemala was attacked and the people submitted to the most violent repression that it has known in its history. And the fact also remains that as a consequence of this aggression, the beneficiaries continue to brandish the false accusation of 'communist' to suffocate any longing for a humane life on the part of Guatemalans.

This would not be so bad had some silly, naïve, sanctimonious, or opportunist revolutionaries not joined the liberationist group to obstruct the efforts of the *pueblo*. For this reason we are obliged to make some observations. During the revolutionary decade, Guatemala had a bit of everything. Among other things there were traitors, bombers, coup plotters, and clowns; all these species now group themselves under the generic name 'liberationists'. Undoubtedly there were also communists. There were, and probably still are, Guatemalan citizens affiliated with the Guatemalan Workers' Party (PGT). But not even the FBI has dared to prove that there were communists in high positions in the executive, with the exception of three or four members of the PGT who formed the limited communist bench in the congress of the republic.

In the revolutionary period, the reactionaries continued to conspire, bombing and agitating under the protection of the nation's laws. Under the protection of these same laws, members of the PGT denounced and combated imperialism in their party's newspaper. But we should not confuse the failed domestic reactionaries with the triumphant armed aggression that destroyed the revolution, in the same way that we should not confuse the October revolution with the activity of communists in Guatemala, which was never proportionately equal to that of communists in the United States nor that of any other civilised country.

Under the protection of our very democratic atmosphere, a few reactionaries burned the constitution, others called our people 'human livestock', others shouted to the four winds that imperialism was winning and put the breaks on our national development. The people guffawed loudly at the first, but joined the chorus of the second, perhaps because of the profound meaning that the anti-imperialist struggle had gained on our soil.

The non-communist revolutionaries have not contented themselves with publicly denouncing imperialism, which commits incalculable abuses in our country. They have gone even further: they have demonstrated the point. They have shown how foreign companies that work in Guatemala enjoy preferential treatment, scoff at the laws, elude taxes, and treat their employees and the nation's authorities abusively. Further, the revolutionaries have indignantly rejected the effronteries of many arrogant gentlemen, and have refused to allow the tinkling of fruit company coins in their pockets, which by now had come to be something like a symbol of 'good understanding'.

The revolutionaries also did not resign themselves to timidly initiating the fight against abusive companies. They went further, as proven by the fact that during the democratic decade there was in Guatemala a certain idea of revolution, with its concomitant effects of social reforms to benefit all citizens interested in the well-being of the nation and particularly in the well-being of masses of workers and labourers in general, of peasants, and the other sectors [who were] extorted by the usury of some Guatemalans and by the whip of some foreigners.

This reason (and no other), and the desperate urgency of the State Department to purposefully find a laboratory [for anti-communist democracy], was the real reason for the fall of the Guatemalan revolution. The North Americans who lived in Guatemala in June 1954 were irritated when they heard it said that fruit companies were invading national territory. 'The fundamental error of Arbenz', they said, 'consisted of believing that he was fighting against the fruit companies, when really he was fighting against the State Department.' The State Department was interested in taking advantage of the feudal landowners and of the Guatemalan usurers to protect the interests of their companies; but they were even more interested in striking a blow to help 'beat Communism' anywhere in the world. Guatemala was not communist and [John] Foster Dulles[11] knew it. But [the accusation] lent itself to the issue. Several reforms that were occurring in Guatemala, along with certain audits of the robberies and abuses of foreign companies were very convenient. The news agencies controlled by the powerful began to give a twisted interpretation of events. Also, domination of regional and international organisations by the State Department was sufficient to silence them during the necessary period. And there was also the detestable work of [John] Peurifoy,[12] the ambition of usurers, and the cowardice of many who in an evil hour obtained 'licence' as Guatemalans to be able to trade and traffic their nation. Now there was no need to take as a pretext the fact that communists hurled insults at the imperialists. It was no longer necessary to recall that the Guatemalan communists had made posthumous homage to [Joseph] Stalin, along with some non-communist revolutionaries; it was no longer necessary to forget that [President Franklin Delano] Roosevelt had participated in various homages to Stalin, and that revolutionaries in a sense had participated in posthumous homage to Roosevelt, without having been accused of being what they were not. The only thing lacking were names of traitorous Guatemalans. And when the imperialists found one, they unleashed their aggression, going as far as a brazen military invasion of national territory.

It all would have gone very well, and the 'communist' accusation would have anointed it forever, if the traitors who lent themselves to humiliating their own land had had a little bit of judgement. But they did not. Cuban journalists visited the national jails when they held more than twenty thousand peasants as prisoners. They were not communists or anything like communists. They were farmers. The smart journalists, surprised, put pressure on representatives of the regime: If the peasants

---

[11] Secretary of State under Dwight D. Eisenhower, advocate of an aggressive approach toward communism, and former lawyer for UFCO. His brother, Allen Dulles, became first director of the CIA and served on the UFCO Board of Directors.

[12] US diplomat in Guatemala from 1953 to 1954. Peurifoy made the US embassy a safe haven for anti-communists and worked with the Dulles brothers to bring about the Arbenz government's collapse.

were not communists, and they were not in prison for being farmers – why were they prisoners?

But what really showed the liberationists' stupidity was the disorder that followed the invasion. The liberationists had not fought. As was clearly said, if there was a group of veterans of the liberation army, they consisted of three mercenary airmen rented by Peurifoy, who were not Guatemalan of origin. The liberationists received power on a silver platter, without pain, without glory, without anything more than the pledge to sell their Fatherland. Peurifoy gave it to them in San Salvador, after treating them rudely in front of some other personalities who have not managed to forget the incident. And they took it like Judas took the thirty coins. Thus began the rearguard action, of all of those who never fought but rather 'pacified' the conquered country when the din of battle was over.[13] Thus began the mass murders perpetrated in the east of the republic and in various departments of the interior. None of these people were communists. Why did they have to die? . . .

Translated by Rachel Nolan

'Association of Law Students Contesting Decree 1215 of the Republic, Declares Carlos Castillo Armas Traitor to the Fatherland'

(1958)

After months of rule by military junta, presidential elections were held in 1957. Many students supported Miguel Ydígoras Fuentes, an USAC Engineering alumnus. In a plainly rigged election, Ydígoras lost to the official candidate, Miguel Ortiz Passarelli, but the results were nullified. A second election held in early 1958 pitted the nation's most powerful social sectors against one another, as a distinct group backed each candidate. José Luis Cruz Salazar and the National Democratic Movement (MDN) represented the nation's traditional land-owning and military elite and many Christian Democrats. Mario Mendez Montenegro had the vote of supporters of Arévalo and some of the centre-left. Ydígoras, who ran for the National Democratic Reconciliation Party (PRDN) appealed to the anti-Arévalo and anti-Arbenz centre, as well as the Catholic Church, military rank-and-file, business sectors, and some urban professionals. Ydígoras

---

[13] This is a shorthand account of the counter-revolution and the support it received from the US government. See Cullather in 'Further Reading'.

won the popular election, but the MDN retained the majority of congres-sional seats and could unilaterally reject the election results. To ensure the MDN's cooperation, Ydígoras agreed to reserve three cabinet posts for MDN members and paid the party a monthly stipend. He made frequent, if strained, attempts to improve his relationship with the university; that he had promoted a pro-USAC stance during his campaign and even promised the return of many exiled San Carlistas made matters worse.[14] While these electoral machinations were under way, the military-dominated Congress proposed Decree 1215, which bestowed special honours on Castillo Armas. Guatemala's oldest student group, the Association of Law Students, opposed this honour in the thorough denunciation of Castillo Armas and the counter-revolution below.

The Association of Students '*El Derecho*', acting within the honourable civic tradition it has maintained in defence of the most beloved interests of the Fatherland, consider it a basic duty of each Guatemalan citizen to protest publicly and energetically against the Congress of the Republic's declaration of Mr Carlos Castillo Armas as 'Liberator of the Fatherland' through Decree 1215.

Through basic logic we may deduce that Mr Castillo Armas not only does not fulfil the most basic requirements to be deserving of that title, but rather very much to the contrary. His public performance in the service of North American imperialist politics and as direct agent of the North American intervention in Guatemala places him squarely in the criminal framework laid out in Article 122 of the Penal Code.

The logic of this last sentence is based on the following deeds, which we may enumerate, without attempting by any means to make the list exhaustive but rather to stress only the most relevant issues.

FIRST: The so-called 'Liberation Movement' had its origins in the fol-lowing facts:

A) Refusal by the revolutionary governments to renegotiate the onerous contracts made by dictatorships of the past with the fol-lowing companies: United Fruit Co., International Railroads of

---

[14] Ydígoras's campaign agenda centred on tax reform, industrial development, the establishment of the Central American Common Market, promotion of public education, and development of the north-western department of Petén. He also advocated penal reform, an adapted agrarian reform law, and revision of strict labour laws of the Castillo Armas regime. Financial resources limited some of these programmes. See Grandin in 'Further Reading'.

Central America, Electric Bond and Share Company, dock building companies, etc.

B) Protection by revolutionary governments of labour movements effected to improve the conditions of life for workers at the afore-mentioned foreign companies.

C) Demands by the revolutionary governments that foreign capital develop its activities within the framework determined by Guatemalan law just as domestic capital does, eliminating the regime of privileges for North American investors.

D) Refusal by the revolutionary government to receive foreign loans that not only jeopardise the country, but also provide foreign inter-vention a foothold on the pretext of protecting investments.

E) Nationalist legislation maintained by both revolutionary govern-ments in the sense of reserving the right to develop the resources of the Guatemalan subsoil – concretely, oil and its derivatives – for the State, companies recognised as Guatemalan, or those whose capital is preponderantly Guatemalan.

F) Development of a revolutionary economic project through which an effort is made to develop the capitalist economy of the country, such as: the Atlantic Highway (competitor for the railway monopoly); National Port of Santo Tomás (competitor for the dock-building companies and maritime transport, all subsidised by fruit compa-nies); Hydroelectric power in Jurún Marinalá (competitor for the Electric Bond and Share Co.), etc.

G) Refusal of the revolutionary government to send Guatemalan troops to fight in fronts outside the American continent, as in the case of Korea.

H) Following a foreign policy without subordination to any foreign power and fully exercising national sovereignty.

I) And finally we will cite the application of the Agrarian Reform to the Agricultural Company of Guatemala (Subsidiary of United Fruit Co.), and the expropriation of 83,929 hectares of unculti-vated land, respecting those that were already in production or in reserved zones. This event provoked an international crisis and the State Department presented a memorandum to the Guatemalan government demanding US$15,800,000 as an indemnity for the land expropriated from the fruit company, which was an immediate pretext for unleashing the intervention.

SECOND: Because of this patriotic policy followed by revolutionary governments, foreign governments were most pointedly interested in conspiring against the regime and taking advantage of the discontent created among the reactionary capitalists and feudal land-holders [because of] the appropriate application of labour legislation and Agrarian Reform. The foreign companies took advantage of these retrograde forces, providing them with money for conspiracies and offering Washington's support for their attempts at sedition. Proof of this lies in the numerous plots the revolutionary governments had to confront.

Finally convinced that an internal reaction was unable to depose the revolutionary regime, and also convinced that the nationalist policies of Guatemala could serve as an example to other Central American and American countries, the foreign companies decided to prepare a direct intervention from the United States, camouflaging it in such a way that Guatemalan traitors would head the intervention, which is how it unfolded, as confirmed by the relevant facts which we will now cite:

A)   Carlos Castillo Armas, a poor Guatemalan immigrant in Honduras, had at his disposal US$150,000 to hire mercenary soldiers, give them modern weapons, and train them. This was money that came from foreign countries established in Guatemala and from the very State Department of the United States.

B)   The tolerance and protection of the governments of Honduras and Nicaragua enjoyed by Castillo Armas, which provided him with training camps, trainers, mercenary soldiers, and even the Toncontín Airport as a base for aeroplanes that bombed and machine-gunned various Guatemalan towns; the radio of San Pedro Sula, extemporised in the 'secret liberation programme', and telegram installations for rapid communication through Honduran territory that borders Guatemala.

C)   The fact that many of the military trainers were Yankees, as were the pilots of planes and the planes themselves, which belonged to the North American Army.

D)   That the North American press unleashed far in advance an intense campaign against the Guatemalan regime, inventing the myth of 'Communism', according to which our country appeared as a threat to the Panama Canal, fostering an intervention that later came to pass.

E)   That top-level North American officials and senators had publicly called for intervention by their country in the internal affairs of Guatemala, as in the cases of Mr Braden and Ms Frances Bolton, representatives of the Republican Party.

F)   That Mr [John] Foster Dulles, Mr [Henry] Cabot Lodge, and Mr [John] Moors Cabot – the most prominent officials of the State

Department – have been lawyers for and shareholders in the United Fruit Company.

G) That foreseeing the possible failure of the attack prepared by Castillo Armas, Secretary of State John Foster Dulles had approved in Caracas a resolution against 'communism', by which the signatories were committed to intervene collectively in any country on the continent whose government was 'dominated by Communists'. This declaration was intended specially for Guatemala, which the Yankee press had made to seem in this situation [of Communist domination] long before the conference.

H) That the intervention was unleashed in June 1954, a month during which it was the turn of delegate Cabot Lodge to be the president of the [United Nations] Security Council, allowing him to prevent this body of the United Nations from taking effective action to avoid North American intervention in Guatemala, which is what ended up happening.

I) That when Castillo Armas's attempt at a US-sponsored invasion of Guatemala failed, the very North American planes which he used bombed Santa Rosa de Copán to provoke a war between Honduras and Guatemala.

J) That because of Ambassador John. E. Peurifoy's pressure and bribery, high-ranking military officers in the national army (among them Colonels Elfego Monzón, José Luis Cruz Salazar, and Mauricio Dubois), decided to and managed to depose Colonel Arbenz's regime, and that of his successor, Colonel Carlos Enrique Díaz.

K) That having had a round disagreement between Colonel Elfego Monzón and Castillo Armas at the Conference of San Salvador, it was Ambassador Peurifoy who dictatorially fixed the system, so that his protégé Castillo Armas would become President of Guatemala.

L) And, finally we will cite, the public recognition by the State Department of the United States of having directly intervened in the overthrow of the Guatemalan government.

THIRD: Having participated in any one of these events is reason enough for Castillo Armas to be tried and convicted of treason, according to Article 122 of the Penal Code, and reason enough to earn the hatred and contempt of all good Guatemalans. Even more so when one is the principal agent that a foreign power uses to make war on a country, to impose privileged treaties for their investors, destroy democratic institutions, and destroy sovereignty by intervening openly in the administration of public affairs.

And this is the case of Mr Castillo Armas. He was the principal agent in the United States' attempt to destroy Guatemala's constitutional regime and destroy national sovereignty. It was also he who, as head of the Executive, was the principal agent of the United States' attempt to reinitiate the colonisation of the country and to impose an iron tyranny over its internal affairs, as the following relevant events demonstrate:

A) Renegotiating contracts that establish privileged treatment for the United Fruit Company and its subsidiaries (IRCA, Agricultural Company of Guatemala, dock-building companies, etc.).

B) Repealing the revolutionary oil legislation and substituting a Petroleum Code written by Mr Roy Merritt, oil advisor to the US State Department, assisted by two North American and two Venezuelan technicians, drafted and published in English and accompanied by a Spanish translation. It concedes all kinds of rights and privileges to oil companies, while it only entangles the State of Guatemala in obligations.

C) Having made concessions for oil exploration and exploitation to subsidiary companies of the powerful trust Standard Oil Company that cover nearly the entire national territory.

D) Having created a 'liberation' tax that served only to pay eight million [US] dollars for the formation and maintenance of the so-called liberation army made up of mercenaries.

E) Accepting huge loans from the United States, which have now reached the astounding quantity of One Hundred million [US] dollars, which will tie the hands of any government that wishes to pursue a nationalist position with respect to the management of natural resources and that has provided cause for North American technicians to run public affairs on the pretext of watching over the use of their investments.

F) Negotiating the anti-patriotic Treaty of the Lago de Gülia, which will deprive Guatemala of the benefits and uses of the water of that lake, its tributaries, and riverbed, which flows throughout the national territory.

G) Paralysing the economic progress that competed with the foreign monopolies, such as: paralysing the construction of hydroelectric works at Jurún Marinalá and continuing the Atlantic Highway with notorious reluctance, leasing out the Port of Santo Tomás and authorising the fruit company to have one branch of the railway system as the only connection from the port to the interior of the country. Transforming the Guatemalan aviation company from a national company to an incorporated company so that Pan American Airways could acquire more than 40% of shares and convert it into a subsidiary, etc.

H) Violently persecuting the labour movement by jailing, torturing, banishing, and destroying its labourers without the protections mandated by the Code on the topic of union leaders, with particular fury directed at the union leaders who work in foreign companies, even to the point of shooting those who work for banana companies as a measure of repression, without trial.

I) Destroying the parcelling of land that favoured 100,000 peasant families in the implementation of the Agrarian Reform, imprisoning and exiling peasants whose only crime was having received a parcel of land.

J) Returning lands to the Agricultural Company of Guatemala that had been expropriated in correct application of the Agrarian Reform, and for which a quantity of 609,800 quetzales in agrarian bonds had already been paid.

K) Destroying the protected rights of workers by persecuting those who unionise and prohibiting the right to strike, which led to a general reduction of salaries and a rise in the number of hours of work without pay for additional hours worked, and the annulment of another series of labour protections, provoking massive layoffs in various companies, particularly in the foreign-owned companies, and creating an acute problem of unemployment and giving rise again to treatment of workers that injures their human dignity.

L) Repealing the Constitution of 1945 and the other revolutionary laws that protected the free organisation of the people, natural resources, free democratic competition between political parties, and freedom of speech and of the press.

M) Violently persecuting the whole citizenry, creating a mass of political prisoners and exiles that is unprecedented in any other era of Guatemalan history.

N) Pursuing an inquisitorial politics in which artistic and cultural organisations are abolished almost entirely, and persecuting the citizenry for simply owning books considered 'communist' that have been included on a blacklist drawn up by the government.

O) Not tolerating political, union, and artistic organisations that officials deem fascist.

P) Not abiding by the Pact of San Salvador, in which Castillo Armas had agreed to promote free elections for representatives and for the Presidency of the Republic, once he was in charge.

Q) Persecuting the student movement with fury, especially that of university students, for its dignified position in defence of national interests and its unwavering campaign of denunciation of the persecution of the public and the continual concessions made to imperialist North American capital, to the extreme point of machine-gunning a peaceful student protest, killing five students, injuring 33, and taking 205 prisoners and deporting 40 people after torturing many of them.

R) Besieging the Faculty of Law with excessive force on 24 June 1956 and violating University Autonomy in every way with a police raid by the forces of law and order with the object of seizing the University Auditorium.

FOURTH: Taking into account the political activities of Castillo Armas and Idigoras [*sic*] Fuentes abroad, who upon placing themselves in the service of foreign intervention committed a crime against Guatemalan sovereignty, the last Congress of the Republic [that was] freely elected by the people and, as such, the last that legitimately represented the people, declared them Traitors to the Fatherland in Legislative Decree Number 1036, of the first of February 1954, which has not been repealed and is in full force as law of the republic.

AS SUCH:

FIRST: The Association of Students '*El Derecho*' publically condemns the attitude of the Congress of the Republic, in pushing through the Decree of 1215 giving the sectarian name 'Liberator of the Republic' to someone who was the agent of North American intervention in Guatemala and executioner of our people, Mr Carlos Castillo Armas.

SECOND: The Association of Students '*El Derecho*' declares those representatives who flaunt academic degrees and lend themselves to the aforementioned antipatriotic manœuvre *personae non grata*.

THIRD: The Association of Students '*El Derecho*' declares Mr Castillo Armas Traitor to the Fatherland and Traitor to the cause of the Hispano-American People.

Guatemala, 17 January 1958

M. F. Martínez   R. Azmitia
President   Secretary

Translated by Rachel Nolan

EL SALVADOR

Moderate reforms, elections, and new political parties hardly concealed the continuity of military leadership in El Salvador. In September 1956, a month before the publication of the edition of *Opinión Estudiantil* that featured the articles below, moderate military leader Colonel José María Lemus was elected by an improbable 95% of the electorate. AGEUS students were sceptical of Colonel Lemus's promise to uphold public safety, despite his public image as a reformer. Four years later, a coup organised by workers, students, and the centre-left would force him into exile. As the documents in Chapter 1 suggest, the AGEUS had long been aligned with workers' organisations and united under the slogan 'Study and Struggle' ('Estudio y Lucha'). *Opinión Estudiantil* was its most widely read publication. Together, the texts below demonstrate the political and social intimacies shared by Salvadoran, Nicaraguan, and Mexican students. This intimacy was often the result of exile, but it also revealed a reinvigorated sense of 'Americanness', which implicitly or explicitly excluded North Americans '*yanqis*'. This particular sense of Americanness is a key feature of Central American students' anti-colonial ideologies throughout the twentieth century and is articulated in many of the documents throughout this collection.

AGEUS, 'Manifesto'

(1956)

This manifesto celebrated Somoza's assassination, hailing López Pérez as a hero for all Americans who suffer under the lash of colonialism and dictatorship. Tucked into the inside of the second page of the edition of *Opinión Estudiantil*, the short manifesto was accompanied by the Pablo Neruda poem, 'Las Satrapias', and an excerpt from former Guatemalan President Juan José Arévalo's book, *Fábula del tiburón y las sardinas (América Latina Estrangulada)*, iconic texts in contemporary anti-colonial Latin American literature.

The Association of Law Students, faithful to the postulates that motivate and the principles that regulate its existence, cannot view with indifference the latest political occurrences in Central America, whose effects have come to unsettle the Salvadoran citizenry.

The student body of Law, by its nature a guardian of legal statutes, [which are] the fundamental basis of the Salvadoran State, [and] in its essence a body with Central American unionist aspirations, has opted to issue a public declaration of its feelings and thoughts.

a) Declares as an illustrious figure of American patriotism the young Nicaraguan Rigoberto López Pérez, considering him a LATIN AMERICAN HERO.

Supports in every way the protests and tributes that the General Association of Salvadoran University Students has made in its true and just recognition of the tremendous holocaust in which he offered his blood for the well-being of his Nation.

b) Protests vigorously the disrespectful terms and pejorative appellations with which the foreign news agencies have described the patriot RIGOBERTO LÓPEZ PÉREZ, intending to diminish his infamous merit which has raised him to a place of honour among the most dignified men of our beloved AMERICA.

c) Protests before the Government of the Republic the abuses suffered by Nicaraguan citizens who are exiled in [El Salvador], on the part of Salvadoran police.

Will recognise that [even] if the positions taken by the authorities are the hypocritical fruit of the diplomatic apparatus, this still does not authorise the flagrant violation of the postulates outlined in our POLITICAL CONSTITUTION;

d) No longer waits for the Salvadoran Government with its mistaken understanding of solidarity [to] once again cunningly violate the fundamental principles of International Law, recognised by our Government, which submits Nicaraguan citizens on our national soil to suffering ostracism by a spurious and America[15]-hating Dictatorship.

e) Condemns the unfortunate meddling of the MINISTER OF NICARAGUA, authorised by the Government of El Salvador, in hopes of diminishing the Rights that we enjoy, in comparison to other countries, as Salvadoran citizens.

The student body of Law, considering this attitude to be perverse, worthy only of a 'SOMOCISTA' henchman, declares the aforemen-

---

[15] By 'America' here, the authors mean Latin America, not North America.

tioned functionary, LEONTE HERDOCIA, to be non grata, and will not cease in its efforts to ensure that he is considered thus by the Government of El Salvador.

San Salvador, 8 October 1956
[Signed]
Fernando A. Mendez A.
President

Rafael Mendoza C.
Secretary

Translated by Heather Vrana

AGEUS, 'Solidarity with Nicaraguan Exiles'

(1956)

This statement of solidarity was published in *Opinión Estudiantil* but it also addressed the transnational alliances of security forces. The AGEUS made public the names of Nicaraguans who were at risk in El Salvador and, in this way, pressured the new Lemus government to ensure their safety. In the event of the disappearance, arrest, or death of one of these men, the students had already suggested a motive and a culprit. Similarly, the letter from Nicaraguan emigrants and exiles in Mexico, signed by some of the most famous Nicaraguan writers of the time, celebrates acts of solidarity organised by Salvadoran students. The writers exalt the youth as the heirs of the dreams of Francisco Morazán, the visionary two-term president of the Republic of Central America, who is remembered as the champion of liberal freedoms – freedom of religion, the press, and speech – in the region. To compare the Salvadoran youth to Morazán was to hold them in the highest esteem. It was also to expect that they would unite and transform Central America.

After the intense commotion that has swept the entire breadth of the American continent, owing to the violent death of the dictator Somoza, the justified acknowledgement of the heroic act of Rigoberto López Pérez has occurred on the part of organisations and persons noted for their democratic thought. But [this] has also carried with it bloody reprisals against the opposition to the military and subhuman regime that nevertheless endures in Nicaragua. As in all dictatorships, the usual reprisals have not only remained within the borders of that long-suffering country, but have sought to spread internationally, endangering the personal security of Nicaraguan exiles who reside in the other Central American nations.

What the exiles in El Salvador have publicly requested is nothing more than the guarantee of their personal safety, especially the safety of Capitan Noel Bermúdez and Lieutenant Alfaro.

We all know of the fatal and tragic experiences of other dictatorships, the case of the assassinations of Dominican exiles in the United States and Cuba is clear. It would not be surprising to find that tomorrow these same tragic events occur in our country and that they lead to the total disgrace of the government of Colonel Lemus.

We are certain that the Somozas, apprentices of jackals and inheritors of the reprehensible pedigree of their father, will not hesitate to coerce the [other] Central American governments into taking violent measures against Nicaraguan exiles and, even more, could even request for them to guarantee impunity for mercenary bandits.

The government has a duty to protect the Nicaraguan exiles, as they have requested, [and] the *pueblo* is awaiting your response. We, the Salvadorans, should uphold our consciousness as free men, independent of these manœuvres by the official Embassies in our nation or of any other sort. This is not, nor are we requesting, a mere act of humanitarianism, but rather an act of dignity and patriotism.

Opinión Estudiantil joins in solidarity with the Nicaraguan exiles in their rightful claim and we demand that the security forces of our nation do all that they can to provide the protection that we have justly requested.

Translated by Heather Vrana

'Communiqué'

(1956)

The Directorate of the AGEUS has received the following communication that we transcribe:

'Mexico, 6 October 1956

The Nicaraguan emigrants in Mexico send a cordial greeting to the General Association of University Students of El Salvador.

As free citizens and as Central Americans that dream of the crystallisation of the ideals of [Francisco] Morazán, we regard with profound satisfaction the actions of the Salvadoran student body in support of the Nicaraguan people, in these transcendental moments of its history.

The Salvadoran student body, strong and determined, has taken an outstanding role in the struggle to maintain dignity in our countries;

This Youth, honest, courageous and sincere, is the greatest voice in our times, from the lands of Central America, to come to the defence of our oppressed people.

Down with the dictatorship!
Long Live Free Nicaragua!

Signatures – Hernán Robleto, V. Godoy R., Lizandro Chávez Alfaro, Juan José Meza, and Ernesto M. Sánchez'

Translated by Heather Vrana

NICARAGUA

The name of the Somoza in power had changed, but little else had. The three short articles below come from an undated edition of *El Universitario*, the official publication of the Student Centre of the National University (CUUN), published some time in late 1960.

'Here are the Murderers and their Victims'

(1960)

This article, 'Here are the Murderers and their Victims,' was an above-the-fold front-page story accompanied by three large photographs of National Guard members in helmets confronting a mass of citizens in shirtsleeves, trousers, and dresses. Below these three photographs were four studio portraits of the four men who were killed in the confrontation. Each young man wore a tuxedo and bow tie, the very image of respectability. The text below was little more than a caption to these images.

The photos and article refer to the confrontation between students and National Guard members on 23 July 1959, wherein troops opened fire on the students who protested against the Nicaraguan and Honduran militaries' coordinated surprise attack on a guerrilla column located on the border in a region called El Chaparral. Under the leadership of Dr Mariano Fiallos Gil, the university had just won autonomy in March and the student body was empowered to oppose the Somoza regime more openly. Students decided to turn their annual '*desfile de los pelones*', a sort of initiation rite for new students, into a funeral-style march. The National Guard, perhaps intimidated by the large mass of students or perhaps under orders of Colonel Juan César Prado, opened fire on the students. The deaths had the immediate effect of radicalising students' dissent and have endured in popular memory.

40 armed guards, as if in a war, opened fire across the backs of the students on 23 July 1959, in the University city of León.

TOTAL: 4 dead and more than 60 wounded. The platoon was led by the cowardly and Lombrosian[16] Tacho Ortiz; Revolutionary Justice calls for the ex-commander of the Plaza of León, César Prado, and the aforementioned sadist.

Br Sergio Saldaña
Br Mauricio Martínez
Br Erick Ramírez
Br José Rubí[17]

Translated by Allessandra Paglia

'COSEC Receives Cablegram from SOMOZA'

(1960)

This text, a second from the same edition of *El Universitario*, demonstrates how Nicaraguan students used their connections with the international student movement to pressure Somoza to permit greater academic freedom

---

[16] Italian criminologist Cesare Lombroso (1835–1909) argued that criminals were of a distinct anthropological type with an observable physical difference from the rest of the population.
[17] These are the names of the young students who were killed by the National Guard.

at the university in the midst of on-going reprisals and campus occupations that were more or less continuous from late 1959 to 1960. This exchange between the Coordinating Secretariat of National Unions of Students (COSEC) and Somoza suggests how widely anti-Somoza sentiment had spread. COSEC was founded in 1952 as a non-communist alternative to the International Union of Students (IUS), which permitted the membership of students from communist countries. Somoza could hardly accuse COSEC of communist sympathies, yet their denunciation was met with denial. The AGEUS responded by reprinting both cablegrams and their own commentary on the exchange, which asserted that Somoza was a liar who perpetrated assaults against defenceless students.

Upon receiving reports of the military occupation of the University, on 1 October, and the persecution unleashed upon the students, the Coordinating Secretariat of National Unions of Students [COSEC] sent a cablegram of protest to the Nicaraguan Government which reads: In the name of the National Unions of Students, of sixty-six countries, [we] express deep concern over the constant threat to Nicaraguan University of León students exercised by the National Guard.

We protest the student imprisonment and demand their immediate release. In response to the protest issued by the Secretariat (COSEC), the following cablegram from Somoza was received:

'Reports received by you are untrue and, although in past cases some people were arrested for being complicit in subversive activities outside the University, currently no university student or professor is [in jail] and I regret the ease with which you accept false news when you should be concerned with finding the truth.'

The cablegram sent by Somoza is fallacious and deceitful because no university student has participated in any subversive activities, the President cannot deny that students were shot in the back, that others have been exiled from the country, as in the case of our comrade Carlos Fonseca Amador, who after being tortured was expelled from the country; Luis Somoza cannot deny that he implemented his infamous Extermination operation on the students, shortly after he implemented Operation '*Limpieza*' in Olama and the Mollejones;[18] there is no denying

---

[18] In Olama and Mollejones in May 1959, a group of Nicaragua revolutionaries launched a general strike that was intended to trigger a national uprising. Some of the combatants included men who would later become the founders of the Sandinista National Liberation Front (FSLN), among them Tomás Borge and Carlos Fonseca Amador. See Ernesto Guevara (1997), *Guerrilla Warfare*, ed. Brian Loveman and Thomas M. Davies, Jr, Lanham, MD: Scholarly Resources, Inc., 348.

that he maintains a constant threat to the university students through his followers, as evidenced by the accounts submitted from Aparicio Artola and José Gustavo Guillén, the last Commander of the City of León, to the University, through which he seeks to intimidate the students; these gentlemen warn that they have enough weapons and National Guard troops to dissolve any student meeting with little equivocation; [but now] we University students will not stand for threats. We know Luis Somoza has a savage army, one that exists in constant training to kill defenceless students.

Translated by Allessandra Paglia

HONDURAS

'National Constitutional Assembly of 1957'

(1957)

Quite different from the texts above, these documents outline in detail the process of securing university autonomy for Honduras's National University (UNAH) in 1957. The juridical processes of securing autonomy, although not at first anti-colonial, provided the space for students across the region to challenge the government while remaining at least somewhat confident that their physical safety would be ensured. More importantly, these debates and the principles of freedom outlined therein set the terms for the decades of dissent that would follow as they outlined the rights and responsibilities of the government, the university as an institution, and students vis-à-vis one another. The key points of contention below were the allocation of the national budget for the university's functions and the degree of control that the government could exercise over the university's functions. Note how the Assemblymen fondly remembered their own years at the university.

On 2 December 1957, the National Constitutional Assembly became familiar with, in a third debate, the contents of Article 146 of the Constitution of the Republic.

On this occasion, present in the session, in the position of invitees, were Br Elvin Ernesto Santos, President of the Federation of University Students of Honduras (FEUH) and Lic. Rubén Mondragón, Financial Advisor of the FEUH.

There were two opposing sides: [on] one [side] was the article in reference to the text of the [Constitutional] Project, which said the following:

'The University of Honduras is an autonomous and legal entity. The State will contribute to insure and increase the university patrimony and will reserve annually the percentage of its budget necessary for [the University's] adequate maintenance. The Law and its Statutes will determine its organisation, function, and attributions.'

The other position was the dictum issued by the Commission, which it conceived in the following terms:

'The University of Honduras is an autonomous and legal entity. The State will contribute to insure and increase the university patrimony and will reserve annually in its budget a guaranteed line of no less than 1%, to tend to its maintenance, development, and expansion, as the guardian of national culture. The Law and its statutes will determine its organisation, function, and attributions.'

The texts transcribed here served as the basis of the discussions that took place in the first and second debates. In the third debate, however, the representative of the Federation of University Students of Honduras, Br Santos, in addition to voicing his disagreement with the terms in which the article in the Project and the dictum were conceived, found it appropriate to suggest to the National Constitutional Assembly the following:

'The National University is an autonomous institution and legal entity. It enjoys the exclusive authority to organise, direct, and develop higher learning and professional education and will contribute to scientific investigation, to the general diffusion of culture, and will participate in the study of national problems. The Law and its statutes will determine its organisation, function, and attributions. Only the academic titles given and recognised by the National University will be valid. The National Autonomous University is the only institution of higher learning that will determine the incorporation of professionals who are alumni of outside universities. The titles that are not of an academic nature but whose conferral corresponds to the State will also be recognised.'

The President of the Students' Federation, explaining his proposal, said among other things that it would be of the utmost importance that the university would enjoy exclusive authority in terms of the organisation of higher education in the Constitution and [he] made additional assessments related to the patrimony of the Highest House of Study. Additionally, he asked the Deputy, Federico Leiva Larios, to sponsor his suggestion and propose a motion, if he was in agreement.

The student representative having taken the initiative, Deputy Leiva Larios presented it in the form of a motion. During the debate different interventions were made that are noted at length in what follows.

Deputy Suazo Alcerro: University autonomy has been a fight that has been taking place for many years; I remember that in the last Regular Congress [that I], along with the Lics Jiménez Castro and Pérez Cadalso, presented a project that was approved in our time; certainly through this autonomy was established.

Br Elvin Santos: Explaining the important advances made by the University in its exclusive authority to organise, direct, and develop higher learning and professional education, [Santos] said the following: 'We have discussed here the aspects by which some universities, of whatever character, whether religious or purely technical, could be founded, later, in our nation; it is wise, or better said, it is perfectly logical, that whatever university that is later founded would remain dependent – in terms of its plans of study – with its organisation and its administration in teaching materials dictated by the Autonomous University.'

Deputy Matute Canizales: 'I will express my complete agreement with the request made by the university students, which we are discussing in terms of the character of the law, as is sponsored by Mr Leiva Larios. I am in agreement because these were my greatest aspirations when in 1935 I took the fifth year of study in Medicine at the University.

Finally, submitted to a vote, Article 146 was unanimously approved in the following terms:

'The National University is an autonomous institution and legal entity. It enjoys the exclusive authority to organise, direct, and develop higher learning and professional education and will contribute to scientific investigation, to the general diffusion of culture, and will participate in the study of national problems. The Law and its statutes will determine its organisation, function, and attributions. Only the academic titles given and recognised by the National University will be [considered] valid. The National Autonomous University is the only institution of higher learning that will determine the incorporation of professionals who are alumni of foreign universities. The titles that are not of an academic nature but whose conferral corresponds to the State will also be recognised.'

Translated by Heather Vrana

'Organic Law of the University of Honduras', Legislative Decree 170

(1958)

Around the same time as the deliberations described above, the National University of Honduras revised its internal Organic Law. The rights and responsibilities described below became law by legislative decree in April 1958. Several articles outline the aims and duties of the institution and the importance of education in the democratic national project. Read together, the Organic Law makes explicit the anti-colonial potential of the autonomy decree, above. The university would prioritise subjects of study that would permit the formation of professionals that could develop unique nationalist forms of knowledge and thus reduce Honduras's foreign dependence. 'On University Extension' outlines ways that the university would seek to promote the diffusion of knowledge nationwide and to strengthen alumni's relationship to the university. 'General Dispositions' attempts to parse out the balance of power between units within the university and between UNAH and the state. The texts in Chapter 3 will further reveal how important university autonomy became to anti-colonial dissent on campus at UNAH.

Chapter I: On the University – Its Aims

Article 1. – The University of Honduras is an autonomous institution and a legal entity and its location is the city of Tegucigalpa, capital of the Republic. Universal problems on the order of science and culture constitute its object of study; of these, especially those that concern Central America; and, in particular, those that concern Honduras.

Article 2. – These preceding aims dictate, as a primordial aim, the cultivation of Science, Technology, Letters, and Arts, by means of *Facultades*, Schools, Institutes, and Research Laboratories for the training and practice of professionals and specialists. Additionally, [the university] will work for the diffusion of culture through magazines, books, and every other medium related to the accomplishment of the recommended aims.

Article 3. – The Autonomous University of Honduras will place its utmost attention on the formation of professionals and technicians, equipped with a broader [intellectual] culture that will prepare them, not just for the efficient exercise of their respective knowledge and professions, but to adequately resolve national problems, with full knowledge of the physical, social, and economic reality of Honduras. As a result, the University Authorities will prepare as well as possible so that the student can acquire the clearest understanding of the world and of life, of the historical process of Humanity and of the structure, function, and economy of Society and of its universal principles.

Article 4. – The university's function extends to the responsibilities and rights of the citizenry, the vital needs of the *pueblo*, the elevation of the patriotic spirit, and the veneration of humanity.

Article 5. – The University will cooperate in the Cultural Unification of Central America, with the goal of achieving the Political Union of Central America as its primordial Aim.

Article 6. – The following *Facultades* make up the National Autonomous University of Honduras:
   Facultad of Juridical and Social Sciences
   Facultad of Medical Sciences
   Facultad of Economic Sciences of Tegucigalpa and San Pedro Sula
   Facultad of Chemical Sciences and Pharmacology
   Facultad of Odontology
   Facultad of Engineering
   National School of Nursing
   National School of Laboratory Technicians

Additionally, the extant *Facultades*, Schools, Institutes, and other centres of investigation and personal training and those that are established in the future and that the University recognises make up the National Autonomous University of Honduras.

Article 7. – The technical functions of the University will be the task of specialised bodies, which will determine instruction, the resolution of

financial questions, the study of administrative Problems, and artistic, sports, and social activities of all sorts. Its Rules will decide in general terms all of the rest of the aspects of its organisation.
[. . .]

Chapter VII: On University Extension

Article 56. – Perfection of learning and the diffusion of culture are the fundamental principles of the University. With these aims [the university] will establish a Department of University Extension that will organise free courses, postgraduate courses, conferences, readings, exhibitions, seminars, interfaculty research, publications, and [radio] transmissions of different sorts.

Article 57. – The Autonomous University of Honduras will conduct the studies necessary for the creation of the Popular University.

Article 58. – The University hopes that the graduates of its *facultades* will connect in a permanent way to the Institution that gave them scientific knowledge and granted or recognised their professional title.

To this end, the University will promote and recognise the professional organisations that its alumni form for the improvement of their respective professions, considering as alumni not only those who had received their title from the University but also those who were incorporated.
[. . .]

Chapter XI: General Dispositions

Article 77. – The Autonomous University of Honduras will cooperate with the State in the study and solution of national problems, in the conservation of historical monuments and works of art, in the creation of museums, libraries, and other centres that make up the cultural patrimony of Hondurans, [and] over which it will exercise jurisdiction.

Article 78. – The Professional *colegios* and university student associations will be subject to, in terms of their connections to the University, the [rules] established in the present Law and in the internal rules [of the university].

Article 79. – The University Council will establish, in the rules referred to in Article 12, everything related to the organisation and function of the *Facultades*, Schools, and Institutes and the rest of the dependencies of the University, as well as those which are not foreseen in the present but which are not opposed to its spirit.

Article 80. – Transitory. At the proposal of the Rector, the University Council will designate a commission of three people to, within the period of no more than six months from when this Law is put into effect, edit [and publish] the rules that this Law reflects.

Article 81. – Transitory. While this does not consolidate the extant Professional *Colegios*, they will have the representation to which this Law refers and which these Rules establish.

Article 82. – The present Decree will go into effect ten days after its publication in the *Gazette*, from this date all of the regulations that oppose them will be revoked.

Granted in the city of Tegucigalpa, Central District, on 15 October 1957. – THE GOVERNMENT OF THE MILITARY JUNTA. HECTOR CARACCIOLI. ROBERTO GALVEZ BARNES.

The Secretary of State in the Office of the Interior and Justice – RAUL FLORES GOMEZ. – The Secretary of State in the Office of Foreign Relations, JORGE FIDEL DURON. – The Secretary of the State in the Office of Defence, O. LOPEZ A. – The Secretary of the State in the Office of Economy and Taxation, GABRIEL A. MEJIA. – The Secretary of the State in the Office of Development, R. CLARE VEGA. – The Secretary of the State in the Office of Health, R. LAZARUS. – The Secretary of the State in the Office of Labour and Social Welfare, ROGELIO MARTINEZ A. – The Secretary of the State in the Office of Natural Resources, A. ALVARADO P.

Translated by Heather Vrana

Works Cited

Almeida, Paul A. (2008), *Waves of Protest: Popular Struggle in El Salvador, 1925–2005*, Minneapolis: University of Minnesota Press.
Dunkerley, James (1988), *Power in the Isthmus*, London: Verso.

González-Rivera, Victoria (2011), *Before the Revolution: Women's Rights and Right-Wing Politics in Nicaragua, 1821–1979*, State College: Pennsylvania State University Press.

Gould, Jeffrey L. (1990), *To Lead as Equals: Rural Protest and Political Consciousness in Chinandega, Nicaragua, 1912–1979*, Chapel Hill: University of North Carolina Press.

Pérez-Brignoli, Héctor (1989), *A Brief History of Central America*, trans. Ricardo B. Sawrey and Susana Stettri De Sawrey, Berkeley: University of California Press.

Chapter 3

Dependency, Development, and New Roles for Student Movements 1960–1981

Introduction

While the Cold War divided Central America, both sides of the geo-political contest could agree that the cause of Central America's social precarity was the unequal distribution of wealth. Some of the factors contributing to this inequality were longstanding, like the power of the landed oligarchy and the region's role as supplier of raw goods; others, like the mechanisation of production or reduction in coffee and banana prices worldwide, were more recent or changeable. But together they meant that, despite generalised economic growth, the majority of Central Americans did not enjoy greater security. Across the 1960–70s, more and more poor rural people moved to cities in search of employment, placing stress on already failing transportation and housing infrastructures, and often settling in unsafe housing in shantytowns. While it is worth remembering that anti-colonial students were only infrequently involved directly in agricultural labour, urbanisation certainly impacted them. Large strikes and smaller protests in urban areas like San Salvador, Guatemala City, Tegucigalpa, and Managua brought urban students into closer contact with rural workers, migrants, and urban industrial labourers.

Meanwhile, in the classroom, dependency and development theory were in vogue. Students and professors were especially interested in work by Guatemalans Severo Martínez Peláez and Edelberto Torres Rivas, Brazilians Fernando Henrique Cardoso and Celso Furtado, Chilean Enzo Faletto, German-American Andre Gunder Frank, and American Paul A. Baran. These thinkers – their points of divergence as well as agreement – helped to explain the differences between Central America and places like the United Kingdom, the United States, and Spain by pointing to their position as exporters in the global economy.

The brief import and industrialisation boom experienced by some parts of Latin America during World War II had not adequately taken root in Central America. Some argued that international economic policies worked to ensure that Central American and other Latin American countries remained exporters of raw materials by discouraging their industrialisation. Some also argued that the inequality experienced day to day by students and their fellow citizens was part of a long history that extended to the extraction of wealth through primitive accumulation since Spanish conquest. Since colonisation, the place of these peripheries in the global economy had scarcely shifted. Unevenness of wealth was endemic, but also deliberate.

If everyone could agree about inequality, they disagreed vehemently about the ideal solution. North American technocrats championed the Alliance for Progress, a ten-year and twenty-billion-dollar plan that sought to industrialise agricultural production and improve literacy and health services throughout Latin America. A witness to the implementation of the programme in Central America, historian Ralph Lee Woodward, Jr, argued that it was also an attempt to decrease communism's appeal among impoverished nations by directing funding and attention toward capitalist development projects and building closer relationships between Latin American and US leaders. In practice, Latin American presidents were able to use the Alliance for Progress funds to support pet projects. The benefits received by the community varied widely. Around the same time, the Central American Common Market (CACM) – or Mercomún, as it is known in Spanish – was established in an effort to promote regional integration, create a free trade zone, provide fiscal incentives for new industries, and set up regional agencies for financing and oversight of development. By the 1970s, it became apparent that industrial development had continued to grow unevenly. As Héctor Pérez-Brignoli has discussed at length, manufacturing jobs became concentrated in places where workers could be paid the lowest wage and industries were developed without regard for the needs and interests of the country or region. For their part, professors, researchers, and students throughout Central America sought to fend off these new incursions by proposing to solve the problem of uneven development without foreign aid or oversight. Curriculum and pedagogy became a site for anti-colonial protest. Public universities expanded their programmes in engineering and agronomy. They redesigned extension programmes that offered new collaborations and opportunities for a broader base of students, including workers and rural *campesinos*, and generally sought to enhance local and national innovations. Of course, many *universitarios* also stressed the culpability of foreign businesses in creating such uneven economic prospects. This admixture of innovation and denunciation characterises the anti-colonial texts below.

Students had plenty to denounce. The Somoza dynasty continued in power and enjoyed the support of the US government, despite its role in creating and maintaining the very economic inequality that US investment plans purportedly sought to mitigate. When, in 1963, Luis Somoza Debayle declined to run for re-election, he ensured someone from the family's vast network of supporters was elected: René Schick (1909–66). While Schick was hand-picked by the Somozas and is often remembered as simply their puppet, his presidency actually brought a brief democratic opening that permitted students to participate in new ways in Nicaraguan political life. Historian James Dunkerley has emphasised how students enthusiastically participated in new political parties and enjoyed civil liberties, like freedom of speech, during these years, even as the Somoza family continued to exert its influence. Schick died in office and one of his vice-presidents, Lorenzo Guerrero Gutiérrez, finished his term. On 1 May 1967, the third Somoza to rule Nicaragua took power.

Anastasio Somoza Debayle ruled with brutal hand until 1979, when the FSLN succeeded in toppling the long-lasting Somoza dynasty. The FSLN grew from small cells throughout Nicaragua (especially in Estelí, Managua, and León) and Honduras across the 1960s. While the guerrilla slowly strengthened and the Somozas' machinations played out, many Nicaraguans reckoned with the land dispossession that industrialisation programmes wrought. The first Nicaraguan text demonstrates the complicated role that privileged university students played in the struggle against *Somocista* social and economic structures. The last, *Imperialism*, is a long study written by the CUUN, Nicaragua's largest student organisation, and it proposes that students take their place at the forefront of the struggle. Students and faculty took a similar position in Guatemala, where some joined the new guerrilla groups that had begun to form since the early 1960s. A far greater number sought to create change from within the university by promoting a new role for students and USAC in national life. Under Rector Roberto Valdeavellano, the university revised its extension programming and night schools, and added additional programmes of study for students unable to attend university full-time. The university sent teams of doctors, engineers, and lawyers into the countryside to exchange techniques with *campesinos*. These development plans promoted by the university were a direct response to North American influence over the nation's intellectual life, but they were also a response to the military government's programmes that interwove agribusiness and counter-insurgent surveillance in areas like the Franja Transversal del Norte (FTN), where the guerrilla forces had begun to consolidate power, as Luis Solano has so astutely argued.

The beginning of the thirty-six-year Guatemalan civil war was marked by a coup attempt against Miguel Ydígoras Fuentes in November 1960, led by young military officers. The coup was unsuccessful, but the core leadership soon formed a new guerrilla organisation, the Revolutionary Movement 13 November (MR-13), and later, the Rebel Armed Forces (FAR). While the strength of the guerrilla grew, so too did the power of the military. Between 1954 and 1986, Guatemala had just one civilian president, Julio César Méndez Montenegro (1915–96), and he was elected only when former president Arévalo's return seemed imminent and after signing an agreement with the military. Intimately aligned with the military, Guatemala's landed oligarchy and a newer business elite saw their fortunes swell. At the same time, widespread distrust of the government grew among the popular sectors of students, professionals, industrial workers, and even some religious groups. The texts below make clear how students, faculty, and administrators understood the poverty of the Guatemalan people to be the result of US intervention in all aspects – economic, military, social, political, and cultural – of life. Making matters even more desperate, a disastrous earthquake struck in 1976, to which the government of Kjell Eugenio Laugerud García responded with reticence and then self-interest. This further catalysed the opposition.

The case of Costa Rica is different. To be sure, Costa Ricans were affected by uneven economic development. But the government of Costa Rica devoted a significant portion of its national budget to softening the blow of export-led growth, mostly through social spending, and carefully developed industry through sustained reforms. The cautious equilibrium reached after the brief civil war of 1948 held strong. When President José Joaquin Trejos accepted an offer from the Aluminum Company of North America (ALCOA) to explore bauxite deposits in southern Costa Rica in 1970, a unified left began to speak out. The Legislative Assembly approved the company's proposal. In response, students at the University of Costa Rica (UCR) joined residents of the region, labour unions, teachers' unions, and various groups on the left in opposition. ALCOA, they argued, represented a dangerous threat to national sovereignty. Students helped to organise daily marches and demonstrations. The protests reached a fever pitch in mid-April as secondary school students and the university's influential Federation of University Students of Costa Rica (FEUCR) joined the protests. On 24 April, a large group of students stormed the Legislative Assembly and waged a battle against the National Guard. These violent confrontations endured for more than a week. In the end, the project was cancelled. This triumph against ALCOA is remembered as a proud moment when Costa Ricans stood up to North American business interests not only to protect national natural resources, but as a matter of anti-colonial resistance. All of the texts below document this struggle and offer an insider's view of an unprecedented achievement.

In Honduras, however, attempts to fend off North American business were more complicated. After the tumultuous politics of the 1950s, order returned to the Honduran executive in the form of José Ramón Adolfo Villeda Morales (1908–71). Then, like Arévalo and Arbenz in Guatemala, Villeda excited the ire of UFCO and the US government when he attempted to implement labour and agrarian reform, a topic discussed at length by James Dunkerley in *Power in the Isthmus*. Relations with the military were also tense, as evidenced – and exacerbated – by an attempted coup in 1959. By the end of his term in 1963, Villeda had alienated many of his supporters for having made significant concessions to the opposing National Party, the military, and the US. The Liberal Party nominated a new candidate, Modesto Rodas Alvarado, for the October presidential election. Then, just ten days before the scheduled election, the army led a violent coup against the government and the Civil Guard. Colonel Oswaldo López Arellano, a nominee hand-picked by former dictator Carías, emerged as supreme leader. For eighteen months, a National Unity Pact united the parties and Ramón Cruz served as president while Honduras recovered from the 'Football War' with El Salvador. Then López Arellano boldly seized the presidency. Surprisingly, López Arellano's second term (1972–5) brought a period of very tepid land reform; all the while, US influence in fruit exports, mining, and banking continued. Throughout this period of dizzying instability, UNAH students and faculty remained steadfastly opposed to the military dictatorship. The documents below, written in 1974 and 1976, demonstrate how students and faculty framed their opposition to the military government in terms of resistance to underdevelopment.

The government of El Salvador also remained squarely in the hands of the military, though, as in Honduras, different factions of the military traded coups and juntas, preventing meaningful social change at all cost. In October 1960, a moderate civilian–military coup succeeded in overthrowing José María Lemus; it was, in turn, overthrown three months later by a far-right military coup. The leaders of this coup ruled for a year before elections were held and one of its members, Colonel Julio Adalberto Rivera Carballo, was elected as president. His presidency marked the beginning of widespread state-sponsored counter-insurgency surveillance and death squads. In 1972, university students rose up in a wave of protest against clear electoral fraud and the imposition of another official candidate, Colonel Arturo Armando Molina (b. 1927), as president. In response, the military invaded campus. The protestors were well organised, but the uprising was quashed swiftly with the help of the Guatemalan Air Force. Fraud also marked the election of Molina's successor, General Carlos Humberto Romero (b. 1924). This time, opposition was met with even more extreme force. In late February 1977, hundreds of protestors in San Salvador were gunned down; para-military death squads and the military's intelligence service expanded their efforts, claiming ever-growing numbers of lives throughout 1978 and 1979. Meanwhile, the Catholic Church documented these human rights abuses and, by doing so, made itself a target.

The victory of the Sandinistas in July 1979 made the Salvadoran military increasingly anxious. A group called the Revolutionary Government Junta launched a successful coup in October 1979, just ahead of another round of presidential elections. In two brief years, the national situation swiftly devolved into civil war, the details of which will be discussed in the next two chapters. The last text in this chapter is from 1981, the year that Ronald Regan was elected President of the US. Reagan's economic plans for the hemisphere were based on the idea that the best way to generate economic growth would be to deregulate domestic markets and promote tax cuts for the high-income earners. In time, the benefits of this overall growth were supposed to 'trickle down' to the most needy. These so-called 'Reaganomics' justified what had, in practice, already characterised US business relations with Central America for decades. Counter to this theory, the AGEUS and the Farabundo Martí National Liberation Front (FMLN) co-authored a pamphlet entitled, 'Healthcare in El Salvador, another reason for the popular struggle', which argued how the deplorable state of medical care, sanitation, and malnutrition in El Salvador was symptomatic of fifty years of oligarchic rule. They outline how even the quality of medical care received by the people was inferior to that received by elites.

In Guatemala, Nicaragua, and El Salvador, the strain of the deep inequalities described below erupted into violent civil wars that would endure into the 1980s, in the cases of El Salvador and Guatemala. Honduras seemed to avoid civil war only by virtue of the military's swift and strong hand. Costa Rica, often the outlier in histories of the region, avoided the violence altogether, largely because the government skilfully absorbed, rather than fought, opposition. As a whole, the texts in this chapter demonstrate how some students and professors understood decades – even centuries – of structural inequality to be the root of regional underdevelopment. Their solutions positioned Central Americans as producers of knowledge and technique, not merely of export crops.

NICARAGUA

'Cuba and Latin America, Yes! Yankees, No!'

(1960)

That young people had a special role to play in the future of their nations was one of the most important rallying cries of student movements throughout Central America across the twentieth century. The anonymously authored article below, published in *El Universitario*, outlines several familiar reasons for this special duty, including their bravery, optimism, and eagerness to learn. But even more, the text likens the people of Latin America who are coming into a particular political consciousness to the figure of youth. Luis Somoza Debayle remained in power and the freedom to demonstrate was quite limited. Nevertheless, students here register their enthusiasm for the success of the Cuban Revolution and their disdain for the US politicians who responded to the revolutionaries like petulant children with attacks, threats, and empty declarations. After the Cuban Revolution, US President Eisenhower drastically cut the import quotas of Cuban sugar to such a degree that the Cuban government under Castro perceived it as an act of economic warfare. Eisenhower, in turn, believed that Cuba represented a Soviet threat in the hemisphere. Eisenhower and Castro took the matter to the Organisation of American States (OAS) and, although the member nations were hesitant to become involved, the group did pass the so-called Declaration of San José, which forbade external influence in the affairs of the American continent and declared that no nation should intervene and impose its political, social, or economic principles on another. This anonymous call to the youth of Cuba and Latin America to fight the Yankee imperialists, articulated with an enthusiastic exclamation mark, was the longest article in this edition of *El Universitario*. Its vision of a pan-Latin American youth movement capable of breaking the yoke of colonialism and feudalism must have been – and remains – quite remarkable to read.

The Latin American youth will always fight on the side of Cuba and its Revolution.

Now, conscious of our historical role as young people, it is our responsibility to struggle for the future dreams of our Latin America *pueblos*, it is necessary to clearly delineate the present conjuncture that we are met with in this part of the world.

We believe that a great sector of the *pueblo* is aware of its responsibility and inevitable tasks, but there also exist – and we do not deny this – many who are disregarding the pitiful call of those who die in darkness, ignored, on the cross of hunger and ignorance. And of course, it is undeniable that now the Youth is divided into two branches: one that relaxes in the breeze and the other that buries its roots in the gracious field of Understanding, Fraternity, and Friendship.

Simply put, previous generations do not want to understand that [it is] the Youth and only the Youth [that] is wholly responsible for the future, just as it is equally true that the Youth is called upon to resolve our immediate problems. It has been traditionally believed – and is it false to believe [this] – that the Youth, in the most pedestrian and vulgar sense of the term, is 'idealistic'. No sirs, among the youth there are truths that history and experience teach us.

And it comes to pass that those who have lived more life, without necessarily more importance, those who have made a vocation and career of complacency and indifference are the ones that fear the Youth and its struggles because they know that it will not fade or give in, since it is incorruptible. Why? Because the youth is principled. Precisely today, Latin America is living through the most decisive moments in the historical process, due to the awakening consciousness of the *pueblo* as in Independent Cuba, fighting for its just demands, the first to forever eradicate from its territory the despotic oligarchy led by the gendarme [Fulgencio] Batista who represented the fifty-seven years before the Constitution of the Revolutionary Government, which is in sum the unshakable base of the New Cuba guided and organised by the principles of reality and not on fictitious and unstable foundations. Because oligarchic power had up until this point been the direct ally of Imperialism and its instruments of oppression, the mercenary army was disbanded on 19 January 1959 by direct action of the Cuban people, replacing it with the Rebel Army formed in its majority by young people, *campesinos*, intellectuals, and dignified workers. And today it liberates [the Cuban people] through the great battle of Economic Independence.

But, consequently, the master imperialist United States has not viewed this with affectionate eyes and is not wasting time in waiting to unleash its system of expansion and tutelage; and on the chessboard of invasions it has begun its attacks, not just bombings in cities and central industries of Cuba, but also economically by reducing the Sugar Quotas, culminating in the hypocritical manœuvre of the Declaration of San José, by which the Presidents, [the] so-called representatives of America, have legalised aggression against Cuba, and it is undeniable that these lackeys of imperialism had received 600 million dollars in an attempt to subdue the indomitable Cubans. It follows that the Presidents did not understand the reality of the present, of the 'Sovereign Public Power of Cuba', which is found in the Legitimate Representatives of their *Pueblo*. We Latin Americans should know, in a word, that the Cuban *pueblo*, for the first time, feels truly sovereign and free, master of its own destiny and capable of pursuing its own economic, social, political, and cultural transformation. Inevitably a radical structural change has proceeded precisely because it goes to the roots, because the relations of land ownership have been diversified by means of the AGRARIAN REVOLUTION and the Cuban returns as owner of the land that he lost years ago. We can say from this point, with or without the OAS, the road towards industrialisation is sure and the productive sectors now feel confident in the steps that have been taken to achieve the basic goals of the REVOLUTION FOR NATIONAL LIBERATION, which is, we underscore, to break with colonialism and feudal vassalage and its greatest backer: Imperialism, so we can enter definitively into the development of industrialisation, a superior phase of the Economic System.

Finally, we make a call to the Youth to lend support to the principles of the Cuban Cause, because the Cuban Cause is the Latin American cause, because yes, no one can deny, the Cuban Revolution is the loyal interpreter of the struggles and the banners of [Simón] Bolívar, [Benito] Juárez, [José] Martí, and [Augusto] Sandino and we are fully convinced that Cuba broke the chains with the same strength and intensity that our Latin American brothers will soon. We declare and advise that in response to any direct or indirect attacks by Imperialism, the Latin American Youth will stand and fight with the Cuban people to deliver the First and Final Independence – definitively, NATIONAL LIBERATION, and that we will be vigilant in the face of the provocations not only of the slanderous information of the UPI [United Press International] and AP [Associated Press] but also the attacks in the circles of the government of the country. Yes, this is the epoch where the cry and the struggle is: Cuba Yes! Yankees No! Latin America Yes! Yankees No!

It is time now that the Latin American youth, indestructible and monolithic fist like Youth worldwide, prepares to join in solidarity and to occupy the place that history chooses for us, [such] that neither prison, misery, nor death can make us retreat in our predestined goals, nor can they hold us back from paying homage to *Truth, Justice, and Friendship*.

Translated by Jorge Cuéllar and Heather Vrana

Excerpts, Student Centre of the National University (CUUN), *Imperialism*

(1971)

By 1970, the university branch of the FSLN, called the Revolutionary Student Federation (FER), had come to dominate leadership of the CUUN and university politics at UNAN-León. Now the FSLN had an even better opportunity to recruit among the student sector and to use the resources available at the university to promote its cause. Students were a great source of support for the Sandinistas, but so, too, were the Sandinistas crucial to empowering students and encouraging their ideological exploration. The text excerpted below comes from a fifty-seven-page treatise that reads like a definitive – if brief – history of imperialism. The text's broad take on imperialism links violent histories of rapacious greed on the part of empires like the US, the UK, and France in places like India, Northern Rhodesia (Zambia), and the Middle East to contemporary underdevelopment and malnutrition in Central America. The CUUN's analysis of imperialism is exemplary of the global student movement that had been flourishing for several decades. They linked local needs to global processes and strengthened their analyses with the use of statistics from internationally recognised bodies. By the time this treatise was published, students had participated publicly and decisively in several acts of opposition to President Anastasio Somoza Debayle, whose contempt and aggression toward dissent resembled those of his father.

INTRODUCTION

Among the labours that have been proposed by the CUUN, in fulfilment of the plan presented by its president to the student body, the most distinguished and primordial tasks are to raise consciousness and politicise the university sector and the whole of the Nicaraguan people.

The mission of raising consciousness has been completed by the CUUN through publications, cultural events, seminars, and above all, by the exemplary actions carried out in 1971, which began on the first of January with protests organised together with the residents of the eastern neighbourhoods to rally against the rise in the bus fares and culminating in the 'taking of the churches' that was executed along with a group of comrades from CEUUCA,[1] revolutionary clergy, and high-school students, to demand the fulfilment of justice in the nation through the liberation of various political prisoners, members of the FSLN.

Today [the CUUN] continues this important mission by offering to all students of the country and the Nicaraguan citizenry, an analytical work about IMPERIALISM, which is one of the most decisive factors of our present situation of exploitation and underdevelopment.
[...]

Octavio A. Rivas G.
President of the CUUN

Managua, 1 June 1971

'I demand freedom for our Homeland or Death'
[...]

IMPERIALISM

Imperialism is a social system by which monopoly capital exercises power.
Imperialism means: As a product of the labour and the deprivation of workers, enormous wealth accumulates in the hands of a small group of monopolists.
Imperialism means: Many people of other countries depend on or are oppressed and plundered by the capitalist monopolies. In these countries, hunger and misery reign.
Imperialism means: A constant struggle between the monopolies for spheres of influence and power, which incessantly generates danger of a new war. We blame imperialism: In an epoch that offers Humanity the possibilities of unprecedented development, millions of men have to drag themselves through a miserable existence filled with terror and fear.
[...]

---

[1] The Centro Estudiantil Universitario de la Universidad Centroamericana, the student group of the new Jesuit university, Universidad Centroamericana (UCA), founded in Managua in 1960.

WE ACCUSE IMPERIALISM OF THE CRIMES COMMITTED BY COLONIALISM

In the resolution of the General Assembly of the UN that condemns colonialism, it is said that 'the subordination of the peoples by the yoke and dominance of a foreign power and its exploitation are a negation of the fundamental rights of man, contradict the Charter of the UN and are an obstacle to the development of collaboration and the establishment of peace worldwide.' The General Assembly of the UN solemnly proclaimed the 'need to immediately and unconditionally end colonialism in all its forms and manifestations'.

This resolution was adopted in 1960 by eighty-nine votes and nine abstentions.

Although the UN condemned colonialism as a crime against humanity, in 1968 the General Assembly found it necessary to confirm that:

The colonisers, with the help of imperialist forces, 'resort to increasingly cruel means, including military operations and the violent imposition of a racist politics in order to suffocate the just struggles of autonomous peoples, aimed at the conquest of liberty and independence'.

Colonialism commits crimes like the annexation of foreign territory by force, violating the rights of the people to self-determination;
It triggers colonial wars, which they carry out with the most illegal methods and with arms prohibited by International Law such as chemical and bacteriological weapons;
It exterminates and assassinates *en masse* the populations of Asia, Africa, and Latin America;
It condemns the local population to a life of hunger;
It undermines the health of entire *pueblos*;
Preserves illiteracy and utilises religious biases for its own ends;
Creates obstacles to the development of education.

All of these crimes are perpetrated in order to secure the colossal benefits of the monopolies of the Imperialist States.

Consequences of exploitation by colonialism

In the [19]50s, the colonies, semi-colonies, and weakly-developed countries, in which two-thirds of the population of the world live, only accounted for 5 per cent of global industrial production.

The average annual salary per person was, in the colonies and semi-colonies, eleven times less than those in the developed capitalist industrial nations.

Colonialism means the extermination of the *pueblos*

Colonialism began its domination by exterminating entire *pueblos*. From the second half of the fifteenth century to the nineteenth century, it took from those countries about 100 million men as slaves. In the French Congo, the population was estimated to be between 12 and 15 million inhabitants in 1900, and in 1921 it was only 2,800,000.

The population of the Belgian Congo, which in 1884 was 30 million inhabitants, was reduced in 1915 to 15 million.

While in the seventeenth century the African continent contained a fifth of the global population, in the period of colonial domination the African people were reduced to a tenth of the human species.

Gains obtained on account of the colonies

During its domination, the imperialists appropriated almost a fourth of the national income of India and approximately a third of that of Indonesia.

The profits obtained in the copper mines of Northern Rhodesia in 1937 came to about 2,000 per cent.

The United States – according to documents of the United Nations in 1967 – obtained a net profit of 7,779 million dollars in the petroleum regions of the Middle East. Meanwhile, their investment of capital into this zone was a mere 747 million dollars.

Diseases and mortality

According to UN statistics, 375 million people live on the edge of death by hunger. Every day 80,000 people perish due to lack of food, that is to say, one person per second!

The magazine of the International Health Organisation says that 'a third of all African children die before having reached 5 years of age.'

The Magazine of the Panamerican Health Organisation informs us 'in the countries of Latin America, about 44 per cent of [annual] mortality is [of] children under five years of age, meanwhile in the United States this is 8 per cent.'

In Africa, the mortality rate is about 22 persons for every thousand inhabitants; in Asia it is 18, in Europe it is 10, and in the United States, 9.5.

The median age in the majority of the countries of Asia, Africa, and Latin America is the same as that of Europe in the seventeenth and eighteenth centuries.

Although in these countries there is devastation resulting from cholera, the plague, smallpox, malaria and other epidemic illnesses, the number of doctors is catastrophically small. For example, in Indonesia there is one doctor for 30,000 people; in Nigeria for every 31,000, and in the Central African States, one for every 25,000 (in the United States, there is one doctor for every 505 inhabitants).

This is one of the terrible consequences of colonial domination.

The illiteracy of the population

After 300 years of domination by Dutch imperialism, only 5 per cent of the inhabitants of Indonesia knew how to read and write. In the colonies of Great Britain only about 8 to 20 per cent of the native children studied in schools. In Angola, 97.3 per cent of inhabitants continue to be illiterate as a consequence of the domination by Portuguese colonialism; in Mozambique it is 98.7 per cent.

Colonial domination in Africa is the cause of 80 to 85 per cent illiteracy in the continent. The number of people dedicated to intellectual work is, on average, 7.5 for every one hundred thousand inhabitants.

In the Belgian Congo, at the moment that independence was conceded, there were only twenty people among the autochthonous population with higher education.

The colonial wars on the African continent

In just Africa and over the last hundred years, the imperialist powers carried out 121 wars and punitive military operations. In these [wars], 5,300,000 Africans were killed.

A majority of the victims corresponds to Algeria (1,600,00), Sudan (1,000,000), Ethiopia (750,000) and Congo-Kinshasa (550,000).

WE BLAME IMPERIALISM FOR PILLAGING AND OPPRESSING OUR PEOPLE IN ITS TURN TOWARDS NEOCOLONIALISM

The liberation struggles of the people made it impossible for imperialism to openly maintain its colonial domination. After the Second World War, the independence of more than 70 States was recognised.

Despite this, imperialism works to maintain and reinstate its *de facto* domination over this part of the world, applying neocolonialist methods.

Neocolonialism makes an effort to oppress the new States by political means, imposing unequal treaties on them or oppressing them through economic and military blockades.

By military means, creating bases or reverting to armed aggression and the exportation of counter-revolution.

And particularly, by economic means, which allows for the pillaging of our peoples:

- appropriating the huge profits of private investment capital and with the exporting of capital;
- collecting growing debts from loans and credits conceded to the government
- imposing unequal business conditions and manipulating prices

Neocolonial politics presents itself as 'aid', but in reality places the new States in a situation of dependency, looting and depriving them of the value created by the peoples' work in proportions that considerably exceed imported capital.

The substance of neocolonialist politics of imperialism consists in maintaining countries in development as providers of raw materials in the global capitalist economy, by which they aim to maintain the division of labour in conditions of servitude.

Pillage of countries in development

[. . .]

The worsening of commercial conditions, among other things, gives rise to injustices like the following:

'With the money obtained by the sale of a ton of cacao, Cameroon was able to purchase 2,700 metres of cloth or 1,200 kilograms of cement in 1960; but in 1965 was only able to acquire 800 metres of cloth or 450 kilograms of cement.' (From the declaration made by the President of the Republic of Niger, Diordi Ammana [*sic*],[2] on the 25th of October 1966 before a commission from the European Economic Community.)

'To import a tractor now we have to export double the quantity of flour or minerals that we did a few years ago.' (From the declaration of Galo Plaza[3], Secretary General of the Organisation of American States in October of 1968 at the National Press Club, USA.)

The returns of the dollar increase

The very imperialists of the United States boast of the earnings provided by neocolonialism.

The president of the North American company 'International Harvester' has declared: 'For every dollar spent on goods outside of the United States in the last five years, we have received 4.67 dollars.'

From 1960 to 1966, the United States has exported a sum of 3,200 million dollars to countries in development. In this same period, the profits gained by the monopolies of the United States from said countries have totalled 16,200 million dollars, of which 13,600 millions have returned to the United States.

A twentieth-century paradox

The new States have a great shortage of specialists: scientists, technicians, doctors, etc. But the new specialists instructed in these States do not remain in the country; instead they are recruited by the imperialists who dedicate themselves to the 'purchase of minds'. This horrible injustice is called a paradox of the twentieth century.

From 1961 to 1965 about 28,714 specialists moved to the United States from the countries of Latin America.

In Latin America there are eighty *facultades* of Medicine. After finishing studies there, a number of doctors equal to those being trained in about twenty of said faculties come to the United States.

Through [these] economised means in the instruction of its own specialists, the United States [accrues] direct gains equal to all of the 'assistance' that it lends to the educational system of the aforementioned countries.

Meanwhile, those countries continue to fall behind in their development.

[. . .]

---

[2] Hamani Diori (1960–74), Niger's first president after independence in August 1960.
[3] President of Ecuador from 1948 to 1952 and of the OAS from 1968 to 1975.

One war after another

After the Second World War, the imperialist powers have supported criminal wars and executed cruel military attacks to ensure or reinstall their domination:

France against Laos and Cambodia (1945–1954)[4]
France against Vietnam (1946–1954)
England against Oman and Yemen (since 1946)
France against Madagascar (1947)
United States against the Movement for National Liberation of the Philippines (1948–1951)
Holland against Indonesia (1945–1949)
The Republic of South Africa against South-west Africa (Namibia 1949)
United States against the Democratic People's Republic of Korea (1950–1953)
England against Kenya (1952–1954)
United States against Guatemala (1954)
France against Algeria (1954–1962)
United States against Laos (since 1954)
England against Cyprus (1955–1959)
France against Tunisia (1956–1958)
England, France, and Israel against Egypt (1956)
United States and England against Jordan (1958)
United States against Lebanon (1958)
United States against China (Gulf of Taiwan – 1958)
United States against Panama (1959)
England against Nyasaland (Malawi – 1959)
Actions by the imperialist countries against the Congo (1960–1962)
United States against the NLF of South Vietnam (since 1960)
United States against Cuba (1961)
Portugal against Angola (since 1961)
France against Tunisia (Bizerte – 1961–1963)
United States against Cuba (Crisis of the Caribbean – 1962)
Portugal against Guinea (Bissau) (since 1962)
United States against Panama (1964)
Portugal against Mozambique (since 1964)
United States against the Democratic Republic of Vietnam (since 1965)
United States against the Dominican Republic (1965)

---

[4] These dates are printed here as they appeared in the original text.

Israel against the Arab countries (1967)
England against Anguilla (1969)
[. . .]

WE BLAME IMPERIALISM FOR THE VIOLENCE AND WAR AGAINST THE PEOPLES OF ITS OWN NATION

[. . .]

WE BLAME IMPERIALISM FOR REVIVING FASCISM AND NAZISM

[. . .]

WE BLAME IMPERIALISM FOR PERPETUATING CRUEL RACISM

The most terrible pages of history concern racial hatred and racial persecution. Racism reached particularly terrible proportions during the Second World War.

After 1945 all forms of racial discrimination and segregation were condemned in a number of international documents: in the Charter of the UN (1945), in the Declaration of Human Rights (1948), in the Declaration on the Elimination of All Forms of Racial Discrimination (1963), in the [International] Convention on the Elimination of All Forms of Racial Discrimination (1965), and in the UNESCO Declaration on Race and Racial Prejudice (1967).

Despite this, in the conditions of imperial domination the discrimination and persecution of millions of people due to their race or colour remains, [and] racial hatred is stirred up and racial crimes are committed.

Racism is artificially stirred up because imperialism, in striving to maintain its exploitation and oppression, seeks to incite some people against others and throw them into bloody massacres.

The progressive forces of all nations are deployed in the fight against racism and imperialism.

Inhumane treatment of the black population in the USA.

In the United States, the foremost imperialist country, twenty-two million blacks live in a state of second-class citizenship. Other national minorities are made the target of discrimination such as Mexicans, Puerto Ricans, and Jews.

Blacks constitute around 11 per cent of the population but are more than 20 per cent of the working class. Despite this, their median salary is only about 53 per cent that of white workers and in the Southern states it does not surpass 30–40 per cent.

Poverty: 39 per cent of blacks in the United States live in poverty. More than 30 per cent of young black people and about 25 per cent of youth from 16 to 21 years of age do not have work. In the black ghettos of the big cities, unemployment affects, in many cases, 50 per cent of inhabitants. (The average percentage of unemployment in the US was 3.8 per cent in 1967.) (From the speech given by [Ramsey] Clark, US Secretary of Justice at the National Press Club, 13 April 1967).

Inequality in life and death: The average life of the black [person] is five years less than that of the white. Mortality among children 'of colour' is 40 per cent higher than that among whites. North American whites go to school, on average, three more years than blacks. The level of unemployment among the non-white population is double that among whites. Fifty-six per cent of the houses in which black people live do not regularly provide conditions to live safely. The income of a black family is on average 40 per cent less than that of a white family. (President Lyndon Johnson, message to Congress on 15 February 1967.)

The ghettos are rising up: From two to two and a half million blacks, about 16 to 20 per cent of the black population from the largest cities in the country live in ghettos, suffering deprivation. (From the report of the Investigative Commission of Civil Disturbances[5] in the USA.)

Imprisoned by desperation and rage, the inhabitants of the ghetto are revolting with increasing frequency. Tear gas, machine guns, and military units: this is what they receive in response.

The inhuman character of South African racism

In South Africa (the South African Republic), 14 million inhabitants 'of colour' live without any rights, in conditions of apartheid, a juridical system conceived to deprive the 'non-white' population of the rights and living conditions enjoyed by whites.

---

[5] Also called the Kerner Commission for its chairman, Illinois governor Otto Kerner, Jr, this presidential advisory committee investigated the causes of civil unrest in African American communities in 1967 and published a report on its findings.

In the countries of Southern Africa (the Republic of South Africa, South-west Africa, Rhodesia, Mozambique, and Angola), whose peoples 'of colour' struggle against colonialism and racism, Europeans account for only 4,400,000 of a total of 35,602,000 inhabitants. In the Republic of South Africa there are 3,600,000 Europeans among a total of 18,700,000 inhabitants. Of the 170 parliamentary deputies in South Africa, 166 represent whites. 1,000 people are arrested daily.

South Africa seeks to extend this system to other territories through the illegal annexation of South-west Africa (Namibia). In Rhodesia, a racist regime holds [executive] power through terror.

These regimes stay in Power thanks to the support of the imperialists. [...]

Extermination of the aboriginal population

The racial persecutions in Latin America are directed, in the first instance, against the aboriginal population: the Indians.

In Bolivia and Brazil, Peru and Ecuador, in Central America, in Mexico and in other countries, more than 30 million Indians live in the same way as they were forced to live during the era of the Spanish and Portuguese colonisers.

In March of 1968, the Brazilian government officially confessed that with the considerable participation of the government service 'for the protection of the Indians', there has been a merciless extermination carried out against the Brazilian Indians to assure the imperial monopolies' access to raw materials (for example, rubber) and minerals. The extermination of the following tribes was confirmed:

Nineteen thousand Munducuras were reduced to 1,200; 5,000 Guaraní to 300; 4,000 Carajas to 400. Of the [group known as the] 'Cinta Larga' that were bombarded from the air, only 500 survived of a tribe of 10,000. Tribes known as 'Cadiveos' and the 'Bororos' now only include groups of 100 to 200 persons. The 'Tapalunas' were totally exterminated through the gratuitous distribution of foodstuffs that had been previously poisoned with arsenic. Brazilian sociologists estimate that in total only about 50,000 to 100,000 survived who will also be surely exterminated by 1980. According to official data of the last decade, the Indians were robbed of livestock and personal property valued at 62 million dollars.

[...]

HISTORY HAS PRONOUNCED ITS SENTENCE AGAINST IMPERIALISM. CARRYING OUT THIS SENTENCE IS THE WORK OF THE *PUEBLOS*

The accusations formulated here against imperialism are irrefutable, even when they are not presented in their entire magnitude and breadth.

The social regime that unceasingly spawns such crimes is a diseased, dying regime, which has been condemned by history to disappear.

Nevertheless, it is the *pueblo* itself that has to execute history's sentence. The people have every opportunity to carry out this historic mission in our time, to prevent imperialism from perpetrating its final and most harrowing crime.

The times of imperialist global domination have gone forever. Against it today rise:

- the power of the working people in the countries where socialism has become a reality;
- the workers of the capitalist countries who increasingly form the majority of the population and who constantly strengthen its organisation and fighting capacities;
- the movements for anti-imperialist national liberation, who unceasingly grow more conscious of the objectives of their struggle.

These unified forces are capable of deciding historical development. In our time there is an abundance of examples of the effectiveness of these unified actions.

The valour and heroism of the Vietnamese people and the struggle of the global solidarity movement have frustrated the military plans of North American imperialism and have created the opportunity to triumph in the struggle for peace and freedom.

Solidarity with the Cuban *pueblo*, that lives only ninety miles from the borders of the imperialist power, has helped these people to maintain and carry out the gains of their revolution, despite all of the provocations and pressures on the part of imperialism.

Solidarity with the people of the Arab States, in the face of Israeli aggression, has blocked the realisation of the imperialist plans, which sought, by means of aggression, to stop the development of those countries through [technological] progress.

The struggles of the *pueblos* in the Portuguese colonies also receive the wide support of international solidarity movements and this situation makes it possible that in the foreseeable future they will eliminate the remains of colonialism in this part of the world.

International solidarity is, finally, a sure support for the people of the Democratic Republic of Germany, submitted to constant attacks by imperialism. International solidarity helps the people of South Korea and East Germany in their struggle against imperialist oppression and war-mongering politics.

International solidarity, cohesion, and aid inspire many other nations in their struggle and protect them from attacks by imperialist forces. Unity and cohesion form the combat weapon with which the nations of the world can defeat the imperialist plans that seek to unleash thermo-nuclear war and launch new military adventures in Europe, Asia, Africa or America.

Translated by Jorge Cuéllar and Heather Vrana

GUATEMALA

Jaime F. Pineda S., 'The Participation of University Students in National Life'

(1962)

Below, an economics student outlines why the university's faculty and students were uniquely equipped to address national problems. Unlike the many other texts in the on-going debate over the university in national political life, this article in the *Tribuna Económica*, the magazine of the Association of Economics Students, ends surprisingly with a call to vote for a particular slate of candidates in an upcoming *facultad*-based election. The party's name is not stated, which suggests that students would have recognised it by Pineda's words alone. It is remarkable how relatively low-level university politics also seem to have involved a foreign policy platform by the early 1960s. Pineda also offers an analysis of the class struggle and secondary school and university students' conscientisation. He writes, 'now we are no longer satisfied by explaining the world, but we seek to transform it.' The middle class was, in his estimation, markedly conformist; but rather than use this to signal their weakness, Pineda argues that this gives the students the opportunity to serve as the vanguard of change. Albeit in the form of a very loose adaptation, Karl Marx's analyses of the political roles of the middle class are reflected below. The text also references the movement of university students at the University of Córdoba in Argentina in 1918, what is often thought of as the first modern student movement in Latin America. The Argentine students began by agitating for better dormitory housing for medical students and, ultimately, achieved university autonomy and territorial sovereignty for their institution. Their platform of autonomy spread throughout the region and became the hallmark of Latin American university student movements for the remainder of the twentieth century. As for Pineda, he disappears from the historical record, aside from writing a brief analysis of tax administration reform, published, ironically, by the International Monetary Fund in 1992.

Writing about this fascinating theme has the effect, I think, of putting student discussions on the table, discussions that should be about the influence of university students in their two dimensions: of student today and professional tomorrow; and about what would be the most dignified attitude he might assume before the largest national problems.

University students are not abstract beings removed from real life, absorbed with themselves, their only desire knowledge for knowledge's sake. On the contrary, students arrive at the University with a whole range of multiple problems and express in their most divergent worries and aspirations the problems of the social organism. Their concrete attitude towards national and student problems reflects the contradictions of their real lives, past, present, and future. Specifically, the comprehension of this reality has caused a change of attitude in a great majority of these university students, who have passed from conformist, contemplative comportment to an attitude of militancy, drive, and action. The combativeness of the Latin American university student body has its roots in the Reform movements of 1918 in Córdoba, Argentina, and in our context has already produced fruits including the 1944 movement that culminated in the Autonomous University. The militancy of Latin American students very much resembles that of students in colonised and dependent countries in Africa and the Middle East, who continue fighting for their independence with much success.

I think that this may be understood as an ideological reflection of the economic–social reality of our peoples. Effectively, the economic backwardness to which we have been subjected, which has made us into simple producers of raw agricultural materials and even importers of [such] goods, the fundamental cause of which is that we are situated within the sphere of influence of a highly industrialised country that seeks a market for its surplus merchandise and capital, which has made our active population, formed by the middle class and other sectors of small proprietors (artisans and businessmen), especially conformist, giving the student population under certain circumstances the opportunity to assume a vanguard role in civil struggles.

These circumstances determine the fact that from the secondary school level on, the student becomes conscious of the most complex social problems that restrict their freedom (understood as the capacity to realise their aspirations and fulfil their material and spiritual needs). Thus students arrive to the bosom of the University filled with anguish and a sense of urgency to find a solution to hunger, illnesses, ignorance, illiteracy, and the other frustrations that tear at the human character.

Thus it is not insignificant that we, Guatemalan university students, assume our historical responsibility with the full consciousness that it is our role to carry out a great transformation according to the local specificities of our economic, geographical, [and] political environment, using our experience and national and universal knowledge.

Without denying the role to be played by other sectors of society in accordance with the place they fill in national life, for us as students – perhaps because we have more access to sources of culture and scientific knowledge, which can be explained by the class configuration of our society – we are more sensitive to the changes produced in the global arena and the first to make ours the banners of social justice and equality among men.

All this necessarily leads us to set forth a hot topic that thoroughly sums up the current student body's explosive conduct. And this is simply their political activity at the University. In effect, regarding this way of being a university student, [some people] have played the most fantastical tricks and have tried to stigmatise [the students] as demonic beings that threaten the sacrosanct sanctuary of the Alma Mater. At the most, they recommend 'higher politics' without defining the concept, which we may guess. But this attitude among the so-called 'apoliticals' has its *raison d'être*. They see a threat to the established 'order', identified with certain interests that are foreign to all social well-being, in the combative and insubordinate conduct of university youth. For this reason, on repeated occasions they condemned the political attitude of the students and suggested to us other conduct, which is also political, but inoffensive to vested interests and the traditional state of affairs.

Aristotle defined man as a 'political animal' and we do not wish to lose the adjective, because we thoroughly understand that we form part of a politically organised society whose political body (the State) voices an economic, social, and political truth that responds to certain interests.

We have arrived, then, to the point where now we are no longer satisfied by explaining the world, but we seek to transform it to meet our present and future needs and above all to maintain the material and spiritual integrity of man.

Given the above, we affirm: we wish to openly discuss our problems without fearing stigma, with bravery and an elevated university spirit, because we will not flee from truth but rather seek it, knowing that as university students we hold the most diverse political ideas.

Fortunately Guatemala cannot be isolated from the rest of the world and Guatemalans are not immune to uncertainties in our thought, and in spite of all the hindrances that they wish to impose on us, the current global dispute affects us. We wish that every one of us could explain the problems that really concern us and offer our own solutions, and that whoever proposed the most just and doable solution would win the sympathy and applause of the student body and of the people.

We have many student[-related] and national problems that require solution. I exhort you, my comrades as students, to tell our truth without prejudice or traps; infuse it with our most noble yearnings and sincerity; help students of Economic Sciences and Accounting to extend their fraternal arms and reach our *pueblo* that remains in pauperism, hunger, ignorance, and depression, without a practical solution to their centuries-long backwardness.

Cheers, Comrades, VOTE FOR A UNITED, DEMOCRATIC, AND RESPONSIBLE PARTY.

Guatemala, June 1962
Faculty of Economic Sciences

Translated by Rachel Nolan

USAC Rector Roberto Valdeavellano Pinot, 'Communiqué'

(1974)

University Rector Roberto Valdeavellano Pinot was elected in 1973 on a platform of democratisation, expanded extension programming, and comprehensive curriculum reform. Although he was not a member of any leftist party, he enjoyed the support of the Communist Party (PGT) and other leftist groups at the university. This made him the object of extra attention from US State Department officials, including being the subject of a telegram from the American Embassy in Guatemala to the US State Department on at least one occasion. Valdeavellano sought to utterly transform the relationship between the university and the people, equipping students with a social conscience as well as technical and scientific skills. The year after he wrote the statement below, Valdeavellano proposed a 'University Development

Plan' that targeted some of these key concerns. It was expansive and would require large sums of money from the government. President Kjell Eugenio Laugerud García urged Valdeavellano to apply for funding from the Interamerican Development Bank (IDB), as other private universities in Guatemala had done. But Valdeavellano refused, reiterating many of the points made below; most importantly, that it was the government's job to finance the public university.

Communiqué of the Rector of the University of San Carlos about the loan that the government of the republic has contracted with the IDB for use at private institutions of higher education, currently under discussion in the Congress of the Republic:

1. The University of San Carlos notes with concern that, given the precarious condition of the national economy and public treasury, external loans were approved to help private institutions of higher education in the context of there being no integral plan for higher education in the country, nor is there a known plan to create one. In this way, the investment that the State actually makes in these private institutions does not amount to anything more than an isolated programme promoted by the Interamerican Development Bank, IDB, in Guatemala.

2. In due course – in March 1971 –, the University of San Carlos decided not to accept the aid that the government had contracted from the IDB 'in the terms and conditions set forth' which were damaging to sovereignty, university autonomy, and the economy of the country.

3. The University of San Carlos is not opposed to the idea that the government of the Republic, if its finances permit, aids private institutions of higher education, if and only if they do so pursuant to an integral plan for higher education, in which priority is given to satisfying the requirements of public higher education, considering also the proportion by which each centre meets the educational needs of the country. With respect to this, recall that the University of San Carlos absorbs approximately thirty per cent of the university student population of Guatemala, and currently its needs are to a large degree unmet.

4. The University of San Carlos of Guatemala will promote a public discussion of this subject, which is of such importance, with the objective of completely elucidating all the aspects of this deal.

Guatemala, 7 June 1974
'GO AND TEACH ALL'

Translated by Rachel Nolan

Excerpts, 'International Monetary Fund, Tentacle of Capitalism'

(1980)

Published in the weekly periodical *7 Días en la USAC*, this article outlines the history of the International Monetary Fund (IMF) in clear terms for a general audience. It also weighs the outcomes of the organisation's plans, in terms of both its own stated aims and their effects for the people it purported to aid. Guatemala is not raised as an example; rather the anonymous author cites Uruguay, Mexico, Bolivia, and Chile as places where even small loans had come with significant proscriptions and demands, forbidding certain social and economic reforms and thereby violating the sovereignty of the debtor nation. Written in 1980, the text describes what has been called 'the lost decade', marked by crushing foreign debt and inflation that affected most of the region. Here, the IMF – called 'the tentacle of capitalism' – appears as the source of instability and debt. Of course, the IMF presented itself as the only solution to the on-going debt crisis. As the text below explains, this forced debtor nations to accept the lending organisation's terms, which favoured the free market and placed strict limits on domestic spending.

THE UNITED STATES CONTROLS GLOBAL COMMERCE

At the end of the Second World War, the United States became the primary creditor to the world. This country lobbied for the creation of an entity that would take as its aim the creation of a new monetary system to propel international commerce, but would primarily facilitate US exports to Europe and the rest of the world.

In 1943, two groups (the group led by [John Maynard] Keynes of Great Britain and [Harry Dexter] White of the United States) were given the task of creating a plan that would adapt to these new conditions of monopoly capitalism. In 1944, through the Convention of Bretton Woods, two new institutions were founded: the International Monetary Fund (IMF) and the International Bank for Reconstruction and Development (IBRD). Because Great Britain was not in any state to force through its conditions, the Keynesian Plan did not prevail. That plan consisted of creating an international currency that was nothing more than the 'unit of international payment'. The 'Bancor' currency was to be used as a medium of payment for any international transaction. In this way global commerce would become balanced. At root, it was about creating automatic credit between countries. Meanwhile, the White Plan – the North American proposal – consisted of the ability of countries to go into debt with an international institution, and proposed the creation of the International Monetary Fund, whose headquarters is in New York. It would always be possible to solicit credit from this institution to correct temporary imbalances in payment, but it ended up creating fundamental imbalances such that countries did not have any other option but to devalue their currency.

[. . .]

One of the goals of the International Monetary Fund was to 'facilitate the expansion and balanced growth of international commerce and thus contribute to the promotion and maintenance of high levels of employment and income and the development of the productive resources of all associated countries'. Other basic objectives included promoting stability in currency exchange, avoiding competitive devaluations of currency, and eliminating currency exchange restrictions that obstruct the growth of international trade.

CREDIT TO INCREASE DEBT

As we know, in practice, participation by percentage of Latin American countries decreased every year, while the exports of industrialised countries increased profitably. They offered us credit so that we could buy their products. Employment levels in countries on their way to development are exaggeratedly low (up to 30 or 40 per cent of the economically active population is unemployed or underemployed), and the inflationary process and international and national speculation reduce the already meagre salaries of workers. What the IMF has achieved is to open the borders of underdeveloped countries to massive exports of products manufactured in hegemonic countries, eliminating export barriers to peripheral countries.

The International Monetary Fund, in constituting a credit institution of great magnitude, has become one of the tentacles of international capitalism, economically subjugating countries on the path of development and imposing economic policies that generally run against the interests of workers.

For precisely this reason, some measures recently adopted by this international body have caused profound agitation in many Latin American countries.

[. . .]

The International Monetary Fund, creditor body controlled by the

United States (this entity has 144 member countries and the United States of America has 21.5 per cent of votes) is among the many mechanisms used by that country to subjugate the developing countries. A nation that solicits a loan from the IMF must permit experts from that organisation to supervise the state of their economy, finances, and reserves; they must also devalue their currency if the IMF so orders; reduce budgetary spending, principally on social programmes, because a reduction in military spending has never been suggested; and open wide the doors of their country to foreign investment.

DISPOSING OF SOVEREIGNTY

No nation that accepts the demands of the IMF can also make profound socio-economic transformations, restrict the activities of multinational corporations, or expand the public sector of the economy to create new State-run businesses.

Governments that unconditionally accept the model imposed by the International Monetary Fund in fact distance themselves from national sovereignty, for example in the case of Uruguay where fascist tyranny has developed the economy in accordance with the IMF [and] accentuated the dependency of that country and created an acute economic crisis, and lowered to unbearable levels the standard of living of the vast majority of the population. Wealth, on the contrary, has been increasingly concentrated in the hands of foreign consortia and the landowning Uruguayan financial oligarchy. According to a newspaper in Montevideo, 'the recipe of the International Monetary Fund has been and continues to be cruel austerity and lack of systematic consideration for all its painful social effects – which, more than recommended, are demanded by this organisation. In giving us advice on inflation and budgetary debt, scorning the results of its recipe of unemployment and misery, the IMF assumes the role of hangman that it has never hesitated in playing.'

In Peru, commitments made to the IMF involved a drastic reduction in fiscal spending, and this required firing thousands of public sector workers. The demands of the IMF also translated into a cut to subsidies of basic goods, which stimulated a wave of speculative price increases, and consequently, an inflationary spiral.

The people of Bolivia, Mexico, and other countries of our America have also been victims of the unfair conditions imposed by the International Monetary Fund. It is worth remembering that at the same time as Somoza's terror was exercised in a brutal genocide against the Nicaraguan people, the International Monetary Fund granted a loan of several dozens of millions of dollars [to the Somoza government]. The United States, which practically has veto power over the decisions of the IMF (they have 8,400 million Special Drawing Rights[6] in the amount of $1.75 each, an amount that represents 21.5 per cent of the global total), asserted on this occasion that they could not oppose the loan because these credits are not provisional based on political conditions; however, the whole world knows that the United States prevented the International Monetary Fund and other financial organisations controlled by Washington from making even a little loan to the Chilean Popular Unity government of President [Salvador] Allende. There is also evidence of [the US's] complicity in the fact that this body, which appears technical, is actually imminently political, and supports submissive regimes of a dictatorial nature.

Translated by Rachel Nolan

'Letter from a Thief to his Neighbours'

(1976)

There is an intriguing document with very little contextual information in the archives of the Centro de Investigaciones Regionales de Mesoamérica (CIRMA). It is signed, simply, 'a thief'. Of its provenance, the brief line after the letter's closing offers a small clue: 'Put forward by Rolando to be published after the earthquake of 4 February 1976.' We can assume that this 'Rolando' is Rolando Morán, the *nom de guerre* of Ricardo Arnoldo Ramírez, an USAC-trained lawyer, friend of Che Guevara, and organiser of the Guerrilla Army of the Poor (EGP). We can also assume that it was a text circulated among the EGP, perhaps written by Rolando himself, as the letter is a complicated critique of the lumpenproletariat, very much in line with Marx in *The German Ideology* (1846) and *Class Struggles in France* (1850). From Marx's perspective, the lumpen were a dangerous class of outcast people defined by their parasitism and susceptibility to fascism. And yet this letter, written from the perspective of one of these dangerous outcasts, becomes a screed against the bourgeoisie and ends with a call to action. It reads as a short dramatisation of a coming to consciousness, pedagogical and demagogical in its prose.

---

[6] Special Drawing Rights is a supplementary international reserve asset created in 1969 to supplement member nations' official reserves after the US dollar and gold proved insufficient in international supply to support the growing world trade.

I am a thief, or to put it better, a <u>member of the lumpenproletariat,</u>[7] one of the socially marginal. I am a product of the disintegration of every class within a society where the regime of exploitation rules. Before, I was a peasant, worker, etc. and there came a moment when I could not continue in those roles. To the lumpen belong thieves, but also prostitutes, people with marginal work (those who guard cars and shine shoes, for example), and, in the lowest sphere, murderers and henchmen. Our principal characteristic is that our 'labour' <u>is not socially productive.</u> We <u>individually</u> appropriate a portion of the work of all, without contributing our own socially productive quota, without generating productive labour.

In some ways and while maintaining some distance, we are similar to the capitalist and landholder, <u>who also do not contribute their appropriate quota of social work in relation to the magnitude of what they rob by means of exploitation.</u>

How did I arrive at this situation? I was not born a thief, but circumstances made one of me. I am not predestined (man is the product of his environment), and neither am I a mental case. I was born neither good nor bad; I was simply born to a given society, whose luck and social circumstances and particulars <u>made of me</u> a thief.

My dear neighbours, do you know what it is like to be non-employed? I am not just talking about <u>unemployment,</u> which is certainly one of the causes that began this marginalisation that thousands of us experience. I am speaking, for example, of the peasant who never learned to do anything but work the earth and one day it failed him, but upon trying to learn another kind of work he found out that there was no opportunity for doing so and to survive he went along inventing 'jobs', in this way becoming one more of the marginal. I am speaking ultimately about the situation when a society concentrates wealth in the hands of a minority and distributes ruin to the rest and thus creates the myth of <u>an excess of citizens.</u> I am one of the arguments used by the capitalist state to reprimand the people in the name of 'conserving the <u>order</u> of the underlings', and at the same time the very product of what this same state defends: social injustice and economic exploitation.

According to bourgeois ideology, my sense of malice makes me aspire to the goods of others. This idea can only come from those who accept as 'just' the exploitation of man by man. In the same way that one who lives in a land infested with mosquitos is prone to malaria, I do not deny that we are closer than ever to the abyss. But is it not possible that this

---

[7] All punctuation and fonts appear here as they do in the original.

society is itself a slope towards the abyss for all those who are exploited? I do not want your goods, for example, to equip my home (I also have a home) with a television or radio. I would like them, of course, but I would rather obtain them as product of my labours, but what happens is that I have become an instinctive being, I no longer struggle to survive, but I fight to live. I do not rob goods, I rob merchandise, which is to say useful things that will help me obtain money (this 'magic' good that opens all doors, even those of 'respectability', to speak the capitalist lingo), and thus to also pay the price of living.

You have organised yourselves to protect your goods. This makes me sad, angry, and also optimistic.

Your alienation makes me sad. From one day to the next you have held up a 'moral' code that is more fragile than adobe. Benevolently deceiving yourselves, you do not want to admit that as soon as you were placed in the same situation of survival [as I have been] you would do the same as I have. When you affirm that 'we must organise because now there will be more thieves' you are alluding to the base issue: not simply more thieves, but essentially more impoverished people lashed by suffering.

How untrue is all this! Some of you are even disposed to suddenly transform into murderers. You do not wish to capture me, but [rather] to assassinate me as a warning! You want to taste the honey of power and think that you have separated from civil society! You even pursue ghosts, unleashing terror among yourselves and you are disposed to end up where others already have: killing <u>in error!</u>

What a strange coincidence? That was the path of the German people at the time of Hitler . . .

I do not doubt your intentions. But you accuse me of injustice . . . towards you! You attack me, you attack the effect and not the cause. I could even accuse you of the cowardice of unilaterally attacking the poorest. You know the abuses committed after the earthquake. The degradation of the Bourgeois State, the corruption of the army and the other repressive forces, in their bureaucracy and servility before the bourgeoisie. They certainly can say that everything has been distributed in an orderly way by the National Emergency Committee! And shout it to the entire world.

Listen fearless ones . . . 'Kill, dear neighbours! The police and army will protect you. If you find a thief – kill him! Kill him with blows, riddle him with bullets, and then proceed like us . . . Throw him on to any roadside!' In the name of preserving the order of the privileged you are exempt from the charge of murder and God also absolves you because

'God is Guatemalan' and he is incarnated in the Archbishop who has received the blessing of the great prophet Tachito Somoza![8]

You are so confused in your role as judges that you do not take into account the grave offences suffered by the whole country. Unfurling their hypocritical white flag of peace, the Yankee imperialists have invaded us. And you consented to it with a silence that was sinful, shameful, and undignified.

I lack the tears to express my rage!

But I, the thief, see a ray of hope . . . is it possible that the bitter taste of ignominy and shame makes us recognise the sweet value of dignity? It is true, to the present your committees have had an impure element, and it's that you do not [truly] see or comprehend it, only unconsciously, and you do not really understand. But your committees also have an untarnished component that has not yet manifested, but is latent. In their seed, neighbourhood committees are proving the value of unity, the unity of all people who are oppressed, abused, and terrified. Terror is the longing for liberty.

Do you really want to get rid of me, does it not matter whether I am named Juan, Pedro, or Miguel? Then help me. There is a dream . . . a dream made real. Have you heard of the countries where there are no liars, no prostitutes, no thieves? There I will prove that I am a useful man, there I want to be, with my people.

Do you want to free yourselves from all oppression? Fight!

Forgive my interruption in your homes, dear neighbours. I came during the day, with open hands to offer you the truth.

Sincerely,

A thief

Put forward by Rolando to be published after the earthquake of 4 February 1976.

Translated by Rachel Nolan

---

[8] The nickname of Anastasio Somoza Debayle, then President of Nicaragua.

COSTA RICA

FEUCR, 'History Signals our Position'

(1970)

The FEUCR, like all student groups by the 1970s, believed that it had a special role to play in the nation's political life. Here, the group's president addresses not just the student body, but also the whole nation to confirm that the students would continue to take a firm stance against the North American-owned ALCOA. Written on 23 April 1970, this text is a strike declaration and FEUCR President González asks for the students' and citizens' support. He writes that the group had first attempted to block ALCOA through legislative means, but this strategy had proven ineffective. The address was reprinted in a May edition of *El Universitario*, which focused exclusively on the strike and the student-led attack on the Legislative Assembly on 24 April. Notice how González's focus shifts to the question of progress and national sovereignty by the end of the text.

Costa Rican citizens;
University comrades:

A major step has been taken today by the youth of Costa Rica. A clarion call has sounded from the pure conscience of the students, who, without prejudice or political commitment, have decided to take part in public life, having as their only goal the highest interests of the Nation.

Our democratic tradition gives us the ammunition of the strike. [This is] a method of pressure and arbitration that many fear, because it certainly can lose its purpose when it is poorly organised, but it is very effective and sincere when one clearly understands its implications.

The Federation of University Students of Costa Rica decreed a General Strike in its classrooms starting this morning. Thousands of secondary school students and citizens from various types of professions have joined it. The stance that we initiated has found support in these sectors because it is powered only by nationalist and democratic designs. It is not the irresponsible street protest that some wish it would degenerate into; it is not the product of spontaneity or of political calculation. It is the most wholesome cry that a large group of students could utter.

In the course of the history of nations, thousands of human lives have been offered to defend [the] sovereignty or the integrity of a territory. Millions of acts, as well, have been proposed in all latitudes in order to use the legislative powers of a Republic in order to contribute to the solution of the problems of affected communities.

The current outlook of the student body of Costa Rica falls into the second category. During the debates about the undertaking that concerns us today, we pointed out to the legislators the need to reform some parts of the law that we considered harmful to national interests; and we achieved this aim, in small part, and this got the deputies to make appropriate requests to the company [ALCOA]. The company, however, rejected the proposal.

At present, it is not possible to make modifications to the contract; there are only two alternatives: approve it or reject it. And we ask that [the deputies] reject it because it does not reflect the most basic standards of sovereignty that ought to define a contract of such importance.

This position must be very clear: we oppose the contract because at its core it is bad. Definitely, we cannot speak out against the progress of the nation, because we would then be the heretics of the twentieth century. We cannot say that the prosperity of the people of San Isidro de El General[9] does not matter to us because we would then be killing our own fellow citizens. But what we can do is cry out, loudly and in all directions, that progress is not subjected to the vortex of economic, traitorous interests that destroy a nation's desire to improve; and that we should elevate above all other interests the prestigious sovereignty of the Nation.

Citizens of Costa Rica: The Federation of University students is conscious of the historical role that it has assumed and is resolute in its position. Today, more than ever, we need your help. We reaffirm the previous statement that we have acted transparently, without corruption or the influence of agitators. We have begun our struggle on the basis of the support of a democratic majority among the youth, the irrefutable legacy of our ancestors.

We are in a position of privilege and responsibility: we are citizens and students. Because of the former, we have every right to participate in political life; because of the latter, we are indebted to the *pueblo*, which we now call on to fill the ranks with their great numbers in order to defend our sacred and inalienable interests.

Rodolfo González Q.
President of the FEUCR

Translated by Heather Vrana

---

[9] San Isidro de El General is the area in southern Costa Rica where ALCOA had proposed a bauxite mine.

'Why I Participated in the Actions on the 24th'

(1970)

Published in the same edition of *El Universitario* as the strike declaration above, this text is a conversation between the newspaper's editors and an anonymous student who participated in the attack on the Legislative Assembly building. The editors ask why the student participated in the strike in the first place, and then how and why the strike turned violent. They also ask about the influence of the Communist Party on the striking students, but the student resolutely rejects communism as a viable path for Costa Rica. They go on to explore the individual student's reasons for participating in the protest once it had turned more violently confrontational. The interview ends with yet another evaluation of the influence of student movements around the globe. Throughout, the anonymous student insists upon the singularity of Costa Rica and its people's unique needs and abilities.

We had the following conversation on Saturday, 25 April, with one of the students who participated actively in the demonstration the day before.

Why did you participate in the fight against Alcoa?
My personal reasons are a little different from those of the other participants. While many of them only see the terms of the contract as terribly unfavourable for the nation, I believe that the problem is much deeper. To me, this contract should be seen as an act of enormous importance for the future economic, social, and political development of the nation, from the [perspective of the] need for an authentic nationalism that defends the interest of our people, first of all.

Would you dare to define yourself as a communist?
Of course not. In general, one can affirm that the international communist movement is undergoing a profound crisis and that it has demonstrated itself to be incapable of reflecting the specific national interests of the diverse nations where it appears.
This can be seen with particular power in the case of the so-called May Revolution in France and in the failed experiment that was the 'Prague Spring'. With regard to Costa Rica, this is definitely not the path to follow. And our youth and our *pueblo* have understood this. Hence the invalidity and political senselessness of the communist movement.

Did you protest with the hope that the deputies [of the Legislative Assembly] would not sign the contract?

To tell the truth, I held on to hopes of this. I thought that, given the document that articulated basic objections to the contract, written by deputies of all Parties who formed the commission charged with this task, it seemed reasonably possible that they would not give it final approval, [also] given Alcoa's refusal to reach any deal with the new Legislative Assembly. Additionally, because [the Legislative Assembly's] political makeup could facilitate negotiations with Alcoa.

Did you have the intention of sparking violence?

Of course not. But that is connected to your previous question. When you see what looks like a '*tamale*[10] ready, wrapped, and tied' – pardon the expression – feelings of impotence and frustration emerge with all their might. The reactions were, of course, individual. But to be frank, when I was among the multitude and I began to hear that it was all 'cooking', that we had all been 'tricked by fools', the idea of doing something more than marching with signs and singing hymns began to take root in my mind. That is what happened, where the idea came from. Not beforehand.

So you participated?

Well, yes. I remember that the first thing that I threw was an ice cream that I had in my hand. You can see from this that we were in no way prepared for this style [of protest]. The multitude approved [of] what had happened in many ways and this prompted us to keep going. Everybody knows what happened next and it was a simple chain reaction, uncontainable, that expressed the ire and the disillusionment of the youth who participated.

Do you think the stoning of the Assembly was reasonable and constructive?

Hmm. Yes and no. Yes, because in some way it has helped make the whole country feel [our] immense rejection of the nationwide selling out that the deputies were sitting there doing [while] acting in the name of the people who they have forgotten about. Yes, because ultimately it was the youth's answer to the violence that it has been subjected to when we have been insulted and slandered by the press, radio, and politicians.

---

[10] A *tamale* is a Mesoamerican food made by steaming corn-based dough containing a filling in a corn husk or banana leaf.

No, because really, nothing was gained with this and the contract was unstoppable. Additionally, this served the politicians, journalists, and radio deejays [who] cast a smokescreen over the very serious truth of what had happened – the approval of the contract – with the pretext of the violence, rocks, and more.

Of course, I do not agree with the attack on businesses. This was an outcome that I do not think anyone wanted and that was simply the outcome of the turn of events.

Do you think the events of April were a copy or imitation of other similar recent events around the world, for instance those in France?

I think there are similarities in some respects, for instance, the desire of the youth to participate in the decisions related to their future; an attitude of scepticism toward the things that are a given and that generations until now have received passively.

But the differences are more glaring. Here what it was about was the defence of national sovereignty, the nation's dignity, and the direct interests of the people. While in France it was about leading to an insurrection, because what it called into question was the very order of things; here no one has denied the validity of the parliamentary system, of the mechanisms of democracy, and respect for the law. Rather, the reaction stemmed from objective disrespect [shown] toward these values of our republican way of life.

It is important, by way of conclusion, to say that this is, of course, only the beginning of the participation of the student body in national problems. Every time they understand better that these are their own problems, that they are linked with the rest of Costa Rica. A great deal of work lay ahead and in it, we, the students, have a big role to play.

Translated by Heather Vrana

Editorial, *El Universitario*

(1970)

In this editorial published in *El Universitario* a few months after the strike, a student journalist explains how the meaning of *universitario* had transformed since the successful protests against ALCOA. Part of the 'rising convulsions of a new order' throughout the 'Third World', they write, the Costa Rican student was called upon to realise their privileged place in society. But the editor argues that every student, more than simply possessing privilege in class structure, was an investment in the future by the *pueblo* through its labour. And yet underdevelopment had also afflicted the classroom and so the author calls for national – and nationalistic – forms of knowledge creation. Underdevelopment occurred when Costa Ricans consumed foreign or even outdated cultural products. Foreign textbooks, too, were to blame. To combat underdevelopment, students must reorient the university and serve as 'an advance guard . . . against dependency'. The student's critique of dependency, growth based on coffee and banana exports, global capitalism, and dispossession is framed in terms of national sovereignty and, even more, integrity.

The significance of their belonging to the institution is not always clear to the young person who comes to the University. In general, they imagine that the basic goal of academic studies is the attainment of a title and the corresponding certification to practise their profession.

Maybe this made sense in the past, when views on national development were narrow and limited. But today, when our nation participates actively in the rising convulsions of a new order of things that [have] stirred to its depths all of the Third World, it is impossible to continue with this short-sighted focus.

The *pueblo* has invested in all of us, the university students, something beyond a simple economic fact. There is an historic investment: that of the inheritance of a socio-cultural heritage to conserve and improve. A social investment: that of creating an effective agent for change. A human investment: that of creating a man [who is] conscious of the limitations of the present and its dated social structures; a man capable of participating actively in the improvement of our *pueblo*.

It is not possible to deny that the university student is a privileged being in this conjuncture of Costa Rican society, but most of the time, he dashes the hopes of the thousands of fellow citizens who struggle in the misery of underdevelopment. However, underdevelopment is not only outside of the University. Underdevelopment also fills our classrooms and makes it impossible to create a complete University like the one that all youth dream of and that the nation needs. Underdevelopment fills the pores of our culture. We are underdeveloped when we consume secondhand cultural material, born of political and historical desires foreign to our nationality. The same narrowness of vision guides the training of our professionals. And when we substitute concrete investigation of our reality for exegesis in fossilised textbooks that are imported from abroad, we are also filling ourselves with underdevelopment and frustration.

For every authentic youth who enters the university classrooms, their principal duty is to look out for the proper orientation of the University; to actively participate in the analysis and solution of national problems that afflict the thousands [within] the institution. And when their participation and experience in the life of the university lead them to question problems down to their deepest roots, this should be the final step of their becoming the citizen that Costa Rica needs and that the University is obliged to generate: an advance guard in the fight against submission, dependency, and backwardness.

Translated by Heather Vrana

HONDURAS

'Joint Declaration by the Federation of Honduran University Students (FEUH) and the General Association of Salvadoran University Students (AGEUS)'

(1974)

The so-called 'Football War' exploded between Honduras and El Salvador on 14 July 1969. In just five days, 6,000 people died and many more were injured. At the root of the conflict was not the World Cup playoff game that catalysed the dispute, but rather the influx of around 300,000 Salvadoran migrants into Honduras in search of work and land. The migrants fled growing population density and escalating dispossession, which were in turn fuelled in part by how El Salvador and Honduras had fared differently in the CACM. A common perception in Honduras was that the economy of El Salvador was inhibiting Honduras's ability to industrialise. Meanwhile, Honduras's politicised peasantry, which was also deeply nationalist, confronted its own land shortage, a crisis that was scarcely improved by a very moderate agrarian reform that failed to appropriate land from the oligarchy of UFCO. The clear solution was to appropriate land from the recent Salvadoran arrivals. Confrontations between Salvadoran and Honduran peasants escalated and the government of Honduras threatened to deport Salvadorans. But the government of El Salvador feared the unrest that 300,000 dispossessed peasants could foment. Five years later, the leaders of four prominent student groups urged their constituencies to reconceptualise the on-going tensions as a struggle of two colonised peoples against the colonial power of North American imperialism and the CACM. They met in El Amatillo, on the border between the two nations, to issue this joint statement, which is reproduced here from the *Boletín del Instituto de Investigaciones Económicas y Sociales* but was surely published in many different periodicals and probably also in pamphlet form.

JOINT STATEMENT FROM THE GENERAL ASSOCIATION OF SALVADORAN STUDENTS (AGEUS), THE FEDERATION OF HONDURAN UNIVERSITY STUDENTS (FEUH) FEDERATION OF SECONDARY EDUCATION STUDENTS (FESE), ASSOCIATION OF HIGH SCHOOL STUDENTS (AES)

The peaceful and just resolution to the conflict between the Republics of Honduras and El Salvador requires the mobilisation of *pueblos* of both countries so that the solution is in accordance with popular interests and not those of the powerful economic sector that caused the conflict between both countries, which culminated in the armed confrontation, bleeding dry not the oligarchic sectors, but [the] exploited and vilified.

A peaceful and just solution is only possible if the popular organisations from both countries mobilise; if the entire *pueblos* from both nations, united into a single force, rise to tie the hands of the oligarchical warmongers of El Salvador and Honduras.

The problem between Honduras and El Salvador is based upon archaic agricultural structures and the crisis of the *Mercomún* [CACM], instrument of neocolonial domination brought on by North American imperialism, which aims to expand and maintain the subjugation of the countries in conflict [by] obstructing those who seek the establishment of a just society, based on the right to self-determination of the people.

For these reasons, and conscious of the historic role that we play in the process of social transformation and the eradication of daily exploitation that our workers and peasants are subjected to, for the final liberation from the domination of North American imperialism,

WE AGREE TO:
1. Strengthen the bonds of fraternity between our National Student Unions and remain in constant mobilisation so that the students of both countries are a force for the peaceful and just resolution of the conflict.
2. Call on other popular organisations in Honduras, El Salvador, and Central America to join a common struggle for peace in both countries.
3. Advocate for the Universities of Central America to actively participate in conflict resolution.

4. Work towards the meeting of a Congress in Central America that will analyse, identify, and propose a concrete solution to the conflict.
5. Demand that the governments of both countries find a peaceful, just, and quick solution to the conflict; and that they shoot down expansionist aims of any kind, taking into account the need to delineate the borders between both countries.
6. Condemn the predatory and bellicose attitude of the Central American oligarchies, which in collusion with US imperialism, keep our *pueblos* oppressed and strive to restore the *Mercomún* in the service of multinational corporations.
7. Grow because our *pueblos* are moving towards total liberation and the establishment of a society without social class, conscious that this is the source of the social problems our people are suffering.
8. Fight for the respect of the right of the people to determine their own economic, social, and political regime, specifically to lift the economic blockade against Cuba and for the vindication of Panamanian sovereignty in the so-called 'canal zone'.

MANUEL FRANCOS
For AGEUS

CARLOS ARITA
For FEUH

TITO BAZAN
For AES

PABLO CARIAS
For FESE

El Amatillo, 24 February 1974

Translated by Allessandra Paglia

'The Murderers of the CIA'

(1976)

From the leftist student newspaper *Presencia Universitaria*, this article summarises the worldwide meddling of the CIA during the Cold War. As printed, the story filled an entire page and featured a large photograph of

US President Richard Nixon alongside the article's punchy title, effectively labelling Nixon a murderer, too. The text elaborates on some of the many moments when the CIA attempted the assassination of high-profile opposition leaders, striking both an informative and an inflammatory tone. Here, as in the *No Nos Tientes* (see Chapter 4) from Guatemala, humour becomes a weapon in the anti-colonial struggle: bumbling and incapable assassins could not manage to carry out their missions.

'We find ourselves before a ruthless enemy, whose aim is world domination by any means necessary and at any cost. A game like this lacks rules. The norms of human behaviour considered up until now to be acceptable cease to be so. If we want the United States to survive, we have to re-examine the idea, customary amongst us, of "fair play".'

This is the foundation of the doctrine formulated in 1954, in the paroxysm of the Cold War, by a special panel of advisors to [US] President [Dwight D.] Eisenhower. The 'implacable enemy' in question is communism; and in order to destroy it all crimes are lawful – provided they have the blessing of the President of the United States, who has never failed them. This is – in short, and without the oratorical caveats from the authors – the conclusion of the report recently published by the United States Senate about the murders and attempted murders carried out by the CIA (Central Intelligence Agency). The report describes, with an aside of horrifying details, a series of plots hatched by the Agency against – amongst others – Fidel Castro, nationalist Congolese leader Patrice Lumumba, South Vietnamese President [*sic*] Ngo Dihn Diem, Dominican President Rafael Leonidas Trujillo[11] (the latter two, after

---

[11] As a leader of the Cuban Revolution and head of state, Fidel Castro (b. 1926) has been the target of many attempted assassinations. Successful assassinations were carried out against the others mentioned. Patrice Lumumba (1925–61), as the text notes, was a leader for the independence of Congo from Belgium. His opponent in the independence struggles, Moishe Tshombe, who is also discussed in the text, enjoyed the support of the Belgian and US government and mining initiatives. On the defensive, Lumumba turned to the USSR for aid. In December 1960, Lumumba was arrested by the military under the orders of Tshombe and killed the following month. Ngo Dinh Diem (1901–63) served as Prime Minister of a US-backed government in South Vietnam from 1955 until a coup in November 1963. His dictatorship famously persecuted Buddhists and communists, a persecution that reached its zenith in May 1963, when four Buddhists self-immolated in protest against his government. He was overthrown by a coup and assassinated a few months later. Like Diem, Rafael Leonidas Trujillo (1891–1961) was an autocratic leader who enjoyed the support of the US government. Like Diem, Trujillo ruled by force, if not always by law, until his assassination. Also like Diem, Trujillo had begun to lose the support of the US by the end of his rule. He was especially cruel to Haitian migrants. All

having served the United States faithfully for many years, had become a liability because of their excesses), and General René Schneider, Commander in Chief of the Chilean army, guilty of refusing to cooperate in an American plot to sabotage Salvador Allende's rise to power.

Miracle Workers

Seized by the crusading spirit, the leaders of the CIA did not hesitate to enrol mercenaries to assassinate Lumumba, nor in contracting assassins from the Mafia to execute Castro, nor in ordering its scientists to release all sorts of poison and weapons worthy of James Bond. They even conceived delusional theological–technological plans in their obsession to topple Castro, as imagined by a renowned expert in the field of psychological warfare, General Edward Lansdale. The crafty General proposed spreading a rumour through Cuba that Christ would return on a specific date to topple Fidel. That day, an American submarine would emerge along the coast of Cuba and release hundreds of flares to announce the miraculous appearance. According to Lansdale, that would suffice for the Cuban people – as credulous and superstitious as those underdeveloped [people] south of the Rio Grande – to rise as one against the Castro regime. However, the project – christened as the 'Elimination through Illumination' – was never executed.

The funniest thing about the Senate report is that according to its conclusion, the criminal plans hatched by the CIA were never carried out. A third party always arrived and killed the intended victim before the Agency experts had time to lift a finger. That's how it happened – according to the report – in the assassinations of Diem, Trujillo, Schneider, and Lumumba. But from this no Senators concluded that the CIA was inept, rather that it was innocent. At most it can be accused of having had ill thoughts. The fact that the victims identified in the report were killed can only be attributed to Providence, which, as is well known in US governmental and corporate circles, is always on the side of the United States.

The Hand of God

The intervention of Providence was clear in the case of Lumumba. According to the report, in August of 1960, Allen Dulles, boss of the

---

of these deaths have been the subject of speculation and investigation, fuelled in part by the on-going secrecy surrounding Cold War geopolitics.

CIA and brother to the Secretary of State John Foster Dulles, told his colleagues that President Eisenhower ordered the elimination of the Congolese leader. According to the senators, it is unclear whether Eisenhower demanded the assassination, or if he limited himself to the mere suggestion, or if in a moment of irritation he simply exclaimed: 'We must do something with that black son of a . . . !' The fact is that Dulles instructed Richard Bissell, chief of the office of Covert Affairs, who in turn forwarded the instructions to Bronson Tweedy, head of the African Section.

Tweedy got to work and instructed one of his scientists, Joseph Schneider, to prepare a discreet poison capable of killing or at least knocking out the Congolese leader. Schneider proposed a transmitter composed of tularaemia (rabbit disease) and another of brucellosis (Malta fever), and travelled to the Congo with his microbe-filled bottles, his rubber gloves, and syringes. Upon arrival he was faced with a problem. UN guards protected Lumumba, who had just led the independence movement that brought freedom to the Congo.

So, the CIA sent a team of professional assassins to help their scientist. Two were ex-convicts, one of whom had been a mercenary in the Congo, which is why the Agency had taken the precaution of having him undergo plastic surgery to change his face so that he would be unrecognisable. Everything was ready. And then the Hand of God intervened: Lumumba was kidnapped by his opposition, [Moise] Tshombe, and taken to the secessionist province of Katanga and executed.[12] Dr Schneider, jilted, took the first plane back home with his microbes, his assassins, and his rubber gloves in tow.

Schneider, Trujillo, Diem

In the case of Chilean General Schneider, the same thing happened. Salvador Allende, victorious in the election of August 1970, lacked only Congressional ratification of his election. President Nixon then ordered Richard Helms, CIA director, to make sure that this would not happen, and even authorised him to spend ten million dollars to fund a military coup. However, René Schneider, Commander in Chief of the Chilean army, refused to cooperate. The CIA decided to neutralise him, and after

---

[12] This reflects the accepted account of Lumumba's death: alongside two other members of the independent government and at the hands of Tshombe and some Belgian army officers, their bodies dismembered and dissolved in sulphuric acid to cover evidence of assassination.

attempting his kidnapping twice, on 9 and 12 October 1970, contracted a group of assassins and provided them with weapons and ammunition. But the hand of the Almighty came forward again, and on 22 October, according to a report from the Senate, it was another group of Chileans who assassinated the general.

The report is emphatic in reference to Dominican dictator Trujillo. The CIA had already taken steps to eliminate him and they had weapons at the ready, when suddenly – bang – another group assassinated him under their noses. With regard to South Vietnamese President Ngo Dinh Diem and his brother Ngo Dinh Nhu, the same: the CIA participated in the plot to eliminate them, organising everything, covering the cost of weapons and ammunition, and at the last minute someone else with no involvement in the project carried out the assassination. Poor CIA, frankly.

Fidel Castro, however, was a different story and things turned out differently, as evidenced by the fact that he is still alive today. However, according to the Senate committee, there is 'formal evidence' that shows that the Agency organised at least eight plots to get rid of him between 1960 and 1965, not including the famous recommendation made to President [John F.] Kennedy about the failed Bay of Pigs invasion. There were, therefore, at least eight opportunities for groups other than the CIA to kill Fidel in the precise moment when [the CIA] was ready to do so. It is surprising that they did not do this.

Translated by Allessandra Paglia

EL SALVADOR

Excerpts, University High Council, *Freedom and Culture with Regard to the Debate about the University*

(1964)

In this long article, several recurrent themes are taken up: the role of the university in national political life, the special duty of students and professors to innovate solutions to local and national problems, and the idea that this knowledge creation would itself be a sort of anti-colonial practice. But the University High Council (CSU) advances these debates by placing them into a global frame and contextualising them within the geopolitics of the Cold War. The catalyst for the article's writing was a trip to Europe taken by UES Rector Dr Fabio Castillo. His travels concluded at the University of Lomonosov, where he contracted two professors for an exchange programme, an action that elicited a histrionic reaction from anti-communists, who began a smear campaign against the Rector. Ultimately, the government of Colonel Julio Adalberto Rivera Caballo forbade the professors' entrance. The text below is a defence of the Rector, issued by the CSU after a university-wide General Assembly. Ironically, Castillo drew from his travels the conclusion that one of the best ways to combat colonialism and imperialism was to build closer relationships with universities worldwide. But the point of the excerpt below is that there were two types of democracies in Central America: democracy in name but not in practice, a type of unjust liberal governance that had changed little since the early nineteenth century and bolstered anti-communist repression of free thinking; and true democracy, which was almost millenarian, and resided in the true hearts of the *pueblo*.

The University and Politics

The University, as a collegiate body, is prohibited from participating in sectarian politics. The current university authorities have sought and will seek to comply with this principle. The promotion of and campaigns for these types of ideas through its organisations is not permitted. But for many, this rule means that the critical problems that affect the society in which we live (the highest concept of 'the political') should not be tackled by *universitarios*; this also means that all critique and protest against government actions ought to be forbidden to professors and students. This position is erroneous. The vital problems of the people concern the University, as a centre of culture. Not only is it permitted, but it is one of the university's duties to confront those problems and propose solutions at the scientific and cultural level. Furthermore, the people's desire for justice, its dream of advancement, and its spirit of rebellion against abuse are represented in the university youth. In the nations of Latin America, it is a phenomenon inherent in the life of the University that the students combat the excesses of leaders; because the students feel in their own flesh, like all loyal citizens ought to feel, the abuses that [the government] commits against the citizenry.

Many dream of a University that is submissive to the government, cowardly and forbearing, if not servile and sycophantic. For these people, the ideal University would be one where the cheapest incense is burned in praise of the rulers.

The University will always be concerned with the core problems of the people; the university youth, flower of the citizenry, will always condemn the government's abuses. It is useless to pretend otherwise.

There is only one way to eliminate these shouts of protest that the youth produce from time to time, and the rulers have it in their hands: it is to submit to the rule of law and to govern their subjects exclusively by the interests of the people.

The journalist who affirmed that the University was a centre of political effervescence should reflect upon his words. It is certain – and rightly so – that within the University there is a deep concern with national problems. It is true – and rightly so for as long as governmental excesses have not been abolished – that students serve in the lofty function of civic guards. But it is not true that the University is a centre of political propaganda for certain credos, nor is it true that its activities have as their objective to proselytise in support of certain groups or individuals.

Fear of Culture

Certain social sectors who wield undue and obsolete privileges [and] who are clinging to the medieval remnants in our social structure are ardent and absolute enemies of our University because in essence they are enemies of culture. They do not want our illiterate masses to emerge from their illiteracy; they do not want our workers to attain technical training or to organise to defend their interests; they do not want access to the University to be open and equal, but rather to reserve it for certain privileged groups; they want a professional who acts in unconditional service to their interests, not one who is attuned to the interests of the people and ready to defend them. They are the direct heirs of those reactionary men who forced Galileo to recant, condemned Copernicus, and carried Harvey to the fire. These groups are those who go to the rulers and propose the closure of the University or its conversion into a new dependent body, in which one cannot say anything except what [the rulers] say should be said, as the solution to all of the nation's problems. Naïvely, they think that social problems will automatically disappear the day when there is no one studying or discussing them. To foster the government's distrust of the University and to distance the university from the people, they tell the rulers that the autonomous University poses a danger because it is 'a State within a State' and that the Universities, like the horse of famous Troy, carry enemies in their womb who will try to wipe out extant 'democratic' society.

They speak of democracy although in reality they pay no attention to the word. They speak of the defence of the dignity of man; but only they, the members of the group, are considered dignified men and deserving of this treatment. They speak of human rights; but only themselves do they consider worthy of this right, because they see society as divided into two groups: theirs, the humans, and that of the great majority, the subhumans.

Thus they appear before the government and before the people as the defenders of democracy and enemies of totalitarian ideas, although they are deep-down practically on fire with totalitarianism. And in the pursuit of their goals, they have found one word with atomic power: 'communist'.

The Communist Threat. The Democracy of the Anti-communists.

Many States – from those who have a system of popular representation to those that are completely unaware of such a system – combat totalitarian ideas, the opposite of democracy, in their laws. Some, like ours, punish the propagation of these ideas. Under this guise the enemies of culture, of inevitable social reforms – the more violent when they are more delayed – the holders of absurd privileges, consider the University to be enemy number one. For these people, the University and communism are synonymous terms for the simple reason that the University is a centre of culture. They are not satisfied that the State punishes subversive manœuvres and the propagation of totalitarian ideas, they want the state to punish everyone who does not think like them, those who in some manner – as minor as it may be – represent a threat to their positions. Communism must be fought, they say, and they ask that the State extend its aggressive efforts to truly irrational limits. The extant repressive laws are not enough for them. They even want to stifle the outbreak of any ideas that might diminish their privileges. The ideal for them would be to equip police agents with a thought detector – (the 'leftometer') – and with an atomic ray, so that this could be applied to anyone who implied the smallest inclination toward social reform, State interventionism, [or] dissatisfaction with governmental actions. For them, the subversive agent of communism; someone who sympathises with any sort of socialist ideals; someone who considers liberalism an outdated approach and calls for some form of State interventionism; someone who even without a defined ideology is outraged by profound the social differences and dreams of a more just social order; someone who condemns the government's excesses; someone who is thirsty for Christian justice; someone who disagrees with the platform of the politicians in power; someone who desires the improvement of government functions; someone who is active in opposition parties; the simple intellectual who in his love of culture draws on all sources of thought; and the *universitario* are identical. Many live under this horrendous confusion of ideas, and with this wretched criterion judge the thinking of Salvadorans who do not share their beliefs.

They speak of the spread of communism into Latin America and the imperative to fight it. Many of those who speak this language are unaware of the real spread of communism because, as already stated, they use this term as a common denominator to label intellectuals, those who critique prevailing governmental regimes, those who denounce injustices, those who are discontented with the subhuman treatment endured in the [current] economic and legal order, especially related to the system of securities. If all of these people are communists, then it is certain that 80% of Latin Americans are communists. Recently, an article published in the editorial page of the *Diario de Hoy* by Juan Vásquez, unknown writer, says in relation to a speech given 'by an ex-Rector' about 'Professional Conduct' that it 'shows an evident Marxist inclination' because in his text 'the word God, Christianity, Christian morals, Christian meaning of life are conspicuous by their absence. However, the author mentions Descartes, Kant, Hegel, and other famous mavericks . . . .' Here is a pathetic example of an imaginary 'communistometer'. To write a discourse on Morals without mentioning God and Christianity and mentioning Kant, Hegel, and Descartes constitutes a clear sign of Marxism. The greater public reads articles like this one, as is the point of the editorial pages, and labels the ex-Rector a communist from here on out. Those who in a totalitarian and insidious manner call those who do not agree with their ideals communists say that they are against communism. They do not realise that they fall into the same bad habits that they attribute to their enemies: cruelty, dogmatism, [and] intransigence. They define anti-communists as democrats. But are they really? Would they receive this label if we were to analyse not just their words, but also their actions? Which democracy do they defend? The sacrosanct democracy of our *pueblos*, they answer. Have these totalitarian anti-communists stopped to think about the form of democracy in which the majority of Latin America lives? Is it not common and normal in our political latitudes to see satrapies dressed in the colourful garb of democracy? Dr Mariano Fiallos Gil, Rector of the University of Nicaragua, recently said: 'Since the Colonial period, we have progressed very little politically with the myth of liberal ideals, with this great paradox that liberalism has brought us the worst dictatorships.' Do we not have multiple examples of [moments when] the people did not vote, nor enjoy the most basic human rights; *pueblos* where dictators are re-elected or where they transmit power within a clique by means of imposition and fraud; *pueblos* where a tyrant dies and his sons inherit power; *pueblos* where the armed forces determine the permissible limit of social reforms, of 'a left turn'; and overthrow popularly elected rulers when, to their judgement, they pass this limit? Without fear of being mistaken, we can affirm that Latin America's radical problem is the absence of democracy and the crisis that the democratic proposition suffers, thanks to the deed and grace of those who preach democracy in their discourses and trample it in their actions. For the most part in our Latin American nations, Constitutions are a collection of declamatory phrases without real practice. Democracy will overcome not because it places ideas in chains, nor because it spreads rumours about who is communist, nor beheads everyone suspected of communism, but by instating it honestly and making sure that the *pueblo*, living it, believes in it, loves it, and defends it.

Translated by Heather Vrana

AGEUS, 'On the Agrarian Problem'

(1979)

The *latifundio* is a form of land tenure dating back to antiquity and brought to the Spanish colonies early in the conquest, characterised by enormous tracts of land organised into commercial estates and farmed by seasonal workers. These large land-holdings and the wage economy they require create a class of landless peasants. Although the economic policies of the CACM were meant to encourage industrialisation and discourage the kind of large-scale export production that was carried out on *latifundios*, the system and its oligarchic owners endured. The ranks of the FMLN included very many of these landless peasants. The article's insistence on the feudal character of the *latifundios* reflects both their history in Europe and the student author's own engagement with a dialectical materialist understanding of social change. This article was published in *El Universitario* by the AGEUS in November 1979, just a month after the Revolutionary Government Junta deposed President General Humberto Romero, marking the very beginning of a twelve-year civil war.

Independent of the historical forms of land ownership, agriculture has comprised the fundamental and chief source of humanity's material progress, [and] the specific characteristics of each stage that society has gone through have been determined in a sense by the predominant social relations of production. In the case of El Salvador, if we cannot consider that the contemporary *latifundio* and *hacienda*, as forms of monopolistic land ownership, are a trace of the historical development of feudal productive forces, their name itself responds to the need to characterise them analogically as forms of property that [developed] as far back as the colony and particularly since the third decade of the last century to the fourth of the present, [and] the violent plunder by today's landowners of the Salvadoran indigenous and *campesino pueblo*, by installing exploitative mercantile relations of production, [have] reinforced semi-servile practices in the extra-economic spheres (religious, political, military, commercial, educational, and ideological, in general), imposing on all of society the bitter flavour of despotism. To the extent that this is successful, many of the features that have historically determined the current situation of Salvadoran society (social, economic, political, institutional, legal, etc.) have their origin, in the final analysis, in the nature of power granted by monopolistic ownership of the land as the main means of agricultural production, features that tend to maintain and impose influence over society that extends beyond control of the land.

The *latifundio*, as a monopolistic form of land ownership, is an expression of the universal class of medieval landowners in the present, and politically, has been and continues to be the embodiment of oppressive and unjust social relations of production. Economically, land ownership has been considered part of the set of values of the landowning class, more than a form of ownership of a means of production that favours the development of agrarian capitalism, and thus it has become a serious obstacle for the expansion of dynamic relations of capitalist agrarian production that suit the growth of an internal market, favourable to accelerating capitalist mercantile production on the global scale.

As was pointed out, monopoly ownership of the land has determined, to a large extent, the general nature of the overall distribution of income in the nation.

It is easy to dismiss the statistical evidence of the extremely unequal distribution of income among different groups and social classes, product of the very extreme inequality in ownership of the means of production (Agricultural Businesses, Industry, etc.). The data obviously do not precisely express the magnitude of the actual concentration of wealth and income and the chain of economic, social, and political privileges enjoyed by the landowners. That a *latifundista* owner of more than 100 hectares owns, on average, 557.6 times more land than a *minifundista*[13] indicates

---

[13] A person who owns a very small parcel of land, called a *minifundio*, which is cultivated for subsistence.

only the extremes of agrarian despotism dominant in Salvadoran agriculture, but it says nothing about the totally unequal and to some extent contradictory relations between them and the rest of society. For the *minifundista*, the fundamental problem is not, economically speaking, the land; obviously, it is very important, but [by] owning land in such a trivial quantity, he still really has nothing. For the *latifundistas*, on the other hand, the ownership of land gives him much more than simple ownership would suggest.

However, capitalism, in the form in which it is advancing, will inevitably push aside the *latifundistas*, limiting their national political hegemony to the communities near to their domains. For many years, this has been expressed by the anti-*latifundista* voices, which have risen up in recognition of the great need for agrarian reforms. Each time with greater consciousness they admonish the agrarian structure for its incapacity to play a more dynamic role in development such that the nation even has to import agricultural foods and other consumer goods that could easily be produced domestically.

That the agricultural structure does not respond in the ways demanded by the development of an internal market for imported agricultural products and raw agricultural materials increasingly necessary for the industrial sector can only be attributed to the presence of economically conservative *latifundios* and the presence of a good number of non-capitalist *minifundios*. This situation, along with the usual social and political problems that agrarian structures perpetually create, constitute the reasons why dominant national and international groups, as well as political parties and organisations of the same imperial stripe, have proposed political alternatives that seek to transform national relations of agrarian property as a way to mitigate the grave social, political, and economic problems that have afflicted the Salvadoran people since the 1970s.

Translated by Heather Vrana

Excerpts, AGEUS, *Healthcare in El Salvador, Another Reason for the Popular Struggle*

(1981)

The AGEUS published this short book with many black and white photographs of public health problems and guerrilla combatants. It outlines how the wages of underdevelopment were borne on the very bodies of the *pueblo*. While the oligarchy enjoyed access to private doctors or the ability to go Europe or the US for medical treatment, the rest of society was forced to go to under-equipped Salvadoran doctors. They suffered from diseases that could be easily treated if more resources were dedicated to public health and education. But more than money, a frank analysis of structural inequality was necessary to truly fix the system. Under the current system, healthcare was motivated by the pursuit of profit rather than community welfare. Thus, the authors argue, healthcare would be a key gain of the revolution. The text concludes with a remarkable observation: rather than wait for reform or revolution, the one million Salvadorans who were left without healthcare had begun to take matters into their own hands. Published for an audience of educated young people, one can imagine that the objective of the book was to infuriate and inspire students to participate in community-based public health programmes.

The health conditions in which the people of El Salvador have lived during the fifty years of military tyranny and fierce oligarchic domination and exploitation have created a terrible scene of suffering, pain, death, and sickness for the Salvadoran people. The Salvadoran oligarchy has a team of medical specialists, with modern private facilities and with sufficient resources to make visits to important North American and European cities for doctor's check-ups to prevent and treat their illnesses, in many instances caused by their idle lives; the working people, on the contrary, are found stuck in a desperate situation and their health indices compete for last place in the world with those of nations like Bangladesh and Haiti.

In an era in which medical science has an answer to the great majority of transmissible illnesses that can be easily ended by preventative means, in El Salvador, these illnesses cause an increased mortality, especially among infants. Malnutrition has affected up to 75% of the population less than five years of age and those who manage to survive the odyssey of those first five years subsequently come face to face with an unfortunate and hostile reality, which brings them a life of suffering and economic exploitation, and therefore, some conditions of life so regrettable that they create a tragic scene, impossible to imagine with only statistics and health indicators.

For the Salvadoran oligarchy, the workers are beasts of burden from whom they must suck the last drop of sweat, not human beings who deserve to have a dignified life; thus, great sums of money are set aside for the maintenance of the military, the national guard, the police corps, the paramilitary corps, the death squads, and intelligence services;

meanwhile, the budget allocated to health is totally insufficient to meet the demands of the people; moreover, in the last two years, the economic resources of the Ministry of Health, like those of Education, have been reduced in order to increase the budget allocated to deepening the war against the *pueblo*.

[. . .]

The FMLN and FDR [Revolutionary Democratic Front] lead and guide the *pueblo*, who, with guns in their hands, fight a war with this final aim: 'The health of the *pueblo* will only be achieved with the triumph of the *pueblo*.'

AGEUS submits to worldwide public opinion the present analysis of the health situation so that they will know yet another facet of the great tragedy to which the oligarchy and military tyranny, backed by the United States, has subjected our population, and so that they understand that this *pueblo*'s dream of freedom and their aspiration to obtain a humane and dignified life, as well as the heroism with which they are confronting the enemy, demand the generous support and solidarity of all the people of the world.

[. . .]

In order to scientifically analyse the health conditions in a country, it is necessary to examine the causes that determine and condition the issue in question. To analyse the indicators and figures of health without correlating them to other indicators about the population's living conditions and without situating them within their structural and political context is to refuse to see the situation of wellness–disease scientifically. This is what many technocrats in the Salvadoran government have become accustomed to doing, and in this way they seek to obscure reality and to present it in such a way as to make it seem as if the situation is less bad than it really is. For this reason, the AGEUS finds it necessary to carry out [its] analysis with scientific rigour, so as to not provide a partial or decontextualised vision of the problem of health, and, on the contrary, [to] objectively consider an explanation of the real factors that bear on the making of diagnoses and treatment.

[. . .]

As regards geographic distribution, we find that in 1976, 77.6% of doctors work in the departments with the country's largest urban population: San Salvador, Santa Ana, and San Miguel. The distribution percentage, indeed constant, fits with the fundamentally urban location of the liberal medicine subsector, which is explained by the greater purchasing power that exists in the cities and, therefore, permits us to infer that liberal medicine exercises hegemony over the other caretaking subsectors and imposes its essential characteristics on the whole health system.

The above helps us to better understand the conclusion reached in the various topics addressed in our analysis: The Salvadoran Health System is not governed by the ethical principles of medicine, nor does it intend to solve the health needs of the majority of the population; on the contrary, it is found to be governed by capitalist laws and its health-care activities entail, as a fundamental principle, the constant pursuit of wealth.

It is widely understood that the motivating principle of the healthcare system is economic, as much with respect to the commodification of the system of medical care as to the repair of the labour force's exhaustion among our compatriots; however, in addition to supporting the economic power of the oligarchy, [the medical establishment] also supports its political power, by privileging the military and paramilitary forces that repress Salvadorans, on the one hand, and, on the other hand, by hoping that their pseudo-therapeutic practice would conceal social injustices [which are] the leading factor in the illnesses that most affect our population.

[. . .]

The economic and political panorama that frames the disastrous health conditions of our people has stimulated collective responses in the heart of the healthcare workers, which were initially about economic demands, as in the case of the strike of alumni of Medicine and medical residents in 1979 and the protests for salary increase of nursing staff. Later, these [protests] took on a political character.

The most important incident occurred in May 1980, when in response to the constant violation of hospital facilities carried out by elements of the military and the military forces of the Government Junta, the health workers in charge of caregiving decided to organise a national strike.

The management of this political strike was in the hands of the National Committee in Defence of Patients, Workers, and Healthcare Institutions, a body comprised of the Societies of Medical Residents, Alumni of Medicine, the Medical *colegio* of El Salvador, Organisation of Teachers in the *Facultad* of Medicine, the National Nurses Association of El Salvador (ANES), Society of Students of Medicine 'Raul Hernández' (SEMRH), and the Workers Union of the Salvadoran Social Security Institute (STISSS). The strike held strong and was suspended after 35 days, upon gaining the attention of the International Red Cross, so that this institution [would] monitor compliance with the Geneva

Conventions, which concern international observation in situations of internal hostilities.

The National Strike Committee published in the *Prensa Gráfica* (10 June 1980), as an argument for the righteousness of their movement, a long and detailed list of armed incursions into hospital centres and aggressions against patients and health workers that, in a more comprehensive manner, included the following: assassinations perpetrated inside of hospitals against nine patients that belonged to popular organisations; the kidnapping perpetrated by the National Guard in the Emergency Room of Rosales Hospital (San Salvador) of Lic. Leonel Hernández Quiroa, ex-Director of the Literature Department of the UCA 'José Simeón Cañas' who later appeared assassinated and with clear signs of torture; and the assassinations of nine doctors, four nurses, and five students of Medicine, because they were believed to be collaborators with the popular organisations.

To continue going through the news in the *Diario de Hoy*, *Prensa Gráfica*, and *El Mundo*, we found that in the following months five other doctors, one nurse, and one Medical student were assassinated, this time for being suspected of providing medical assistance to FMLN combatants.

Popular power and health

As we can see, the health sector has not remained on the margins of the economic and political situation of the country. However, the participation of health workers in the process of popular liberation remains to be discussed.

We noted in the previous pages that more than 1 million Salvadorans are without coverage by the healthcare system, therefore this unprotected population has been forced to respond to its own healthcare needs. It is in this manner that healthcare workers more identified with the suffering of the people appeared on the scene to play a very important role in the development of a new type of care, [one] that is based on the participation of the residents of communities affected by the popular war, in close relationship with the revolutionary combatants. Integral to the creation of revolutionary structures of popular power is the existence of a body that coordinates, trains, and incorporates people into the work of healthcare; managing, through constant creativity, solidarity, and great sacrifice, to counteract the dearth of necessary surgical and medical supplies.

This manner of tackling the problem of health and illness, governed by the principle of popular participation, is being formed in the midst of the development of the war of liberation as the objective of the creative potential of the working class; and [it] opposes, in essence, the elite, corrupt, and inefficient system of the Democratic Christian Military Junta. In conclusion, we find ourselves before the heroism of a people who, unconscious of the limits of suffering, insist on directing their own destiny and responding to their health problems with an unbreakable determination to win the final victory and to set up a truly popular and revolutionary government.

Translated by Heather Vrana

Works Cited

Dunkerley, James (1988), *Power in the Isthmus*, London: Verso.

Solano, Luis (2013), 'Development and/as Dispossession: Elite Networks and Extractive Industry in the Franja Transversal del Norte', in Carlota McAllister and Diane M. Nelson, eds, *War by Other Means: Aftermath in Post-Genocide Guatemala*, Durham, NC: Duke University Press, pp. 119–41.

Telegram, American Embassy in Guatemala to Secretary of State, 'Valdeavellano Elected Rector of San Carlos University', 23 November 1973, WikiLeaks, <https://www.wikileaks.org/plusd/cables/1974GUATEM00456_b.html>. Accessed online 15 January 2016.

Woodward, Ralph Lee (1999), *Central America: A Nation Divided*, 3rd edn, Oxford: Oxford University Press.

Chapter 4

Revolution and Civil War 1966–1981

Introduction

Military dictatorships in the region viewed the growing power of the guerrilla in the 1960s as a dangerous disease that needed to be stamped out. New strategies of repression followed. So, too, did greater resistance. But, as the decades of Anastasio Somoza's rule in Nicaragua made so painfully clear, resistance need not follow from repression. Why, then, did growing numbers of Central American students, workers, and peasants come to see the guerrilla as their best hope for a prosperous future? The texts below offer some clues. They suggest that students' belief in their own unique responsibility to lead the *pueblo* was important. They also show the impact of research in the social sciences, public health, and engineering that explained inequality and its effects. Faculty and students delivered eulogies for their friends and also found in their grief a way to speak of revolutionary futures. On the whole, these texts demonstrate how many of the themes from the previous chapters came together to link the struggle for social justice in the present to longer global histories of colonialism and capitalism.

Across the 1960s, the FSLN developed an extensive system of safe houses in the western part of Nicaragua. These homes and farms became important sites for training, planning, and intellectual exchange. The group also developed a careful and elaborate security culture, including pseudonyms, disguises, passwords, codes, and strict hierarchies of command and intelligence. Although Carlos Fonseca and many other leaders spent considerable periods of time in exile or prison, these security measures generally succeeded in keeping clandestine combatants safe. FSLN recruitment at UNAN expanded, as Fonseca's address illustrates, below. At that time the FSLN counted only about a hundred members, though its influence far exceeded its numbers. In the mid- and late 1960s, the Sandinistas experienced some victories and some major defeats, like the operations at the Coco and Bocay rivers in 1964 and at Pancasán in 1967. Historian Matilde Zimmerman has also demonstrated how the 1970s were also difficult because the group grew divided over strategy. Making matters worse, its leadership was spread out across Latin America and the Caribbean in exile, weakening their connections with contacts in Nicaragua and contributing to ideological disagreements. In early 1975, Fonseca decided to return to Nicaragua from Havana to attempt to heal some of these wounds, but was killed in an ambush on 8 November 1976.

Even among moderates, the Somoza regime made more enemies than friends as the 1970s progressed. By possessing a third of the nation's assets, the family not only controlled wages and prices, but also limited the wealth and mobility of the business sector. Finally, after decades of violence in violation of human rights, the Somozas had begun to alienate their supporters in the US government. The Sandinistas, on the other hand, gained support from the governments of Cuba, Venezuela, Mexico, Costa Rica, and Panama. The Somozas' embezzlement of earthquake relief funds in 1972 and the assassination of journalist Pedro Joaquín Chamorro Cardenal in 1978, likely at the behest of the Somozas, further distanced professional and white-collar sectors. The Sandinistas also attracted international attention. All of these factors contributed to the Sandinistas' victory in mid-1979, a topic taken up at length in the next chapter.

After his own disastrous mismanagement of the 1976 earthquake relief effort, President Kjell Eugenio Laugerud García attempted to save face by developing a new strategy to neutralise solidarities between the popular sectors, interweaving war, development, and the military state into what J. T. Way calls a 'pure, military modernism'. Paramilitary and parapolice forces operating in the capital city targeted individuals who represented a threat to order, especially people like Mario López Larrave, a beloved Law professor, advisor to urban unions, and founder of the Labour Orientation School, who was gunned down in his car at midday on 8 June 1977. In hindsight, his death signalled the beginning of the most difficult years at USAC, when successful marches and demonstrations united some students with *campesino* and labour groups, while the student movement itself splintered and undercover informants called *orejas* infiltrated the autonomous university. One student group called FRENTE responded to the deepening crisis by forming a broad alliance of student parties across the centre and left, and building relationships with major labour federations. Many of its leaders were members of the youth branch of the Communist Party (Juventud Patriótica Trabajador [JPT]). On the whole, the group focused on university issues and organised peaceful marches and demonstrations. Yet this strategy depended upon a rule of law and the students' positive reputation in society. These conditions changed dramatically at the end of the decade. Failing to adapt, many of its leaders were killed. Another student group, later called the Robin García Student Front (Frente Estudiantil Robin García [FERG]) in memory of one of its slain members, took the opposite approach, and turned away from university-based politics, instead building closer relationships with the guerrilla, especially the Guerrilla Army of the Poor (EGP), Rebel Armed Forces (FAR), and *Campesino* Unity Committee (CUC). Then, in 1978, newly elected president General Fernando Romeo Lucas García (1924–2006) responded to the leftist florescence by declaring in Mexican newspaper *El Excelsior* that the university was a cradle of subversives who planned to overthrow the government. Partisans of the right viewed this as an opportunity to gain international support for their counter-insurgency; on the left, professors, students, and parents worried that this pronouncement would justify more surveillance and violence on campus. Indeed, as the texts below indicate, their fears were well-founded.

The on-going counter-insurgency war in Guatemala and the FSLN victory in 1979 meant that El Salvador endured an atmosphere of uncertainty. North American interests in Central America turned an even more critical eye toward El Salvador. That the Salvadoran guerrilla had become increasingly powerful among a broader sector of the population was without question. The cycle of resistance, repression, and death that had taken hold since 1971 was only swelling the ranks of the guerrilla. For this reason, the October 1979 coup seemed a boon for the right and for the US. The coup was carried out by a coalition junta representing military and business interests, Christian and Social Democrats, and less radical sectors of the Catholic Church. This new junta focused its attention on restoring the rule of law and diminishing the appeal of the guerrilla by dismantling paramilitary death squads, freeing political prisoners, and accounting for the many disappeared, thereby incorporating many of the demands of the popular organisations into a moderate reform package. This tactic might have succeeded, had the far-right groups within the military and oligarchy cooperated. Instead, the passage of reforms was combined with yet another wave of violence, this one claiming the life of Archbishop Oscar Arnulfo Romero. Romero's death put a fine point on the deteriorating situation. The Social Democrats withdrew from the junta with some Christian

Democrats, and joined other popular groups to form the Revolutionary Democratic Front (FDR), committed to effecting change by participating in the political system. Their efforts were rewarded with still another wave of kidnappings and assassinations. Meanwhile, the ranks of the guerrilla grew, organised under the umbrella group the Farabundo Martí National Liberation Front (FMLN), founded in October 1980. Given the government's wilful rejection of the path of electoral change and reform, growing numbers of Salvadorans began to see the guerrilla as their only hope.

On the whole, in Nicaragua, Guatemala, and El Salvador, the changing stakes of opposition to the government and the experience of organising general strikes and neighbourhood-based protests meant that students who had perhaps before seen themselves as acolytes of knowledge began to build closer relationships to workers, *campesinos*, and the rural and urban poor. These alliances were hard-won, forged in protest and experiences of repression. In several texts below, young men and women killed by military, police, or paramilitary forces are remembered and celebrated as martyrs for the people's struggle against imperialism. In less dramatic ways, too, these commitments impacted the texture of daily life. Among radicalised students, there was a pitched debate about popular culture, informed by the media critique offered by the Frankfurt School. Cinema and literature from outside of Latin America were often scorned, viewed as mere distraction, or worse, moral defilement.

In Honduras, the military's hold on national political life tightened. Foregoing any appearance of democratic rule, factions within the military simply traded the presidency. López Arellano lost power in almost the same way he had gained it. The López Arellano government had been largely discredited when it was discovered that they had accepted over 1 million dollars in bribes from the United Brands Company (the successor of UFCO). In April 1975, a *coup d'état* installed General Juan Alberto Melgar Castro as head of state. Melgar Castro, under pressure from the landowning oligarchy, put an end to the modest reforms that had improved the quality of life for Hondurans. While disunity within the military continued, power remained resolutely in its hands. For their part, students continued to resist the military and its perennial allies, the landowning oligarchy, foreign business, and North American politicians. Before long, Melgar Castro, like his predecessor, was overthrown in a military coup in 1978. This time it was Policarpo Juan Paz García (1932–2000) who took the reins. Paz's presidency brought even more political violence and corruption, highlighted by a growing role in the hemispheric drug trade and support for the Nicaraguan counter-insurgency forces, the 'Contras'. It is now well documented by anthropologist Lesley Gill that the secret paramilitary death squad Battalion 316 expanded its efforts to quash any dissent following the training it received from counter-insurgency experts of the CIA and the School of the Americas.

The texts below reflect an array of revolutionary experiences in four nations across nearly two decades. Some are full of promise, while others reflect a stunning depth of hopelessness. As the political situation in Nicaragua, Guatemala, and El Salvador deteriorated, many more young men and young women quit the classroom for the countryside or served in urban guerrilla cells. Some remained enrolled in university or secondary school, acting as recruiters for their classmates and leading discussion or reading groups. It is important to note how young men were remembered, as opposed to young women; and how young students were mourned differently to young workers or peasants. The rhetorics of national knowledge and patrimony against foreign incursion that comprised the previous chapter shaped martyrdom in classed and gendered terms. Young men were held up as especially Christ-like while young women were mourned as mothers and nurturers of the nation. Together, these texts make clear that much of the youth of Central America was prepared to offer their life in the struggle against North American and European colonialism and neocolonialism.

NICARAGUA

Carlos Fonseca, 'A Message to Revolutionary Students'

(1968)

Ideologue and General Secretary Carlos Fonseca had been exposed to various debates in Marxism from a young age and was radicalised as a secondary school student. At fourteen, he started a student group and newspaper called *Segovia* at his school in Matagalpa. Six years later, when he enrolled at UNAN, Fonseca brought with him the same dedication to organising and was soon named the editor of *El Universitario*, the newspaper in which many of the Nicaraguan texts contained in this volume were printed. The text below is one of Fonseca's better-known writings, a message to revolutionary students who were much like him. By the time it was written in 1968, the FSLN had lost many of its founding members in military defeats. The global rumblings of May 1968, the death of Che Guevara, and the massacre of students at Tlatelolco plaza in Mexico City also served as a backdrop for Fonseca's call to students. The text is familiar in that it asserts once more the belief that has driven all of the anti-colonial texts in this volume: that students have a special obligation to lead the cultural and intellectual life of the nation. But Fonseca also emphasises some of the contradictions that had come to define the anti-Somoza movement at the university, including the tensions between calls for revolution or reform; disconnection between those who left campus to join the struggle in the mountains versus those who remained on campus; and the *foco* question. The *foco* theory of Marxism, or *foquismo*, holds that groups need not wait for the appropriate conditions to launch the revolution, but rather small insurrectionary bands could foment revolutionary conditions by their example, becoming a revolutionary vanguard and focus, or focal point, of the struggle. Che Guevara developed this idea in *Guerrilla Warfare*, but not all revolutionaries ascribed to it. The vision of social struggle that Fonseca offers here highlights the ideological and strategic disagreements that plagued the FSLN at this time.

My dear brothers,

In the name of the leadership of the Sandinista National Liberation Front, the FSLN, I address this note to the revolutionary students of Nicaragua. This message is directed as much to the students who are studying in the university as it is to students at the intermediary level. This message is directed as much to the women as it is to the men, who, being students, sustain revolutionary ideals.

The <u>Record</u> of Student Martyrs

In these lines, we propose to emphasise the lofty mission that falls to the students who are fighting to propagate Nicaragua's liberation, to forge a country that only has room for justice. Liberation, justice: two words that embody the ideal of the popular, labour, and peasant revolution, and for which no small number of Nicaraguan patriots have heroically offered their lives.

Among these patriots, we can count the following: Casimiro Sotelo, Francisco Moreno, Silvio Mayorga, Fausto García, Otto Casco, René Carrión, Roberto Amaya, Jorge Navarro, Modesto Duarte, Francisco Buitrago. To this list of martyred student militants of the Sandinista Liberation Front, we must add the name of the young professor and doctor, Danilo Rosales Argüello.

Other students who have fallen [while] fighting for the defence of dignity during the course of the last decade are the following: Mauricio

Martínez, Julio Oscar Romero, Ajax Delgado, Jesús Mendoza, Manuel Baldizón, Antonio Barbosa, Victor Arbizú, Eduardo Medina, Hector Zelaya.

These student martyrs constitute a luminous example for the revolutionary students who, full of courage, intend to continue fighting for a radical change to the capitalist system – a system of exploitation and oppression that rules the land of Nicaragua and almost all of Latin America.

[. . .]

The Two Faces of the Students' Position

In the past ten years, student combatants have occupied a distinguished place in the emergence and growth of the armed struggle. This is not to say that the student movement has met the demands of the revolutionary movement. The situation is such that while student militants have given the most they can give, even offering their lives, revolutionary students have not been required to contribute the share of sacrifices that corresponds to them in this struggle for sowing justice in Nicaragua. That is to say that while student guerrillas have shed their blood, the revolutionary students have essentially stayed in the classroom with their arms crossed.

One example clearly illustrates the problem we have just described. Before the deaths of Silvio Mayorga and other comrades in the mountains of Pancasán and of Casimiro Sotelo and other comrades in the city, the organised student movement's solidarity was limited to offering simple proclamations of condolences. The students did not gather in fraternal assemblies, they had not declared their identification with the noble ideals of the *pueblo*'s soldiers in the streets.

And it is necessary to emphasise that the cause of this situation is not the students' indifference to the desires of those fighters. The truth is that the majority of students, like the large masses of the *pueblo*, approve of the combatants' rebellion. [Rather] the root of the students' inactivity underlines the revolutionary students' lack of political discipline and the capitalist penetration of the nation's two universities.

Another example illustrates the same problem: the student movement's inaction upon the death of Commander Ernesto Che Guevara. This also was not the result of student apathy because Che Guevara's example generates profound respect and admiration among student youth. [This] arises from the lack of revolutionary discipline, from the penetration of capitalism.

Overcoming the disregard for the students' demands

The inactivity that we have mentioned is not only demonstrated in terms of their national and revolutionary commitments. It happens that the nation's educational system is suffering tremendous problems: the majority of children do not attend school, [for] they limit the enrolments at specific university departments. What is happening is that the government slashes the university's budget, refusing to finance the construction of necessary buildings. Meanwhile, the student movement, including the revolutionary sector, sits back and does nothing.

Overcoming the tendency of the student movement and its revolutionary sector to do nothing is necessary to strengthen the battle to transform the evil political and social system that dominates Nicaragua. This should be possible so long as the student movement in Nicaragua continues to be loyal to the ranks of students who have not shied away from offering personal sacrifices to fulfil their duty of defending the people.

The history of the Nicaraguan student movement assures us that they will be loyal to the people. The 23rd of July 1959 represents a key date, the date when the forces of the GN [National Guard] attacked a student demonstration. That day plainly demonstrates that students are among the greatest enemies of the *pueblo*'s oppressors.

A deceptive vision of the university

Our demand for a resolute revolutionary militancy among students is naturally repudiated by the democratic–capitalist ideologues, who are, of course, more capitalist than democrat. The document entitled 'Development Plan', published by the National University of Nicaragua, contains such deceptive ideas as: 'Today the primary issue is peaceful coexistence, which means living in close proximity without destroying each other. It means understanding, discussion, compromise, mutual respect.' Such ideas attempt to do away with both the university and the student movement. They believe the struggle, which is the answer, is something that demeans the university. And they speak of coexisting not just with the capitalist oligarchy but also with the Yankee empire. The authors of these ideas are adamantly opposed to the culture of struggle. They dare to deny that the foundation of this culture is complete national liberation. The reactionary view that we have just described reveals that misguidance in the student movement and in the university is not an accidental and spontaneous phenomenon. Instead, it follows the concrete plans of those university authorities that serve the capitalist system.

Any action that the revolutionary students take should be accompanied by a clear explanation of the reasons why they are obligated to practise revolutionary militancy.

The backward attempt to isolate students from [their] historical challenge for the benefit of a dying society has led them to apply pedagogical theories from *Life*, the yankee [*sic*] magazine that has little to do with the university. According to this magazine, educational programmes should occupy as much of the students' time as possible, irrespective of the students' well-rounded scientific education. The object is to prevent students from having the time to participate in the popular struggle.

Students today should be the champions of the people
Our student brothers need to remember that the country they live in is called Nicaragua. In this country, the immense majority of the population lives in the darkness of illiteracy. The people who reach secondary and university studies need to consider themselves privileged. This minority sector of the population who has access to secondary and higher education cannot turn its back on the oppressed popular majority.

Educated youth can more easily recognise the causes of the problems that plague the nation. That is to say that education multiplies the students' responsibility to fight in the popular struggle. Because of their education, they represent the sector of the population with the greatest capacity, with the most opportunities, to encounter the ideas that accurately explain the root cause of social problems.

The Historical Reason for the Students' Decision
The revolutionary students should have a clear understanding of the reason why the popular sector, of which they are part, is at the front lines of the battle for the transformation of our society. Because of their young age, students are individuals with spirits that have not been deeply penetrated by the lies and the vices engendered by a corrupt capitalist society. Today students represent the popular sector that has the most difficulty detaching itself from the dominant capitalist regime. This explains to a large degree the important role youth always play in the great revolutionary moments of history. It has even been said that when the revolutionary struggle gains strength, the tyrants, enemies of the people, consider it a crime just to be young.

It must also be said that the relationship between politics and student movements is inevitable. Those who oppose the students' support for the *pueblo* say that students should not participate in politics. But they are being hypocrites, and they do not actually propose separating students from politics. Their true and hidden intention is to use students for the worst kind of politics, that is, reactionary politics. This is confirmed by the act celebrated on 14 September 1967, the date on which thousands of secondary students were required to parade before Anastasio Somoza D., who was giving one of his absurd speeches.

The importance of the students' role in the current historical process is a phenomenon we see more broadly in Asia, Africa, and Latin America. On top of this reality, in Nicaragua, there are certain characteristics that make the students' militancy more critical.

In our country, the industrial proletariat is very young and the overwhelming majority is not part of a union, which means that their capacity to fight is limited. Likewise, a *campesino* movement with class demands has emerged only recently. Due to the dialectic process, it is the student sector of the population that most enthusiastically embraces the ideals of revolution in the first stage. Within a certain period of time, students should be the force that leads the popular struggle.

The students' alliance with workers and *campesinos*

The previous statement does not deny, but rather qualifies the role that the labour and *campesino* sectors should play. Revolutionary students, students with a proletarian consciousness, should establish ties with the working class and the *campesino* class. These links should include a detailed investigation into the problems of both sectors. It is important that the revolutionary student go to the factory and the neighbourhood, the district and the *latifundio*. This research is essential for mobilising the popular masses against their enemies.

The universal experiences of both traditional and modern societies demonstrate over and over again the essential role of the guerrilla movement in the mountains. Nevertheless, it is good to emphasise the role cities must play. In *Guerrilla War: A Method*, Ernesto Che Guevara says, 'The urban forces, directed by the staff of the people's army, can undertake actions of incalculable importance.' These words are of special importance to the Nicaraguan revolutionaries.

In Nicaragua, as the rural guerrilla organisation develops, the political forces of the opposition that identify with capitalism (Conservative Party, Social Christian Party) will not remain unmoved. Upon the growth of the revolutionary worker's movement, they will begin to mobilise.

The incalculable importance of the urban forces

In effect, in the face of the political upsurge that will create the guerrilla movement, the capitalist political forces with influence among certain sectors of the people will propose a change based on compromises, which will only remove Somoza's name from the state apparatus, [and] will essentially preserve intact the economic power of the foreign and domestic capitalist class. Naturally, revolutionaries must fight such ploys. This is where the incalculable importance of the urban forces comes in. And because the organisation of the labour sector is weak right now, the role of the student sector becomes more critical.

The aforementioned 'development plan' of the National University also says the following: 'Connect the university with the development plans.' That is, that the capitalist professors, at the same time that they are trying to separate the university and the students from the political struggle, are declaring that the university should link itself to [national] development plans. In order to underscore the significance of this declaration, it is necessary to explain that in the quote above 'development plans' means the plans elaborated by Yankee imperialism and its agents in the Nicaraguan government. We already know the state of affairs to which such plans have led the country. Considering this experience, it is more appropriate to term those development plans proposals of backwardness and misery.

As in all of America, the progress of Nicaragua, the development of its economy, the destruction of such dreadful misery can only be achieved with a new system – a system of complete national liberation. And until the university and the students participate in that struggle for liberation, it is absurd and hypocritical to speak of a single legitimate link to development.

Also utilising academic resources

Speaking of the university and the students' role in fighting for a new Nicaragua, we do not only suggest that they use methods that mobilise the student popular masses. We also think they should employ methods that are strictly academic, such as the publication of materials that examine national problems, debates around those issues, conference proceedings, etc. It is said that the National University has left behind its provincial origins and is becoming a modern university. We would do well to say that this is not true and that the progress of the university is not based on the use of novel terms to call forth a bureaucracy. The university will only be as modern as its ability to connect itself to the culture that longs for social revolution.

Combat and root out capitalist penetration in education and in the university
Faced with the capitalist penetration – frequently disguised as Christian Socialism – of education, the student movement, and the university, the revolutionary students must adopt a firm stance.

The rectors of the universities of Nicaragua maintain that the goal of these institutions is the formation of cultured men. To this purpose, we must respond that there exists a greater goal: the formation of a patriot, of a conscious human being who will put his knowledge to the service of the nation, to the service of humanity. The esteemed rectors should remember that cultured officials abound in the court of the despots that oppress Nicaragua, whose anti-patriotic mentality largely originated in the reactionary education they received when they were students.

The university as victim of imperialism
We urge you to pay attention to the deals that the leaders of this country's universities are making. For one, the authorities refuse to forcibly demand that the state provide the necessary funds. And because the state does not provide that budget, the university becomes the victim of institutions controlled by the United States.

University authorities and certain capitalist entities like the INDE (Nicaraguan Institute for Development), INPRHU (Nicaraguan Institute for Human Development) know that student unrest over the problems of the *pueblo* is inevitable. In light of this fact, they have decided to divert that unrest towards innocuous activities.

One example of this manœuvre is the organisation of student campaigns to teach people to read. We are not saying that it is bad that students teach literacy to some people. What we contend is that this is a trick that diverts student unrest because it is ridiculous to believe that the students will be able to resolve the central problems of the *pueblo* by using such methods.

So long as the state does not take the solution to the problem of illiteracy into its own hands, this problem will continue to affect the great majority of the people. The students' attitude regarding illiteracy should revolve around demanding that the government dedicate an appropriate budget to resolving the problem.
[. . .]

The student movement of 1944 did not break with the traditional parties
The events of 1944 illustrate the experiences of the student movement in the first twenty years of the Somoza regime. On that occasion, the

students expressed their repudiation of the Somoza regime in the streets. But it is important to highlight one feature that characterised student action in those times. This feature is that the student movement was unable to break with the traditional political parties and, in the end, the student action unfolded under the banners of antiquated liberaloid objectives. The student actions of 1944 lacked social fervour.

The weakness of the movements of 1944, which were certainly not led by the individuals who today most frequently recall them, lasted for many more years. So when we arrive at 1953, the best representation of student [political] activity was a group whose stated goal was to ponder the nation's problems from an intellectual Mount Olympia and [who] renounced popular struggle as a solution to those problems.

It is only since 1956, or more precisely 1958, that a student movement emerged with revolutionary clarity, understanding that the solution to the university's problems is inextricably linked to the ills of the antiquated social system that governs the country.

Let us lift up the ideals of Marx and Sandino, the ideals of Camilo Torres and Che Guevara

One of the defects of Nicaragua's revolutionary student movement is the hesitation to support a revolutionary programme that clearly proclaims the ideals of the great historical revolutionaries: Karl Marx, Augusto Cesar Sandino, Camilo Torres,[1] and Ernesto Che Guevara.

This hesitancy comes from the influence of the oppositional sector that has allied with the capitalist class in the contemporary national struggle. To tell the truth, even our revolutionary organisation has suffered that influence, which in certain moments has led us to delay adopting an unequivocally radical revolutionary line. The current attitude of the revolutionary students is probably related to the attitude our own organisation once had on this issue, but it is a moment we have now overcome. [. . .]

Armed struggle and mass struggle

Often, the popular struggle in the classroom and the struggle in the

---

[1] Camilo Torres Restrepo (1929–66) was a Colombian socialist priest whose writings would inspire Liberation Theology. Like so many of the young people featured in this volume, Torres was born to an elite family and arrived at his political convictions after studying the poverty of his fellow citizens in school. In late 1965, Torres abandoned his efforts to organise among the Church, student body, and neighbourhood organisations in Bogotá and went to the countryside to join the guerrilla National Liberation Army. He died four months later in combat and soon became a larger-than-life symbol of revolutionary sacrifice.

streets do not present the same level of danger as fighting in the trenches with gun in hand. The comrades who, in a given moment, ally with the popular masses without taking up arms should do so without losing sight of the fact that the struggle does not end with speeches and pamphlets; and that there will come a time when those comrades will take their place in the trenches. We say this because we wish to take advantage of the opportunities to fight that do not involve guns; and we want to do away with its disadvantages, such as the illusion that the guerrillas' weapons are not essential. In our strategy, popular masses without guns are defeated, just like guns without the masses are defeated.

The path to victory has to include the parallel strengthening of both mass struggle and armed struggle. It will not do to first organise the masses and postpone the armed struggle. We propose shortening the timeframe, to get to the armed struggle as fast as possible, so that the mass struggle and the armed struggle can occur dialectically.

Secondary school students

This message, as we expressed in the beginning, is directed to the various sectors of revolutionary students, including secondary education. It is apparent that the social origins of each individual student are a very important factor in his or her decision to rebel against the reactionary system in force. It happens that most secondary students come from the popular and exploited sectors – much more so than among the university students. The secondary students who are forced to abandon their studies because of economic obstacles constitute an immense majority.

There are more than 20,000 secondary students and approximately 5,000 university students. That is to say that secondary students constitute the vast majority of students in this country, which logically makes them the most important. Additionally, while the university students are concentrated in León and Managua, plus some in Jinotepe, secondary students are distributed throughout all of the country's departmental capitals. These conditions mean that their actions can have effects on a wider portion of the country's territory and population.

Finally, we want to discuss how the mobilisation of secondary students guarantees the revolutionary future of the university student movement. In the future, those who are able to enrol in the university will arrive with a certain political education. In general, in Nicaragua, students begin their political activity when they enter the university, which partly explains many of the weaknesses the university student movement must overcome.

Rescue the university for the *pueblo*

One of the calls for student action that we are making in this message is the duty to recover the university for the *pueblo*. The sweat of the working people sustains the university. Culture comes from thousands of years of the *pueblo*'s labour. Thus, the legitimate owner of the university is the *pueblo*.

Authentic autonomy, within the conditions of a capitalist society, opens up the possibility of the *pueblo*'s participation in the university's direction. Autonomy in Nicaragua is a farce. With a thousand ruses, the reactionary and despotic government has imposed its arrogance on the university. To make the situation worse, there are professors who, passing for democrats, affirm: 'It is an abuse when autonomy is interpreted to be a magic sentiment, like the physical inviolability of the buildings or people – the taboo of the sacred campus.' These words appear in the aforementioned document from the National University of Nicaragua, 'Development Plan 1966–1967'. These words, we believe, exemplify the intervention of the brutal force of the reactionary state in the university.

The fulfilment of all of the duties we have suggested is only possible if the student movement works arduously day after day. This means ending the electioneering habits that limit the student movement's activities to when the student elections are coming up. Meanwhile, most of the time, they do not do anything. The revolutionary student movement's goal, its reason for being, cannot be limited exclusively to winning positions on student councils. In the name of the ability to gain supporters during student elections, students have renounced their revolutionary demands as well as [their] alliance with the broader masses. For the student movement to bear the glorious title of revolutionary and to admirably defend the *pueblo*, these aberrations must disappear.

Once more, I invoke the names of the sacred martyrs of the Sandinista National Liberation Front, FSLN, and the names of our student martyrs. In their name, I call on the revolutionary students, men and women, of secondary schools and universities, to faithfully carry out their patriotic duties – their revolutionary duties.

A Free Fatherland or Death
By the leadership of the Sandinista National Liberation Front
Carlos Fonseca

Translated by Claudia Rueda

GUATEMALA

Editorial, *No Nos Tientes*

(1966)

In characteristic lewd and meandering style, the student organisers of the Honourable Committee of the Huelga de Dolores, an annual carnivalesque tradition celebrated the week before Holy Week, trace a long history of Guatemala's political corruption in this editorial from 1966. Along with performances and competitions, the Huelga de Dolores included a costume parade and the publication of a newspaper called the *No Nos Tientes*, and several bulletins. The *No Nos Tientes*, loosely translated as 'do not mess with us,' is modelled on the daily newspaper and usually includes an editorial, fake interviews, bawdy humour, and other features like crossword puzzles and film listings. Here the student authors frame Guatemalan history as a transcendent parable of *chafarotes* versus honourable students. Here, *chafarote* is translated as swine, but it could be understood to mean pig in the sense of a derogatory term for police officer. The students lead their readers through a history of the nation from colonisation to the presidency of Ydígoras Fuentes, identifying as *chafarotes*, or swine, the agents of imperialism and self-interest. Most of the time, military leaders are singled out, but the editorial invites young military cadets, who may not yet be corrupted by the doctrine of imperial greed, to join them. In the end, duplicity and dishonesty define the swine. By contrast, the students are defined by their principled defiance of the *chafarotes* and their commitment to the *pueblo*. Ultimately, the editorial ends with a call to the people. The students are prepared to rise up – and soon.

Tortured, hooded, gassed, sometimes shot, possibly 'marinated'[2] and always hungry, dear *Pueblo* of Guatemala: on this Friday of all Sorrows, in the Year of misfortune of 1966, the Voice of the University Student – this student in the Autonomous University of San Carlos, who dies for you – , on this occasion of even more than a handful of contagious happiness, we come to offer you a COMMEMORATION, that you cannot simply relegate to silence:

---

[2] As in drowned.

THE SWINE OF GUATEMALA, WERE AND CONTINUE BEING THE SAME!

To demonstrate this affirmation of ours, we will do a bit of History while they continue shitting on this very thing.

We will show with few words that during the time that we were a Colony of Spain, just like the time we have spent as colony of the United States, the swine are the same.

Today's swine are the same ones who during the Spanish Conquest betrayed their expeditions' Bosses.

Today's swine are the same as those who during the Colonial years betrayed the Captaincy General.[3]

Today's swine are the same as those who should have resisted and imprisoned the invader [Vincente] Filísola, but instead welcomed him and kissed the entire ass of the so-called 'Emperor' Iturbide.[4]

Today's swine are the same as those who with their endemic ignorance and traditional servility deformed the [ideals] of [President] Justo Rufino Barrios up to converting them into the abject pseudo-liberal dictatorships of [Presidents] Estrada Cabrera and Jorge Ubico.

Today's swine are the same as those who tried to resuscitate the putrid cadaver of *Ubiquismo*, supporting General Ponce Vaides.

Today's swine are the same as those graced by the October Revolution who, in gratitude, betrayed it through more than 50 plots against President Arévalo.

Today's swine are the same as those who prostrated themselves in adulation at the feet of Arbenz swearing loyalty to the Agrarian Reform, but who instead of seeing them taking up their rifles – being professionals of arms – when faced with the Yankee intervention of 1954, they had no qualms about betraying it, kissing the short blond gangster Mr Peurifoy, arranging the shameful betrayal that in technical and highly trained military terms was known as the 'Colonels' Pact'.[5]

They are the same swine as those who, after having been humili-

---

[3] The colonial administrative unit encompassing present-day Guatemala, Nicaragua, El Salvador, Honduras, Costa Rica, and the Mexican state of Chiapas.

[4] Filísola was an Italian-born military commander who served in the wars of independence in Mexico and under Agustín de Iturbide, Mexican military general and statesman; together, they invaded the Republic of Central America and present-day east Texas in order to expand the Mexican state.

[5] Pact between Colonels Monzón and Castillo Armas after the 1954 counter-revolution, which assured Castillo Armas's ascension to the presidency; Peurifoy supervised and, by some accounts, arranged the pact in order to ensure that the US's favourite would emerge as president.

ated by Castillo Armas, wasted no time in shamefully changing sides.

They are the same military leaders who in 1957 eliminated the afore-mentioned quadruped (stealing the show from the Koch bacillus), an act that if the swine who were accomplices of the deceased had not commit-ted it, would have merited the eternal gratitude of the Fatherland.

They are the same men of kepi and epaulets who share the great trades of embezzlement, bribery, and bullshit as unconditional servants of that thief of high status and clown of little reputation who is called Miguel Ramón Ydígoras Fuentes.

They are the same swine who, avoiding throughout their history a fight with any enemy army (anything at any price, not to fight), in March and April of 1962 massacred the unarmed *Pueblo* in defence of Ydígorist corruption.[6]

They are the same swine who, after being reviled, protected, bribed, ascended, decorated and enriched by Ydígoras Fuentes, with the same dirty hands as concupiscent Ydígorism, had not even the smallest scruple in betraying the old criminal before allowing him to hold presi-dential elections.

They are exactly the same ones as those who, with Peralta Azurdia, under the dung-coloured flag of 'Operation Honesty', have trampled on Intelligence, have hoarded all of the profitable opportunities, drawing the highest salaries while they haggle with the *Pueblo* over minimum wage; control the mafia of contraband through Aviateca [airlines] and the Army Commissary and in sum form this caste of insatiable '*nouveau riche*' who are old – lifelong – sons of a bitch.

They are the same as those who show off their 'Model Platoon' – models of armies that occupy their own Fatherland, assassinating and robbing the peasants' harvest in the mountains, torturing and imprison-ing the worker in the city.

They are, in short, Pueblo of Guatemala, the swine who all their lives, today like yesterday, sought to screw up the elections on the sixth of March, cheating the wishes of the people with fraud, and as a last resort, turning to a military coup!

Yes, people of Guatemala, you should never forget that the swine

---

[6] In response to the State of Siege declared by Ydígoras in late February, university and secondary school students organised a series of escalating protests that were met with fierce opposition from the National Police and paramilitary forces. Students called into the question the legitimacy of the government and, in turn, paid with their lives. As the vio-lence escalated, capital city schools were closed and at least thirteen students were killed.

continue to be the same as ever, they have distorted their mission, and coming from low strata of the *Pueblo*, they reject their humble origins to become the bitches of the creole Oligarchy, allied to the reactionary Clergy and marionettes of Imperialism, so that all together [they] stifle Sovereignty and asphyxiate you.

They continue, then, to be the same . . . but also We . . .

WE THE STUDENTS ALSO CONTINUE BEING THE SAME!

We are the same ones as those who in 1821 responded to the wake-up call of Pedro Molina and that old lady, Mrs Dolores Bedoya de Molina.[7]

We are the same ones as those who supported the visionary ideas of don Mariano Gálvez.[8]

We are the same ones who lent force and substance to the Revolution of 1871,[9] before it was corrupted.

We are the same ones who, in a heroic salad of blood and balls, brought down Cabrera's 22-year dictatorship.

We are the same ones who in 1944 sent the fourteen-year Ubico–Ponce dictatorship to hell (United States of North America), to the peace of the cemetery that the mulatto Ponce[10] longed for.

We are the same ones who openly fought the submissive dictatorship of Castillo Armas – who gave our ass without them even asking for it – and spilled the young blood of the university martyrs of 11th Street at 6th Avenue in June 1956 for you, the *Pueblo*.[11]

We are the same ones who organised resistance against corrupt

---

[7] A professor of medicine and innovator of treatments for epilepsy and other ailments at the colonial USAC, Molina was also a fervent supporter of independence for the Provinces of Central America; his wife, Dolores Bedoya de Molina, held a rally to gather the citizens of Guatemala City on the day that the act of independence was signed.

[8] Mariano Gálvez studied law at the colonial USAC; as a Liberal, he was a key figure in limiting the power of the Catholic Church in education and instituted a number of judicial reforms. Both Molina and Gálvez are considered founding fathers.

[9] The Revolution of 1871 was a Liberal revolution waged against the Conservatives who had ruled Guatemala for more than two decades. Miguel García Granados and Justo Rufino Barrios led the revolt, which sought to further limit the power of the Catholic Church, provide for public schools, and, in sum, rule by the tenets of order, science, and progress. However, both men became the prototype for a series of Liberal dictators with Rufino Barrios serving as president for twelve years.

[10] Because Ponce was president so briefly and to such little effect, biographical information about him is quite scarce; there does not seem to be, however, any indication that he was actually mulatto. The appellation 'mulatto' should be read critically when coming from San Carlistas who were of the non-indigenous and non-black urban elite.

[11] Four university students and one secondary school student were killed in front of a popular cinema, Teatro Lux, during a protest by members of the National Police and the army.

Ydígorism, in March and April 1962, with another tribute of young blood, which soiled the hands of the swine who were 'acquitted'.

We are the same ones who fought the asinine assault on Public Power by the Peraltas[12] (Pollito and his herd of nieces) in the public eye, on the open street, on the mountain, and anywhere the nose could smell out some khakis, with our bare chest as our only shield.

We are the same ones, our *Pueblo*, who, if the swine once more persist in profiting off of your rags, WILL BEAT THEM DOWN WITH YOUR UNWAVERING ETERNAL SUPPORT just as we did in 1920 and again in 1944!

Traditional swine, do not make the mistake of clinging on to your dick![13]

Military youth who are still not corrupted, align yourselves with your *Pueblo* while there is still time!

AND YOU THE CHAPÍN[14] *PUEBLO*: UNTIL SOON!

TAKE GOOD CARE OF YOUR BALLS – do not let them get too hot in the [Holy Week] Processions – , BECAUSE IT IS POSSIBLE THAT VERY SOON YOU WILL HAVE TO PLAY WITH THEM AGAIN. AT OUR SIDE!

THE BOYS
Good Friday of 1966[15]

Translated by Rachel Nolan

JPT, 'Who Will Benefit from the War in Belize?'

(1977)

The longstanding territorial dispute between Guatemala and Belize actually predated independence from Spain, dating to the 1763 Treaty of Paris after the Seven Years' War, or even earlier to the failures of Spanish colonisation to fend off British piracy in the sixteenth and seventeenth centuries. When

---

[12] Colonel Enrique Peralta Azurdia deposed Ydígoras by military coup in 1963 and held power as president for six years.

[13] In Spanish, '*aferraros a la guayaba*'.

[14] 'Chapín' is an affectionate slang term for Guatemalans.

[15] In Spanish, Good Friday is called Viernes de Dolores, or Friday of Sorrows. This is the day that Jesus Christ was crucified and Guatemalan students often played with this meaning, referring to students and professors who were killed in the anti-government struggle.

Spain, France, and the UK traded colonies in an effort to restore their tenuous balance of global imperial power in the eighteenth century, Belize (or British Honduras) frequently changed hands. By 1933, Guatemalan claims on Belize had been promoted by military heads of state as a type of *cause célèbre* in order to unite the people in moments of domestic dissension. In 1933, 1940, and then from 1945 to 85, Guatemala claimed Belize to be its sovereign territory. Of course, until 1981, Belize was itself a colony of the UK. From the perspective of the Guatemalan government, the territorial dispute was not resolved until 1992, when the Constitutional Court upheld the decision by President Jorge Serrano Elías to affirm Belize's right to self-determination. Yet, as recently as 2015, Guatemala and Belize continued to negotiate a boundary dispute in the OAS. This article from *Juventud*, the newspaper of the JPT, decries the conflict as a war for profit that was counter to the needs of the people of Belize and Guatemala. This text stands out as an instance of colonial aggression from Guatemala, so often framed as a victim of European and North American colonisers by anti-colonial students.

In his third year report, the dictatorial president Laugerud García reiterated the intentions of the most aggressive sectors of the army and Guatemalan reactionaries to start an armed conflict against the right of the Belizean people to self-determination.

Given the danger involved for the country in the irresponsible acts of the government, the cliques of the army high command, and Guatemalan reactionaries, young workers, peasants, and students should be alert so that we do not become cannon fodder for the dubious interests of a handful of national and foreign exploiters.

WHY DO THEY WANT WAR?
We Communists have been reporting that new anti-popular measures are hidden behind the warmongering plans developed by the military clique that governs the country. The dictatorial president took it upon himself to announce what should happen in the case of war when in his report he said that the civilian population 'should prepare itself to confront deprivations and sacrifices'. Which means: more hunger, more misery, even higher prices for basic goods, more repression, [and] prohibition on any movement that tends to value the rights of the people.

To the bourgeois, to the large speculators, to those who traffic in the hunger of the *pueblo*, however, this [war] will bring more profits. In the recent [period of] warmongering alarmism, the greedy withheld many products from the market in order to create scarcity and sell them at higher prices.

Moreover, we have said more than once that behind the problem of Belize we find the economic interests of North American imperialists, which Laugerud García plainly confirmed in his report to Congress upon pointing out that the issue of Belize is 'a purely territorial question, but one in which Guatemala is involved not only because of legal and historical factors, but also because of critically important interests of the highest importance for our development'.

As Guatemalan workers, we know from our own experience that for the government to talk about 'development' is to talk about the surrender of our natural resources to Yankee imperialism as it has already done with oil and nickel.

There are also clear reactionary political interests behind the problem of Belize: contradictions in the heart of the dominant classes are ever sharper, at the same time as the people's struggle for their rights continues to grow. Those who encourage the conflict try, through it, to reduce the acute contradictions that wear at them, uniting around interventionism, installing an open military dictatorship in the country, getting rid of the pseudo-democratic façade with which it is now veiled, and permitting the continuity of the new escalation in repression and reactionary terror in the hopes of ending the popular struggle.

TASKS FOR THE YOUTH AND PEOPLE OF GUATEMALA
Youth and the Guatemalan people should not be deceived by the chauvinist demagoguery that the government and army are expounding. War cannot bring anything good to the *pueblo*. War interests our exploiters and oppressors. For this reason we must struggle against the reactionary war that they are preparing against the Belizean people. Youth, particularly youth in the countryside, should be very clear about this situation and not allow themselves to be pressed into [military] service. Conscious youth who have already been recruited and are serving in the army should abandon the ranks, if possible deserting with all their equipment and keeping it for when it will serve the people, against exploiters and oppressors.

The working people should continue waging their struggle, continue organising themselves to defend and increase their rights, to demand the satisfaction of their most urgent needs. Together we should defeat the warmongering plans of the government and the fascist military clique that runs the army.

NO TO THE FASCIST MILITARY ENTERPRISE IN BELIZE!!
RESPECT FOR THE RIGHT OF SELF-DETERMINATION FOR
THE BELIZEAN PEOPLE!!

Translated by Rachel Nolan

AEU, 'The Guatemalan Student Movement in the Struggle for the Respect of Democratic and Human Rights . . .'

(1977)

Two young students named Anibal Caballeros and Robin García were kidnapped on 28 July 1977 while on a short trip from Guatemala City to nearby Mixco for a memorial service for three young EGP comrades. Caballeros's body appeared two days later in a neighbourhood near the university. Denunciations of his kidnapping and death turned into protests demanding García's appearance. Following days of demonstrations, his body appeared with signs of torture and strangulation, and wearing nothing but a stranger's trousers with two items in the pockets: his identification card and a note from the Secret Anti-communist Army (ESA). The deaths sparked a month of protests, the protests of August referred to below, after groups like the AEU published denunciations in paid political advertisements in the daily newspapers. Nearly every academic unit and student organisation paid to publish a memorial or denunciation. This longer account was written months later, at the end of September. Throughout the text, the AEU identifies the deaths as part of the labours of the oligarchy and North American imperialists to silence the popular opposition.

THE GUATEMALAN STUDENT MOVEMENT IN THE STRUGGLE
FOR THE RESPECT OF DEMOCRATIC AND HUMAN RIGHTS
AND TO STOP THE ESCALATION OF FASCIST TERROR IN
GUATEMALA.

The Association of University Students – AEU – , organisation that is deeply committed to the struggles of our people, confronting the repressive escalation currently carried out by so-called '*paramilitary groups*' (actually fascist gangs that act with the government's sponsorship and consent, as part of the '*institutionalised violence*') against the popular organisations, submits to international and national public opinion the following testimonial summary that condenses the repudiation of governmental policies [expressed] during the '*Protests of August of 1977*'.

Unions, guilds, teachers', university, and high school students' organisations, and groups of professors and university authorities express their repudiation of the capture and assassination of students ANIBAL LEONEL CABALLEROS and ROBIN MAYRO GARCIA DAVILA, perpetrated in the last week of July and the first week of August, respectively.

Of all of the pronouncements we reproduce [only] those published as paid advertisements in local newspapers.

This compendium is a historical testimony of the violence, repression, and terror employed by an unpopular government and the dominant classes in order to quiet the righteous protests and demands of the popular organisations. It is also testimony to the high degree of development of the struggles of the popular masses that resolutely speak out and struggle against the new repressive and terroristic escalation of the reactionaries in power, for the respect of democratic and human rights in Guatemala.

The kidnappings and assassinations of LEONEL ANIBAL CABALLEROS and ROBIN MAYRO GARCIA DAVILA are part of this new repressive terrorist escalation that is ever-greater evidence of the fascist solution to the current economic crisis sought by the bourgeois–landowner oligarchy and United States imperialism.

This escalation has its corollary in the economic, political, military, and ideological spheres. In the economic sphere it is expressed as a complete surrender of all the nation's non-renewable natural resources and shameless concessions to large multinational monopolies, against the will of the majority, including the national university. In the political sphere, it appears as the imposition of the interests of the oligarchy on the interests of the country, manipulating international politics behind the backs of the people, preventing the political organisation of popular and even moderate centrist sectors, and imposing a gag rule on the few political organisations that the pro-fascist regime has authorised in more than twenty years of military dictatorship. In the ideological sphere it mechanically reproduces imperialist models of propaganda and has come to control nearly all of the means of communication through which it develops expensive campaigns 'against violence' and in exaltation of an exaggerated patriotism, in order to lay the groundwork for a fascist coup; at the same time, the reactionary government sustains a constant attack against any form of organisation or struggle on the part of the popular classes; attacks that this year have reached extremes never seen before: the government accused the popular Guatemalan movement of being part of an 'international plot against Guatemala', '*in cahoots with British imperialism and the regimes of Panama and Cuba*'. This unprecedented accusation also carries the threat of the death penalty for those who oppose governmental politics and was pronounced in a moment when all national sectors protested the cowardly assassination of the distinguished trade unionist MARIO RENE LOPEZ LARRAVE, which helped accelerate the nationwide protest among the public sector workers, educators, health workers, and communications workers, the workers of many factories, those of the banking system, and the paralysation of fourteen institutes of secondary education who demonstrated in the streets of the city and in front of the Governmental Palace to demand that the repressive minister of education, Guillermo Putzeys Alvarez, stop the authorities' repression against them, that the government respect their freedom of organisation, and that the minister comply with the post-earthquake laws, in which he promised to build classrooms, provide desks to the institutes, and appoint a large number of needed teachers. The maturity and high level of development of the popular masses allowed them to confront and bravely and determinedly reject this dictatorial threat and so force the unpopular government to retreat. In the military sphere, the arms race is encouraged with the support of Zionism and imperialism, placing the country further into debt and aggravating the current economic crisis; it also interferes in and supports repression against the Nicaraguan and Salvadoran people and seeks the support of the fascist dictatorships of the Southern Cone for a likely confrontation in the territorial dispute over Belize.

In spite of the repressive escalation and the fact that the unpopular government of Kjell Laugerud García supports the formation of para-military forces in order to conceal the actions of the police forces of the government and the army, especially the Regional Police (thus called because it is subordinate to Regional Telecommunications) and the G2[16] in the city and the countryside, the people have not been intimidated. The massive response of the workers and peasants has found support in other sectors of the population. The student movement has contributed to elevating the spirit of the unified and organised struggle, through its immediate demands for respect for democratic and human rights and for an end to repression, [while] at the same time maintaining constant

---

[16] The G2 was a military intelligence unit, also called the Intelligence Section of the Joint Chiefs of Staff. As the civil war progressed into the late 1970s and 1980s, the G2 carried out misinformation campaigns and interrogations of captured combatants, tortured and killed their prisoners, and singled out the Mayan population for especially harsh treatment.

support for all sectors who fight for their own demands. The politics of repression and governmental terror receives constant repudiation from the most diverse sectors of our community and has not managed to contain the struggles and demands of factory workers, agricultural workers, public sector workers, bank workers, and the students who have been repressed by police forces.

The students' pugnacity is directed by the Association of University Students – AEU – and the Coordinating Body of High School Students – CEEM. Comrade ANIBAL LEONEL CABALLEROS (twenty years old), who was captured by security forces along with ROBIN MAYRO GARCIA on Thursday, 28 July at night, belonged to the latter [as] Vice President of the Association of Students of the Rafael Aqueche Institute.

On Friday the 29th the family of ANIBAL LEONEL CABALLEROS began to search for him in detention centres and hospitals without success.

On Saturday the 30th in the early morning his body was discarded on a public street with signs of inhumane torture and strangulation, on land neighbouring the University City, located in zone 12 of the capital. This way the reactionary forces knew that the student body could not manifest its repudiation *en masse*, since the burial would be held on a non-business day. [Nevertheless,] four hundred people accompanied the coffin of ANIBAL LEONEL CABALLEROS to the Rafael Aqueche Institute, in whose auditorium the thunderous notes of the students' band sounded, and hundreds of fists clenched in a sign of indignation and repudiation [and] paid homage and afterwards accompanied him, walking to the general cemetery. Speakers from various organisations bade him farewell and renounced this latest barbaric act by the forces that repress and exploit Guatemalans.

The same Saturday, the student organisations and family of ROBIN MAYRO GARCIA reported his '*disappearance*' (capture), and given the possibility that he would meet the same fate as ANIBAL LEONEL CABALLEROS, student organisations took desperate measures to save his life.

These measures led to progressive strikes and general assemblies in most of the middle and secondary schools and the *facultades* of the National University.

On Monday, 1 August in the morning, ten thousand middle- and high-school students protested on streets in the city centre and gathered in front of the Governmental Palace to demand information about the assassination of ANIBAL LEONAL CABALLEROS and the appearance of ROBIN MAYRO GARCIA (nineteen years [of age]), ex-director of the

Association of Students of the National School of Commercial Sciences and currently student in the *Facultad* of Agronomy at the (National) University of San Carlos. The same Monday during the night, a caravan of cars organised by the Association of University Students – AEU – departed from campus joining the night-school students and organised a gathering in front of the Governmental Palace and afterwards a demonstration on the main [6th] avenue. The Ministry of the Interior tried to intimidate the participants in the caravan and illegally issued an arrest order against the leaders and vehicles that participated, publishing a false list of people who had been arrested the next day.

On Tuesday, 2 August there were general assemblies in the majority of the institutes that began to call for a general strike of academic work; in the University there were rallies and general assemblies that denounced the assassination of LEONEL CABALLEROS and demanded the appearance, alive, of ROBIN GARCIA. At night there was a demonstration by night-school students, who left the National Central Institute for Young Men [INCV] and installed themselves in front of the Governmental Palace to demand the appearance of ROBIN GARCIA and then marched down the main [6th] avenue. Under the banner of 'WE WANT ROBIN ALIVE,' other popular sectors joined the movement, and the first to demonstrate in the interior of the country were students in Quetzaltenango. In all parts of the city, the sign 'WE WANT ROBIN ALIVE' was painted on walls and it was also painted on a considerable number of buses; the Ministry of the Interior tried to punish the bus drivers for the latter action.

On Wednesday, 3 August, Robin's family had a meeting with the Minister of the Interior, Donaldo Alvarez Ruiz, and with the director of the police, who cynically claimed that the government and security forces would do their best to clarify the incidents. In the National University this was the day of [the] greatest unrest because the students of the *Facultad* of Agronomy still did not return to their regular classes, [and] instead held a general assembly led by the Association of University Students – AEU – which repudiated the claims of the government and demanded that ROBIN GARCIA appear alive; at the end of this assembly a group of students, shouting the slogan 'WE WANT ROBIN ALIVE,' marched around the various *facultades*, interrupting classes and general assemblies until they amassed in a huge demonstration, when they decided to turn it into a march to the centre of the city. This act was very significant, since for the first time a march of university students from all *facultades* centred on the university campus: four thousand university students protested on Wednesday night, trudging five kilometres until arriving in the city centre, to Bolívar Avenue, where they held a rally demanding that the government respect the life of ROBIN GARCIA. That same day there were rumours that the matter would be dropped because the government, through the Ministry of the Interior, had announced that further marches would be suppressed. Apparently this announcement was an attempt to counteract the growing mood of contempt and the huge demonstration planned by all of the popular sectors for Friday; but ultimately, the tactic for the resolution of all conflicts perfunctorily used by the government was to make a threat one day and cede to petitions put forward the next.

On Thursday, 4 August, while preparations for Friday's large protest were under way, our premonitions came true: THAT DAY ROBIN GARCIA APPEARED, his cadaver appeared with signs of inhumane torture and strangulation on kilometre 48 of the highway to Palín, Escuintla. In the afternoon ROBIN GARCIA'S COFFIN was taken to the rectory of the National University, where homage was paid and all *universitarios* expressed their repudiation of the act. Thousands of students, professionals, workers, and humble people went on foot to accompany the coffin from the university campus to the Rafael Aqueche Institute, which is located not far from the Governmental Palace. After the coffin entered the Rafael Aqueche Institute, speakers from the Association of University Students – AEU – , the National Committee of Labour Unity – CNUS – , the Coordinating Committee of Educational Workers of Guatemala – CCTEG – , and the Coordinating Body of High School Students – CEEM – repudiated the government's policies and held the government of Kjell Laugerud García responsible for the brutal assassination.

All groups demanded the appearance of three trade unionists who had been captured the same day as the two assassinated students and who, initially, the government had denied having in their custody. Facing the fear that the present unrest would lead the movement to broader aspirations, the government had to recognise that they had the three trade unionists, who were fighting an important struggle to win a collective bargaining agreement in their factory and had been dispatched to the courts on ridiculous charges of theft. There were also demonstrations of support for the student movements in Quetzaltenango, Mazatenango, Jutiapa, Huehuetenango, and Chimaltenango.

On Friday, 5 August at eight o'clock, 20,000 high school students accompanied the coffin [of Robin García] from the Rafael Aqueche Institute to the National School of Commercial Sciences. And at four o'clock the coffin was brought to the general cemetery with an impressive march of 70,000 people, predominantly youth. Carrying banners and signs repudiating the government and demanding an end to repression, this demonstration wove through the streets of the city centre. The distinctive feature of this march was that most of those who participated carried a red carnation in their hands, and when they passed the national police they observed a striking minute of silence and all raised their carnations in a sign of protest and outrage, youth who protested respectfully but [who were] confident that the future belonged to them. In the general cemetery there was a farewell like none ever seen before, and one single [voice], of a young student, representing all of the popular organisations that were present, read 'BY WAY OF A FUNERAL PRAYER', a proletarian song dotted with lyricism and a popular hue that celebrated the life and struggle of ROBIN GARCIA and bade him farewell as one bids farewell to a son of the *pueblo*.

Facing the labour stoppage of all of the sectors [in the strike] and the pressure exerted by the media and political sectors, President Kjell Laugerud García called for a meeting with the leaders of the high-school and university students and the parents of the assassinated students.

Student sectors attended this meeting without any delusion that we would obtain a positive outcome. As further evidence of the government's and the president's demagoguery, we presented a list of demands that summarised the principal demands of the popular sectors and requested concrete actions from the government to dismantle the paramilitary groups that operate with impunity in the country. Only by meeting the requests of this list of demands would the government have avoided falling, once again, into demagogic action.

The government mounted a whole publicity campaign to take advantage of the meeting. The very president misrepresented what was discussed at the meeting in declarations that were offered to the press at the meeting's end. As connoisseurs of the demagoguery that would transpire in the proceedings with the president, we had arranged a press conference beforehand, which took place on the same day as the meeting and where we clarified what the real substance of the meeting had been.

Faced with the upsurge in the repressive and terrorist escalation that in the month of August claimed more than thirty victims (not including the 'disappeared'), the majority of whom were agricultural workers and peasants, whose cadavers were found with signs of the most inhumane tortures (several were burned alive or marked with very hot metals) [*sic*]. This, along with total non-compliance with the set of demands [that we] presented, were the reasons why on 1 September the Association of University Students – AEU – published a pronouncement the headline of which was: 'THE LAUGERUD GOVERNMENT HAS TWO OPTIONS: EITHER IT CONTINUES COVERING UP CRIMES AGAINST THE *PUEBLO*; OR IT DISMANTLES THE PLAN OF FASCIST SECTORS.'

Guatemala, 21 September 1977

Association of University Students
-AEU-

Translated by Rachel Nolan

Oliverio Castañeda de León, Speech to the AEU

(1978)

Around the time that García and Caballeros were killed, economics student Oliverio Castañeda de León was elected to serve as Treasurer of the AEU, a position he held until his election as AEU General Secretary in May 1978. A detailed biography by Ricardo Sáenz de Tejada notes that Castañeda de León had not been radicalised as a secondary school student like Carlos Fonseca, Anibal Caballeros, and Robin García. Rather he was radicalised on a trip to London with his sister, who wished to study English at King's College. The Castañeda de León siblings had a homestay with a family of British trade unionists. In post-dinner discussions, the two siblings learned the history of English workers, unions, and party politics. Thus inspired, Castañeda de León finished secondary school and enrolled at USAC to study economics. In his first year at USAC, he took a course on Guatemalan economic history with Severo Martínez Peláez, the author of *La patria del criollo*, a book that argued Guatemala remained a colonial society. Castañeda de León soon joined informal reading groups with JPT members. In 1976, he began writing for the JPT's *Juventud*. Often called simply 'Oliverio', Castañeda de León is the most famous martyr of the Guatemalan student movement. He was killed on 20 October 1978 after a demonstration in observance of the thirty-fourth anniversary of the democratic revolution against Ubico that coincided with escalating citywide protests against a bus fare hike. From an acoustic bandstand near Central Park, Castañeda de León delivered a speech that implicated top national leaders in more than a decade of disappearances and assassinations. His speech ended with the prophetic assertion: 'They can kill the best sons of the *pueblo*, but they never have and they never could kill the revolution . . . As long as there is a *pueblo*, there will be revolution!' He died minutes later. The speech below is Castañeda de León's inaugural address as AEU Secretary General as reproduced in *Oliverio Vive!*, edited by Rebeca Alonzo.

Young Guatemalan students, representatives of the most advanced progressive and anti-dictatorial thought of this epoch, which emanated and arose from a Latin American and global movement in favour of reform and democratisation, saw the necessity of founding a Students' Association, an organisation that would form a representative [body] of Guatemalan university students and that would fight and lead the struggle for a university and higher education that was democratic, popular, and attuned to the political conceptions of our time.

Today, fifty-eight years after the glorious 22 May 1920, on this university campus with more than fifty-eight times more students than at that time, we may say: The Association of University Students stands up and will march steadfastly towards the outlined objectives of an education at the service of the Guatemalan people and for an education counter to the interests of the indoctrination[17] of the Guatemalan student body.

Today, as has been mentioned, thousands of young Guatemalans have taken on the struggle for a right that is denied and trampled upon in our country on a daily basis, human rights, which do not represent a utopia for our people, they do not represent a utopia, but rather represent a real reason for their daily and constant struggle, a reason for their quotidian struggle; and for us, the university youth, the struggle for the right of Guatemalan youth to education represents the very reason for being of our work at the university.

Thus, in the situation in which our country is [presently] involved, currently subjugated to the cruel exploitation of some sectors of the bourgeoisie allied with imperialists, subjected to cruel exploitation in which our most basic rights are trampled upon, we wish to record for posterity on this occasion that the Association of University Students, far from backing off, will march onwards [and] follow the combative example of so many martyrs fallen in the struggle, and will continue forward, loyal

---

[17] Castañeda de León is marking a subtle difference between education (*educación*) and formation or indoctrination (*formación*).

to their commitment to the student body and the Guatemalan *pueblo*, leading the students' struggle for a scientific, democratic, popular university and for a Guatemala that answers to and is the property of its real inheritors – the Guatemalan labourers, peasants, workers, intellectuals, and students.[18]

Our commitment is interpreted as it has always been and in the only way that it may be, that of leading the struggle of the Guatemalan youth for an education in the service of the *pueblo* and uniting it with the struggle of the Guatemalan *pueblo* against exploiters and against the assassins who trample upon our rights and repress our country on a daily basis.

On this 58th anniversary of the founding of the Association of University Students, I would only like to express in the name of the 1978–79 secretariat, in the name of 35,000 university students, that we are prepared, as has been demonstrated, to carry on the struggle for a scientific and democratic university, the struggle for the rights of the Guatemalan people to education, and the constant struggle for the transformation that our society needs to become a democratic Guatemala of the people.

Long live the Association of University Students!

Long live the Guatemalan student body's fifty-eight years of struggle!

Translated by Rachel Nolan

EL SALVADOR

'Declaration of the University of El Salvador's High Council on the National Situation'

(1979)

While the October 1979 coup hoped to return El Salvador to the rule of law, before long it became clear how little had been done in that direction. This lengthy declaration from the High University Council (CSU) of the University of El Salvador was printed in the centrefold of *El Universitario* in mid-December. It outlines the many ways that the university's autonomy and the nation's sovereignty had been endangered by the October coup

---

[18] Labourers (*obreros*) here are distinguished from workers (*trabajadores*) by the type of labour they perform. *Obrero* generally refers to those who do physical or manual labour.

and offers yet another critique of North American incursion in the region, noting how, over a period of fifty years, the increase in investments had only deepened the contradictions of capitalism. Much of the text excluded from this excerpted version lists the names of fifteen people who had been disappeared or imprisoned in at least thirty repressive actions carried out by the government between the coup and mid-November 1979. Notice how the CSU carefully negotiates its own role in an unjust society, seeking to clarify its advocacy for the needs of the *pueblo* despite its imbrication in what it calls 'the System', as the highest administrative body of the public university.

DECLARATION OF THE UNIVERSITY OF EL SALVADOR'S HIGH COUNCIL, ON THE NATIONAL SITUATION

1. The developed countries of the so-called Western World use the enormous surpluses that they extract at the cost of the popular sectors and dependent countries for the purpose of broadening and deepening investments in the production of war. The countries of the North Atlantic Treaty Organisation (NATO) have invested in military expenditures of nearly 19 billion dollars in 1949 [and] more than 106 billion dollars in 1971; among these, the United States of America has spent nearly 78 billion dollars. The World helps to guarantee the financial–economic survival of the great Western powers, furthering the accelerated development of militarisation for the purpose of maintaining a climate of 'permanent war' promoted by these same powers.
2. The progression of North American investment in Latin America is notable, in 1929 it was 3.519 billion dollars, in 1966 it was 9.752 billion dollars, and in 1976 it was 23.536 billion dollars. This means that during the decade 1966–1976, the aforementioned investments nearly tripled. During the period between 1929 and 1976 the sum of imperialist investments in the secondary materials processing industry increased from 6% to 39%.

[. . .]

In ten years North American monopolies extracted from our continent 10.047 billion dollars, which is 2.500 billion dollars more than their own 'capital' investments.

These investments have not done much more than develop the contradictions of capitalism in the dependent countries, [for] the influx of capital into the agricultural industry brings with it the displacement of the small producer [in order] to create large capitalist firms creating, at the same time, a larger agricultural proletariat; moreover, the small producer that survives suffers an acute financial crisis where he must go into debt to produce. Satisfied, investing more, companies emerge that unite the working class, and they start fighting for their most deeply held needs, at the same time, a sector of society that is salaried like teachers, bureaucrats, etc. emerges and develops ... small trade intensifies, which also supports the inflation inherent in capitalist development, etc.

3. The decade of the 1970s, in our country, represents a political surge coming from the socio-economic difference of the previous two decades. No one is unaware that at the beginning of the 70s, politico-military organisations emerged, and by the middle of the same decade, mass revolutionary organisations of the same sort [also emerged] that now capture the public's attention nationally and internationally. As a result of the peculiar conditions of El Salvador, having a high rate of proletarianisation as a product of massive displacement initiated during the middle of the nineteenth century, its small geography, and its considerable population density, the popular movement marches along, with greater collective consciousness, towards the eradication of the existing social–economic system; but for this reason, too, the combination of capitalist reforms and military repression by the monopoly capital and its allies, the local dominant class, tends to quickly overcome the popular movements.

Also monopoly capital acquires experience in its confrontation with popular sectors, and, in our case, similar to Vietnam, Cuba, and Nicaragua, has influenced the current government's model of political reforms and repression. In Vietnam not even the so-called strategic hamlets (that have been copied here in Aguilares, San Pedro Perulapán, and Soyapango, for example) and in Cuba not even the period of waiting after the first Agrarian Reform Decree could stop the popular desire for change in the system. Here in El Salvador, these manoeuvres have not side-tracked the popular movement from its objectives.

4. In our country, monopoly capital and the dominant classes have been able neither to resolve the economic crisis nor to stop the development of the popular revolutionary movement, which forms the intensification of class conflict [and] faced with this situation,

imperialistic monopoly capital and the dominant classes have devised a new way of keeping the popular movement from realising its objectives [and] in order to ease class conflict:

On 15 October 1979, the coup took place, making itself known through a proclamation for the apparent benefit of the *Pueblo*, repackaged at both a national and international level through extensive propaganda regarding its character.

This coup represents the interests of the dominant class and of imperialism and thus its practices from the 15 October 1979 until now have shown its anti-popular character . . .

[. . .]

The Government Junta seeks to provide a way out of the current economic, political, and social crisis through tepid reforms that will not resolve the fundamental problems of the *pueblo*.

To resolve the problems of the *pueblo*, profound economic, political, and social changes need to be implemented, like, for example, a Radical Agrarian Reform. And even when those reforms impact [the *pueblo*], for example, land tenancy, foreign commerce, the banking system, even the nationalisation of all the land, they continue being reforms in the service of the bourgeoisie that in the end do not resolve the problems of the *pueblo*.

On the other hand, the *pueblo* has seen clearly that [the government] has never satisfied their most pressing needs: political prisoners have not been liberated; war criminals have not been prosecuted; the price of basic necessities for popular consumption has not been controlled; a radical Agrarian Reform has not been developed; the price of energy has not fallen. Instead, the people have been repressed: factories on strike have been violently evicted; civilians have been massacred – developing a type of slaughter without precedent in the previous repressive regimes; etc.

The second half of the decade of the 1970s demonstrates reformist and repressive efforts to contain the growth of the popular movement in its just aspirations.

5. The University, as an institution of the 'System', has an operating range limited to the realm of culture; even so, it expresses the will of professors, workers, and students that do not restrict their political labour organising to the institution. The university sectors, as part of the *pueblo*, also fight for its most pressing needs, like the transformation of the socio-economic system. In this sense,

the institution of the University should express to the best of its ability the interests of the university sectors as a part of the broader *pueblo*, [and] thus, the University makes their own just popular aspirations and so we demand:

1) The immediate liberation of all political prisoners and the disappeared and compensation for the affected families.
2) The trial of those responsible for crimes against the people.
3) The expropriation of the property of the oligarchic families:
   —Regalado Dueñas
   —Hill
   —De Sola.
4) The immediate dissolution of paramilitary organisations and security forces (National Guard, Treasury Police, National Police).
5) The demilitarisation of workplaces.
6) Ending the repression against the *pueblo*; ending military incursions in *campesino* zones like Cinquera, Chalatenango, La Paz, Opico; ending searches, roadblocks, etc.
7) Withdrawing Israeli and North American military advisers [from El Salvador].
8) The right to free organisation of the *pueblo*.
9) Respect for the mobilisation of the *pueblo*.
10) Actual guarantee of the immediate return of exiles.
11) That popular organisations can serve in state agencies.
12) Actual compliance with the just economic, social, and political demands of the different sectors of the *pueblo*.
13) Open access for all people to the University, popular organisations, and to all mass media: Radio, Press, [and] TV without censorship.
14) The repeal of the Decree that permitted the theft of funds from other Ministries to increase Defence Ministry spending.

Translated by Vikram Tamboli

Communiqué

(1980)

The two texts below, a communiqué and a statement of solidarity with the people of Guatemala, were printed in the AGEUS's *Opinión Estudiantil* in July 1980. The edition featured a photograph of Farabundo Martí on the cover and below Martí's image were his words: 'When history cannot be written with the pen, you must write it with the gun.' By this time, the combative spirit of the students was quite clear. The editorial that opens the edition states without equivocation that its intention is to tell the Salvadoran people and the world about the political, economic, and social conditions of the *pueblo* of El Salvador, while at the same time affirming, 'sooner than later, our *pueblo* will gain its final liberation [and] Yankee Imperialism and its internal allies will take desperate steps to maintain the present system.' This radicalisation reflected the mounting opposition to the government in other sectors, especially after the assassination of Monsignor Oscar Arnulfo Romero in March. Continuing its millenarian bent, this edition of *Opinión Estudiantil* is dedicated 'to the hundreds of university students, teachers, and workers who with their blood have maintained a combative presence in the classroom and books and who in this moment are abandoning them in order to join the ranks of the Popular Army of Liberation'. Several pages are filled with brief summaries of battles and victories, entitled 'International and National Affairs'. Printed in this way, the two texts below articulate quite powerfully the belief that the Salvadoran left was engaged in a global struggle against global imperial power.

COMMUNIQUE
TO ALL THE PUEBLOS OF LATIN AMERICA AND THE WORLD:

The university students of Central America and Panama assembled in the IV Central American Congress of Sociology 'Blas Real Espinales', held from 1 to 5 June in the city of Managua, Nicaragua, [and] conscious of what this entails AGREE:

1. To demonstrate our unwavering solidarity with the heroic struggle for liberation of our brother countries of Guatemala and El Salvador.

2. To condemn the military intervention and massacre to which the militant University of El Salvador has fallen victim.

3. To repudiate the claims of imperialism and the local reactionary groups of Honduras and Panama that want to convert these territories into bases of the counter-revolution to stop the advance of the wars of liberation of the *pueblos* of Central America.

4. To fraternally and revolutionarily salute the people of Nicaragua in celebration of the First Anniversary of the triumph of the Sandinista popular revolution and to reiterate our solidarity with the process of transformation.

5. For the transcendental events that have occurred in Central America and Panama, to make an urgent call for the unity of all students of Social Sciences of the Region, that they join the Central American Association

of Students of Social Sciences in order to develop a vigorous campaign of solidarity with the struggles for the liberation of our *pueblos*.

Translated by Vikram Tamboli

'Guatemala: In the Difficult Struggle for its Freedom . . .'

(1980)

With the ascension to power of General Lucas García, the State returns to intensifying its politics of terrorism; once again hundreds of representatives of the popular movement in the countryside and city are assassinated.

The past few months of this year have been, for the students, workers, *campesinos*, and professionals, a palpable display of the most sinister escalation in terror. [This includes] the complicity of the repressive forces in directing their actions against labour and political leaders whose principal crime has been to demand better conditions of life and work, and thus the establishment of a regime that guarantees the security of the people and their rights, the right to life, education, housing, work, union organisation, etc.

The escalation in repression includes innumerable kidnappings, assassinations, intimidations, etc., all of this orchestrated under a broad plan that involves, on the one hand, the execution of illegal military operations, registries and searches, illegal detention of citizens, black lists, etc., as well as the application of measures aimed at generating a climate of terror amongst the Guatemalan citizenry.

Among the events that demonstrate the present escalation of terror in various sectors of the population, we highlight cases like the following:
Students
– Julio Alvarado Solórzano
  student of psychology
  assassinated
– Ana María Mendoza
  student of psychology
  tortured and assassinated
– Roberto Moreno
  student of the Law *Facultad*
  assassinated
– Members of the Executive Committee of the Association of
  University Students (AEU)
  threatened with death.

Professionals
- University Graduate [Lic.] Felipe Mendizábal
  university employee
  machine-gunned
- University Graduate [Lic.] José A. Bay
  Legal Advisor to the Movement of Urban Residents
  assassinated
- University Graduate [Lic.] Rita Navarro
  Professor of English and university employee
  machine-gunned
- University Graduate [Lic.] Roberto Ortíz M.
  University Professor
  assassinated.

Journalists
- Manuel René Polanco
  assassinated
- Marco Antonio Cacao
  Member of the Social Democratic Party (PSD)
  assassinated

Trade Unionists
- 27 trade unionists of the
  National Workers' Centre (CNT)
  captured and 'disappeared'
  (women were among those trade unionists, one of them from the
  General Secretariat of one of the unions that form the CNT, was six
  months pregnant).
- José Emilio Escobar and María Adelaida González
  Representatives of the Guatemalan Social Security Workers' Union
  (STIGSS)
  assassinated

Campesinos
- 100 farmers from the northern zone of the country
  captured and disappeared

Given the current condition of generalised terror in which Guatemala currently lives, it is necessary to deploy an international campaign aimed at increasingly isolating the fascist military regime that rules in Guatemala.

Thus, we demand that all international popular organisations promote this great campaign in support of the struggle that is liberating our heroic pueblo.

LONG LIVE THE HEROIC STRUGGLE OF THE GUATEMALAN PUEBLO!
LONG LIVE INTERNATIONAL SOLIDARITY!

Translated by Vikram Tamboli

José María Cuellar, '1932' and 'Wars in My Country'

(1971)

Poet José María Cuellar was part of a large movement of Central American poets and artists in the late 1960s, later called the 'Committed Generation' (*'Generación Comprometida'*). As historian Héctor Lindo-Fuentes so carefully demonstrates, this generation inspired the ranks of the FMLN and students and workers who continued to struggle through everyday life. Amidst repression and military threat, Cuellar and a number of other students at UES formed the group 'Piedra y Siglo', which published newspapers and small books, held readings in San Salvador cafés and bars, and met with labour unions. The group demonstrated how visual art, radio, music, and poetry could be used reach the *pueblo*. Cuellar was killed in October 1980 when he was hit by a bus. His death occurred just before the wave of kidnappings and assassinations that decimated the leadership of the FDR and radicalised the FMLN. Cuellar's children, Claudia María and José, were also involved in the popular struggle and died at the hands of the government. His poems are marked by their political and historical content, as well as their lyricism. The first poem below, '1932', refers to *La Matanza*, the massacre of *campesinos* in western El Salvador in January 1932, which was carried out by the Salvadoran army on the orders of President Hernández Martínez. Augusto Farabundo Martí led the *campesinos* and was himself killed in the fighting alongside between 10,000 and 40,000 others. The uprising is held dear in popular memory as evidence of the state's rapacious violence, the economic elite's grasp on the state, and the peasants' ill-fated bravery. 'Wars in my Country', in turn, depicts El Salvador as a nation destined for violence and loss.

1932
Forever the memory of punctured flesh and the land full of flies.
Of people hanging from telephone poles and piled

On the side of the highway like animals.
Forever the memory of knives stuck in the waist.
Of men, and of death that circles in the secrets of migratory
Birds descending from the blackened thatch roofs of the ranches
like a dove of San Juan;
Spreading his word like an iron gauntlet
of an Ancient Horseman; over the ribs or femurs of all of these young men
Dying from hunger, those who rose up in 1932;
Who extinguished the hearths of the old estates and went up
To the cities to switch on all the lights.
Forever the memory of those elders, of those women,
Of those children, who died with a clump of dirt between their lips . . .

Wars in My Country
In my country there were wars where rifles were born
From shadows
And the planes of nineteen forty
Flew overhead drying the goats' milk.
Everything was uppercase and small gestures became
Golden
In my country there was a war
With generals and battlefields
With heroes and anti-heroes
With blood
And tearful goodbyes at the doors to bedrooms
With silent bayonet strikes
And the machine-gunning of women and children
In my country there were many wars
(and bullets formed aerial rivers)
In my country there were many wars
But this one my eyes did see
And my nerves felt
And my senses throbbed
In my country there was the war for independence
And the war of Anastasio Aquino[19]
And the war of the confederates[20]

---

[19] Aquino was a Nonualco indigenous man who led an insurrection against large land-owners in 1833. He was invoked and revered in the 1932 insurrection.

[20] From 1823 to about 1840, the territories of present-day Nicaragua, El Salvador, Honduras, Costa Rica, Guatemala, and parts of Chiapas formed an unstable republic called the Federal Republic of Central America; the confederates were the supporters of this united government. First threatened with Mexican annexation, then with dissension from within the ranks, the united provinces were short-lived. But the dream of a unified Central America endured and inspired subsequent experiments in regional state-making

And the war of the idealists[21]
And the war of a hundred hours[22]
And the war of the *guerreros*[23]
And there were never winners or losers
Only women without breasts
Men without testicles
Children with their tongues removed
Huddled together in terror
Like an ancient statue
Like a wasteland
Like the most sorrowful landscape of the Second World War.

Translated by Vikram Tamboli

'Poetry from a Heroic Woman from our *Pueblo*'

(1981)

Delfina ('Delfy') Góchez Fernandez was a young UCA student who became involved with the AGEUS in 1977. She was killed in May 1979 at the protest outside of the Venezuelan Embassy. Just days before her death, she wrote the poem below. The poem was reprinted in the AGEUS's *Opinión Estudiantil* under the title, 'Poetry from a Heroic Woman from our *Pueblo*'. The tragedy of the poem's foreboding is stunning, but even more so is Góchez's vision of the future after her death, where a lifetime of suffering would give way to hope and nourishment. The masculine heroics of the 'New Man'[24] may be reflected in the mother homeland's hope for her son, but too the revolutionary woman's sacrifice becomes an honourable death borne 'in the most natural way'.

(What follows is a poem from our comrade, university student
Delfy Góchez, who heroically fell in combat on 22 May 1979 in
San Salvador)

---

in 1842, the 1850s, 1880s, 1896–8, and the 1920s.

[21] The meaning of this is unclear, but it may refer to these subsequent efforts at establishing a united Central American Republic.

[22] The 1969 war between Honduras and El Salvador was called alternately the 'Football War' or the 'Hundred-Hour War'.

[23] Probably referring to the combatants in the on-going Salvadoran civil war.

[24] Guevara wrote that a New Man (*Hombre Nuevo*) was needed to build a socialist society and that he would emerge alongside new economic forms after the revolution, as a new relationship to the means of production would free him from alienation and the fulfilment of his basest needs.

With Pleasure I Will Die
They are going to kill me
when?
I don't know . . .
What I do know is that I will die
Like that, cut down by the enemy.

Because I want to continue fighting
I will always be fighting to die in this way.

Because I want to die with the *pueblo*
I will never leave it.
Because it is our cry that will come some day
One must always shout it.

Because the future and history
are with us
I will never stray from the path.

Because I aspire to be revolutionary
My points of view
and all my aspirations
will start from that.

I will never be afraid
all that I do
must be a strike against the enemy
in whatever way possible.

I will always be active.

What is certain
is that they are going to kill me.

and my blood will water our land
and the flowers of freedom will grow

and the future will open its arms
and warm, full of love,

our mother,
our homeland,
will bring us to her breast

she will laugh joyfully for she is again with her son
with her *pueblo*
with the boy who yesterday cried for a piece of bread
and who today
grows like a river.

with the mother that was dying slowly
and today lives yesterday's wildest dreams.

with the eternal combatant
whose blood
nourished the day
that one day will come.

Yes, with pleasure I will die, full of love,
I want to die in the most natural way in these days
and in my country:
assassinated by the enemy of my *pueblo*.

Delfy Góchez
Santa Tecla, 19 May 1979

Translated by Vikram Tamboli

HONDURAS

'Honduras–Nicaragua: Form a Solidarity Committee'

(1976)

Under President Melgar Castro, Honduran students continued to resist the military and its allies among the landowning oligarchy, foreign businesses, and North American politicians. But one of the most effective ways to register their opposition was to manifest their support for their peers in Guatemala and Nicaragua in paid political advertisements and articles like this one, published in *Presencia Universitaria*. UNAH students argued that these military governments were merely proxies for North American interests. They formed solidarity committees, as the article below describes, and exchanged supportive telegrams and letters. This solidarity committee between Honduras and Nicaragua was formed in early 1976 at a time when the FSLN leadership struggled to maintain unity amidst divides over strategy and military tactics while Anastasio Somoza Debayle unleashed an offensive that left the guerrilla forces decimated.

Recently, and with the initiative of a group of Honduran professionals and intellectuals, the Honduran Committee of Solidarity with the People of Nicaragua was formally established. *Presencia Universitaria* reproduces [below] the complete text of the founding communiqué and the names of those who signed the copy that circulated in the University

City. Other copies have been distributed in certain locations throughout the nation and they have collected numerous signatures.

The solidarity of the Honduran people with the people of Nicaragua is now an old tradition. It is enough to remember the times of General [Augusto] Sandino and his heroic feat in the Segovias. We Hondurans understood [that we ought] to be in solidarity, in every moment and place, with Sandino's struggle against the North American occupation.

Presently, the *pueblo* of Nicaragua endures one of the most despotic and cruel tyrannies known to political history on our continent. Through forty-one long and terrible years, the Somoza dynasty has sunk our brother nation into misery and ignominy. *Somocismo* constitutes an abominable excrescence stuck on to the living organism of Nicaraguan society.

We, the below-signed, conscious of the need to translate into concrete actions our active solidarity with the people of Nicaragua, testify through this document our decision to form the Honduran Committee of Solidarity with the People of Nicaragua. We will carry out an expansive effort of awareness-raising and denunciation of the crimes and capriciousness of the Somoza dynasty and will supply the Honduran people with the best information possible about the struggle against it that will free the *pueblo* of Nicaragua from its oppressors.

Eduardo Villeda Soto, Abraham Andonie, Manuel Antonio Santos, Aníbal Delgado Fiallos, Rolando Valerio H., Mario López Soto, Fernando Villar, Santiago David Amador, Ernesto Paz Aguilar, Juan Antonio Martell, Edgardo Cáceres C., Arturo Morales, Medardo Zúniga Rosa, Ramiro Colíndres, Mario Argueta, Jubal Valerio H., Jorge Arturo Reina, René Murillo, Marco Virgilio Carías, and more signatures follow . . .

Translated by Heather Vrana

Excerpts, Armando Valladares, 'Achievements and Meaning of Our University Autonomy' in *Universidad y autonomía: un encuentro del presente*

(1978)

In honour of the twentieth anniversary of university autonomy, the UNAH University Press published a short book by Armando Valladares[25] entitled

---

[25] Not to be confused with the Cuban Armando Valladares, who was incarcerated

University and Autonomy: An Encounter with the Present. In this excerpt, Valladares celebrates the modest gains made by the autonomous university and rails against the reformist tendencies within the university. He argues that these reformists have compromised true autonomy by accepting loans and donations, while yielding to what he calls the 'ideological solvent' of anti-communism. Under pressure from North American imperialists, even the effort to create a peaceful and discrete University City away from the busyness of the city centre was a manœuvre by individuals who sought to depoliticise the university.

If on a *sui generis* scale, built of perfect materials, we place on one plate, say on the right one, the 110 years of the university without autonomy and, on the left, the product of its four years of autonomy, the resulting balance regarding growth and development would actually be identical.

Religious, utilitarian, oligarchic, the centenarian university learned to be loyal to this path, above the hopes of the people. It was not [the university's] fault obviously, but rather that of the dominant system that used her, impregnating her with its abuses of social class, making her a mouthpiece for the ideology [of class] and a preacher of *order*.

However, remitted to the museum of history – an expression that should be understood in its most relative sense – we concretise the question of the *new* university, the reformist university, the autonomous university.

First and foremost, let us say without paraphrase that if twenty years of university life are celebrated this 15 October, this is only in a formal, not actual, sense. Let us explain by saying that not everything achieved in the period in question was a consequence of [university] autonomy. In fact: there were 'reforms' that in their moment and profundity entailed an abuse of autonomy itself.

It is certain as well that autonomy 'emerges as the fruit of concrete struggle'; but this fruit does not ripen immediately, rather it tended to dry out in the hands of professorial groups who, save for honourable exceptions, were props of the dictatorship of the 'blessed peace'.[26]

In terms of the faculty, the teacher continued to be the indisputable

---

in 1960 for accusing the government of Fidel Castro of human rights abuses and later became Ronald Reagan's appointee to the United Nations Commission on Human Rights.

[26] The period of peace during the Carías dictatorship, which Carías was fond of claiming as a political victory and evidence of his meritorious leadership; in fact, the extended period of peace was the result of the strong-armed rule of Carías himself and UFCO's purchase of Cuyamel Fruit Company.

owner of the professorship, from which he inculcated every student with [the idea of] his sole responsibility to 'devote himself to study' if he wanted to become a 'good professional'. Regarding the political, he continued advocating that the University not be antagonistic, believing that 'active militancy annihilates its scientific spirit', its 'impartial' character prohibits it from 'taking sides and mixing itself in the struggles and interests of the street'.

'There is no age, perhaps, like ours wherein we find an implacable struggle for the domination of man and the world by *so many dangerous doctrines*; it has become necessary to fight with decisiveness and bravery for the *permanent values of man* in his transcendental purpose,' said the autonomous university of old.

[. . .]

The international reactionaries and their local agents are motivated by the presence and above all, the example, of the Cubans. [They argue] the revolution moves dangerously and it is necessary to 'contain it'. One of its centres is the University; from there it is necessary to arrest it in radical fashion. The press will be responsible for agitating anti-communist slogans and its common expressions: the 'Moscow bear', 'defending the democratic institutions and the Western Christian way of life', Castrocommunist subversion . . .

This strategy costs great dividends. The autonomous University is practically totally absorbed by the sectors dedicated to dependency. In the name of its autonomy, loans are celebrated, and 'help' is accepted from foundations and North American universities that co-sign the interventions made by North American consultants with the stamp of 'university reform'.

Under these auspices, the construction of the University City, praiseworthy aspiration of the reformist university movement, was initiated, which after passing through the sieve of foreign intervention and its ideological solvent, is stripped in great measure of its democratic ends. We ought to understand its political implications, above and beyond its relative academic advantages.

With the necessary forethought – neocolonial cultural planning – the new Autonomous University is physically removed from the centre of the city to a depopulated suburban zone, with the unspoken objective of isolating it and separating it from contact with the social environment.

The argument presented here is that the student and professor need a calm environment and more ample space so that the University can faithfully meet its 'specific missions', that is, cultural and professional formation and scientific research. The real goals are of a political nature: to neutralise the mission of the university as a lever of change in Honduran society. This seeks, moreover, for the student to distance himself from the street, [so] that he forgets the rallies and popular demonstrations, that he reverts to submission, [becoming] egoistical and pragmatic; that he dedicate himself to, in sum, his *modern campus*, to utilitarian study in order to '*make a career*'.

In another no less important sense, the student body coming from economically limited households or that studies inconsistently due to the need to work in order to survive suffers the consequences of this distancing, compounded daily by the anarchic congestion of vehicles and increasingly deficient, insufficient, and onerous public transit services.

Zigzagging, contradictory, without keeping to a defined course, however, the autonomous university has yielded merely poor results. It has also borne singularly substantial fruits, the result of a state of innovative conscience, blooming in recent years.

Through self-critique the University itself recognises its various deficiencies, '*in its form: the institutional structure is not favourable for the scientific development of knowledge, among other things; in its content: its programmes and actual systems of teaching do not promote creative activity, they are disconnected from the national reality, they do not permit the serious formation of social conscience*'; in spite of this – we reiterate – we point out some of the reformist measures that have been implemented:

– An increase in the number of degrees, now up to thirty-two are presently offered.
– Progressive elimination of the anachronistic system of hourly pay for professors who were routinely ill-prepared. At the moment, 64% of professors can be full-time, 16% part-time, and only 19% hourly.
– Adjustment of study to work, with the intended effect of lessening the unjust incompatibility [of work and study] and the elitist character of the oligarchic university.
– Suppression of the rigid [system of] enrolment of annual courses and its replacement by a system of passed courses, with more flexible hours; the division of semesters into a lecture period and a corresponding exam period.
– Construction of modern laboratories and [the] renovation of all others, in order to make theory and practice more coherent.
– Improvement of library services. The central Library holds a collection of approximately 100,000 volumes and attends to roughly 3,000 requests daily, the majority from students.
– Proportional increase of the number of scholarships for poor students.

In 1976 the institution financed 246 of these to the same number of students [*sic*].
- Improving the ratio of the number of students to professors, conducive to encouraging the performance of both . . .

Of the transcribed sample one can infer that the reformist university movement has focused its efforts on the implementation of a process of educational transformation, qualitatively necessary to the cultural and professional mission and function of the UNAH.

However, as the same House of Study states, 'it is not enough to reform its internal structures or to completely revise and substitute its programmes.'

It is necessary to surpass the limits of an autonomy that is legal, valorised, accepted and as such conceded by the oppressive state, if in truth one wants to make of [the university] something more than just a means of academic transformation. In the resulting practice, autonomy acquires its own dynamic and becomes more contradictory inasmuch as it moves away from its restrictive legal code through the deliberate and conscious action of the university man.

In fact, it acquires a broader reach and a more substantial meaning, whose major implications we summarise as follows:

1) If in its *stricto sensu* university autonomy is not thoroughly questioned, when we ascribe to it greater militancy, it is necessarily rebuked by reactionary groups, scattered throughout public and private spheres and in the bosom of the University. Political power accepts it in its basic sense, so long as it is under *control* and is not 'dangerous' to their rule. The economic forces 'swallow' as long as it does not become an instrument of 'social agitation', [and] the university sectors opposed to social change defend the word and send it up in smoke in practice; as professors, they want an elitist and *quota*-based University, deaf to the clamour of the people but obsequious to the interference of the 'unsettled and brutal north that despises us', as Martí said; as students, they want autonomy as such, for their groups and interests and for the preservation of the *Facultades*.

The economic dependency that immutably afflicts the University is another enemy of its autonomy. Insufficient to and subject to government force, the financial factor is perhaps the most limiting to the growth of a democratic autonomy.

The apathy and indifference of a great number of alumni is another negative feature.

2) More than these limitations that without question weigh on the development of autonomy, it is reasonable to ask: is the University fully convinced that it is necessary for academic self-governance to be anything more than what it is? That autonomy should be broadened, more just, less *literal*? Because without clear conscience of what is wanted, without clear definition of the reasons and aims that are sought, all intended action will become sterile, if not demagogic. 'The unity of action – said Lenin during the student struggles in Russia of 1912 – is only possible when there exists an authentic unity of conviction that a specific action is necessary.'

In search of a 'new course' at the end of 1974, the university authorities organised the *First Meeting of the University Community* in accordance with their goals, in order to critically review and specify 'the ends, objectives, and functions of the UNAH in relation to the development of the country'. With the participation of students, professors, employees, and authorities, the event debated the university problem in two interrelated senses: 'The role of the University in the present historical stage' and 'Tenor and scope of the autonomous university in contemporary Honduran society'.

With regard to the second topic, the head of the university, Lic. Jorge Arturo Reina, in his inaugural address, declared, 'autonomy is the opportunity for more advanced action beyond that propelled by the dominant system. To not make use of this opportunity for action results in not wanting to utilise the potential for constructive work implied by a concept such as university autonomy. In other words, the University needs to defend and utilise to the utmost, in this stage, the possibilities that this entails.'

In the analysis of this theme, the *Meeting* underscored: 'a university that has not defined its fundamental tasks and is adrift regarding a topic of such importance as its *principal function*, is not capable of fully utilising its autonomy and actually limits its reach, reducing it to a simple act of administrative self-determination . . . There also exists a constant and systemic pressure from official sectors, the same ones who believe themselves obliged to concede university autonomy, which seek to limit its reach and reduce to a minimum the possibilities that it implies . . . Official pressure and the lack of definition of its objectives join to complicate the expansion of the scope and possibilities that autonomy imparts to the University.'

In signalling that this event marks a new stage in the historical development of the Institution in terms of its traditional objectives: the formation of professionals, conservation and diffusion of culture, and scientific research and technological development [. . .] as subordinate to 'the primordial function accorded to its role in the present historical moment of our country: *to contribute to social transformation*', [the *Meeting*] establishes moreover that the new approach involves the task of *learning by doing and learning by transforming*.

Thus defined, the objectives and principal tasks of the UNAH and the 'new course that today orients university activity' were formalised, by virtue of being approved *unanimously* and *without debate* (! ! !) by the Full Senate, [and] the only thing that remains is the crystallisation on the solid ground of actions.

And it is on these grounds – on this one must be clear – where the new university action shall truly begin. Because to 'contribute to social transformation' requires something more than words and attitudes of protest; because to 'learn by doing and learn by transforming', more than a rhetorical formula, demands the assumption of clear positions and correct political commitment to those social forces [that are] hostile to dependency and underdevelopment.

In these active processes – coming soon – the Autonomous University will need to identify itself with the autonomous politics and economics that the people seek. This brings us to our point of departure: autonomy contains in itself 'the germ of its own contradiction', ever more acute as it makes those class interests that gave rise to it more uncomfortable.

If the Honduran State as a political expression of order and dependent capitalist production configured the limits of Autonomy as the law says, objective and scientific analysis of it might give the University and its vanguard student movement the frame of reference necessary to expand its reach and significance, in its *possible* terms and in its *concrete reality*.

In the present moment – twenty years since its conquest – the dominant sectors that conceded [autonomy] strive now to nullify it – attempting to make it disappear as [merely] a constitutionally sanctioned right – . Absolute Autonomy is a necessity in the present historical stage of our society, [thus] its *encounter* with the University indicates we must protect it with both our fists and mind, so long as the Honduran people do not say otherwise.

Translated by Jorge Cuéllar

Works Cited

Gill, Lesley (2004), *The School of the Americas: Military Training and Political Violence in the Americas*, Durham, NC: Duke University Press.

Guevara, Ernesto, Brian Loveman, and Thomas M. Davies, Jr, eds (1997), *Guerrilla Warfare*, Lanham, MD: Scholarly Resources.

'La Universidad de San Carlos es un "foco subversivo", dice el Presidente de Guatemala', *El Excelsior*, 18 November 1978. Hemeroteca Nacional (HN).

Lindo-Fuentes, Héctor, Erik Ching, and Rafael Lara Martínez (2007), *Remembering a Massacre in El Salvador: The Insurrection of 1932, Roque Dalton, and the Politics of Historical Memory*, Albuquerque: University of New Mexico Press.

Martínez Peláez, Severo (1970), *La patria del criollo: ensayo de interpretación de la realidad colonial guatemalteca*, Guatemala City: Editorial Universitaria.

Sáenz de Tejada, Ricardo (2011), *Oliverio: una biografía del secretario general de la AEU, 1978–1979*, Guatemala: FLACSO.

Way, J. T. (2012), *The Mayan in the Mall: Globalization, Development, and the Making of Modern Guatemala*, Durham, NC: Duke University Press.

Chapter 5

Revolutionary Futures 1976–1983

Introduction

One of the most iconic images of the Central American civil wars is that of the thousands of exuberant Nicaraguans who filled the large plaza between the old cathedral and the Presidential Palace on 19 July 1979. Some combatants dressed in fatigues or khakis embraced and grinned while others simply stared, perhaps too exhausted and hungry to smile. Somoza and his closest cronies were on a plane bound for Miami. On the whole, the optimism on the faces of the crowd is breath-taking. Many of the texts in this final chapter were written around the same time as those of the previous chapter, but these stand out for their imaginations of revolutionary futures, sometimes millennial, sometimes remarkably detailed and even practical while utopian.

In contrast to the victorious scene in Managua, civil wars raged on in Guatemala and El Salvador. Both nations suffered economic stagnation as a result of the warfare. The level of violence endured by these communities was exacerbated by the comprehensive approach to hemispheric leftists adopted by the administration of US President Ronald Reagan (1911–2004). At the UES, the AGEUS became increasingly outspoken against the successive military regimes and, as a result, faced escalating violence. The university campus frequently was closed or occupied by the military. In 1972, the military invaded campus and arrested several members of the National Revolutionary Movement (MNR), a predecessor to the FDR. One of those arrested, Félix Ulloa, was elected university Rector in 1979, just seven years later. With a known leftist at the helm, the UES came under close scrutiny. The Revolutionary Government Junta led by José Napoleón Duarte kept a watchful eye and sent troops to occupy the university campus in late June. Just four months later, Ulloa was assassinated, some ten metres from campus.

The Jesuit Universidad Centroamericana 'José Simeón Cañas' (UCA) had also been labelled a haven for subversive proponents of Liberation Theology and endured comparable repression. Simply to be a student made one suspect. Duarte, a Christian Democrat and leading figure in the anti-communist counter-insurgency, served as interim president while elections to the Constituent Assembly were planned. The FMLN took advantage of the potential opening and went public in late 1980; in response, the US funnelled money, aid, and equipment into El Salvador to support the Duarte government. Two years later, in March 1982, the far-right parties dominated a democratic charade of Constituent Assembly elections. Once instated, the Assemblymen relentlessly shot down any attempt at reform and dismantled the surviving traces of even the most moderate reforms. The last Salvadoran text below, a homage to Agustín Farabundo Martí, was published in February 1982 on the eve of the Constituent Assembly.

USAC students in Guatemala confronted the toughest years of the civil war yet. The four largest guerrilla groups – the Rebel Armed Forces (FAR), Guerrilla Army of the Poor (EGP), Revolutionary Organisation of the People in Arms (ORPA), and Guatemalan Communist Party (PGT) – joined together to form the Guatemalan National Revolutionary Unity (URNG), demonstrating a more organised plan of defence. Meanwhile, the military shored its reserves. The guerrilla expanded its recruitment at the university and secondary schools nationwide. Interviews conducted years later by Byron Renato Barillas, Carlos Alberto Enríquez, and Luis Pedro Taracena indicated how student life was interrupted by the presence of infiltrators and informants (*orejas*) who reported to the National Police and Army intelligence services. These *orejas* received payments and favours – sometimes even homes and cars – for information about students or faculty purported to be part of the guerrilla. The infiltrators and misinformation campaigns exacerbated divisions between and within student groups, inhibiting a united student front and endangering the lives of student leaders. As in El Salvador, being a student or associating with students could make one the target of assault or surveillance. In a horrific display of violence, President Lucas García's government responded with growing ferocity to protests, demonstrations, and guerrilla offensives. Anthropologist Paul Kobrak has counted many dozens of students and professors who died in 1980 alone. In March 1982, Lucas García was deposed by a coup led by another general, Efraín Rios Montt (b. 1926). Rios Montt ushered in more death squad violence, especially singling out for attack anyone involved in any attempt at alliance between workers, *campesinos*, and the university. The severity of violence during his brief presidency triggered a refugee crisis as many Guatemalans fled for Mexico or Honduras.

Meanwhile, in Sandinista-led Nicaragua, the elation of triumph quickly gave way to difficult work: transitioning the economy, building constructive cross-class alliances, implementing literacy and public education programmes, restructuring the National Guard, and soon, fending off the US threat and fighting the counter-revolutionary armies. Much of this counter-revolutionary threat came from Honduras, where the US government took advantage of the presidency of Policarpo Paz García to create an anti-communist outpost in the region. Countless counter-insurgent offences against Guatemalans, Salvadorans, and Nicaraguans were launched from within Honduran borders. Since the mid-1950s, an almost constant stream of military strongmen had ruled Honduras (Ramón Villeda Morales and Ramón Ernesto Cruz Uclés are notable exceptions). Only in 1982 was the chain of Honduran military presidents broken with election of Roberto Suazo Córdova, a USAC-trained medical doctor. Yet even after his election, Hondurans remained, in the words of the student newspaper below, 'endlessly screwed'.

Again the outlier, Costa Rica continued to enjoy political and economic stability, but the first text below serves as a reminder of the bonds between Central American students and other student struggles worldwide and the sense of purpose that drove all Central American anti-colonial students. As author R. Morua writes, 'We take on, proudly, the responsibility that history has offered us.' The texts collected in this chapter suggest some of the ways that Central American students found hope – sometimes in the midst of victory, but usually whilst enduring great losses – in revolutionary futures. By 1982, the outcome of anti-colonial struggles in El Salvador and Guatemala remained unclear. What had been a decisive Sandinista victory in 1979 had, by 1982, turned into a bitter battle against the US-funded Contras. Honduras marched forward under the military regime of Paz, then under the civilian leadership of Suazo. Costa Rica remained exceptional in the region, somehow unable to help resolve the problems immiserating its neighbours.

COSTA RICA

R. Morua, 'We the Students Say: "We Want to Build our Tomorrow"'

(1970)

This article was published in *El Universitario* just a week after the strike against ALCOA had turned violent with the students' attack on the Legislative Assembly. Two years after the global surge of the summer of 1968 and just a week after this landmark moment for Costa Rican youth, the author notes how resistance to specific demands – exams, pedagogy, and natural resources – spurred larger struggles. The hopefulness of this Costa Rican moment provides a powerful counterpoint to the violence endured by their peers in El Salvador, Guatemala, and Nicaragua.

The surprise demonstrated by certain sectors of our society regarding the events that culminated on 24 April only serves to demonstrate the shortage – if not total lack – of knowledge that informs many people who to this day have been playing the role of leaders in our society.

To be surprised by the irruption of the study body as an active factor in national politics and to immediately assume that this was caused by a small and well-organised minority only indicates total confusion about the trends and determinant socio-political factors of modern life.

Latent in all of our societies is the cry of the youth, ever more conscious, against an order of things, an international system, and a sequence of phenomena that although valid in their essence have been twisted in practice and from positive elements of social and national improvement have resulted in significant obstacles for economic development and the effective solution of the urgent social labours that our *pueblos* demand.

On the other hand, the events among students in recent years – Mexico, France, Czechoslovakia – are the greatest testimony that the Youth no longer want their tomorrow to be made by others, as an unchangeable inheritance that they ought to simply accept. The myth that the future belongs to the Youth has been revealed before their eyes in its true meaning: the Youth do not belong in the present or in the future. The present because this is for the 'mature and conscientious' adults; the future because this is nothing more than the result of the actions of the past.

Many are the errors that are carried from generation to generation and by accepting them one after the other, responsibility has extended equally over everyone.

The youth of the world, because of exams and methods of teaching in France; for assassinated students or the celebration of a historic date in Mexico; or for the refusal to surrender national riches and the mutilation of our sovereignty, in Costa Rica, have turned to direct action, which permits them to actively affect the construction of their future.

[The Youth] has therefore turned its eyes, wide open and without cobwebs, to the surrounding reality. As did the best men of their time – then exceptional, now multitudinous – we subject what exists, that which we inherited, and that which we want to leave behind to open and well-founded critique. We demand the fairness of institutions, pure and simple truth as the foundation of existing [structures], and the recognition of our rights as men of today and tomorrow.

We want a defence of the institutional democracy of our nation, not as a set of untouchable and static dogmas, but as a harmonious and coordinated structure, with rational, justified, practical, functional, dynamic, and vibrant foundations.

No one has attacked parliamentarism [sic]. No one the freedom of the press, of opinion, of conscience. No one attacks democracy. This we can say clearly, that we, the students, in defence of national interests and of our convictions have fought actively against the nefarious and shameful contract with Alcoa.

But can those who have attacked us say this? Can those who have used the freedom of the press to denigrate us and to make us look like ruffians or tools say this? Can those who have threatened the [public] University with the creation of a private University, just because we are becoming a stronghold for the defence of national interest, without political, commercial, or electoral predispositions, say this?

Obviously, no. Thus, conscious of the transcendence and the duty of this historic struggle, with the FEUCR we declare: we take on, proudly, the responsibility that history offers us.

Translated by Heather Vrana

HONDURAS

Federation of Honduran University Students (FEUH), 'Public Declaration'

(1976)

In this 'Public Declaration' in *Presencia Universitaria* the leadership of the FEUH presents a careful analysis of the situations confronting their *pueblo* at a moment when the government of General Juan Alberto Melgar Castro proposed a 'great national dialogue' to root out corruption and, ultimately, reduce the appeal of the left. As if to proffer a counter-argument to the government's inevitable assessment of the situation, the group gives an account of several recent acts of violence and neocolonial incursions, including the massacre at Talanquera, where six *campesinos* were killed when they attempted to occupy land held by large landowners in February 1972. This protest was part of a longer campaign of *campesino* organising in the region. In turn, the 'fresh blood' of Olancho refers to the 1975 torture and murder of six people – two priests, two young people, and two *campesinos* – for their purported subversion. While the students distrusted the government's call for a 'great national dialogue', they seized the moment to push the government to make good on its claim, inviting 'Workers, Peasants, Teachers, Businessmen, Journalists, Cooperative workers, Bosses, and Students' to join in. After so many years of lying in wait, the students were prepared to take advantage of the opportunity.

The Federation of University Students of Honduras – FEUH – loyal to our tradition of fighting for popular causes, will outline our position with respect to the critical situation experienced by the country.

On this occasion, we university students outline a brief but objective analysis of the challenges that trouble us as a nation and propose solutions, alternatives, and suggestions to overcome them.

The structural crisis bringing down Honduran society is the historical consequence of global capitalist development, the result of centuries of exploitation and looting of our resources by developed capitalist societies, especially the United States of America. The Honduran people, like other people of the earth, make possible the luxury, opulence, and well-being of the imperialists, at the cost of our own misery and nakedness. To this we must add that the reigning anarchy, which translates into the inflation and deflation that erodes the foundations of the capitalist system, directly affects our dependent and underdeveloped economy. In sum, the national crisis is nothing more than the reflection of capital-ism's resistance to its complete collapse as a social system.

The political economy of the regime has not managed to move beyond the strict framework of bourgeois reformism and developmentalism, which imposes great limits on tangible changes. In the regime's bosom a marked tendency to appease their adversaries has developed for some time, which logically has awakened a growing lack of confidence among the popular sectors who could, potentially, turn into their social base. To achieve this, the government should reactivate and expand its initial inten-tion to establish a state sector of the economy that is strong and powerful. This, the implementation of a policy of drastic, rigorous price controls that would safeguard the consumer from the voracity of intermediaries, is urgent. It is incredible that those who could arrange a set of economic poli-cies favourable to the majority do not go forward with the nationalisation of foreign banks and the democratisation of the national bank.

On the other hand, the Government acknowledges grave errors that will certainly lead to paralysis, chaos, and failure. The threatening presence of corrupt bureaucrats, hindrances by the oligarchic parties in the governmental apparatus, and the shameful dismissal of honest, upright officials makes it impossible to have a capable, agile, and honest administration. If we look back, we can easily see that national sover-eignty and dignity have been tainted and stomped on by the petulance and pride of the octopus banana company[1] that oppresses our country with the complicity of undignified Hondurans with a Phoenician voca-tion.[2] Where are the punishments for the bribers and the bribed? We cannot hide our distrust of the results of the court case against those implicated in the crimes of Olancho. Will they walk free like those of La Talanquera? Why has no case been opened against the robbers of the national treasury identified by the Yllescas Report? Why have they tried to hide the scandalous traffic in basic grains by the BANAFOM?[3] It is evident that the regime supposedly led by General Melgar Castro is splattered with the fresh blood of the martyrs of Olancho and that bribes and corruption are constants in its growth, while honesty and probity in administration have dragged their heels.

---

[1] UFCO was often called *el pulpo*, the octopus, by journalists and the left because it seemingly had a hand in every industry in every nation.

[2] The Phoenicians built a thriving economy by selling timber to their neighbours, just as some Hondurans made tremendous profits on selling bananas to foreigners.

[3] BANAFOM, the National Agricultural Development Bank, controlled the financing of agricultural development and thus had tremendous power over the pricing of basic grains.

The situation of Honduran agriculture has never reached such high levels of social intensity [as those] produced by the terror sowed by armed bands in the service of landowners and in certain zones with the complicity of some members of the National Army. As a result, it has frequently happened that class conflicts turn violent; the government's intention to implement a capitalist agrarian reform within the guide-lines of dependency has been slowed by the ferocity of attacks by the reactionary press, by the seditious preaching of the decrepit heads of the oligarchic parties, and by the pressure of hoodlum governments in El Salvador and Guatemala, and most especially by the satrap Somoza Debayle of Nicaragua, gendarme of the most reactionary capitalist inter-ests in Central America. The process of agrarian reform has suffered ebbs and flows thanks to the combativeness of the peasant movement through its central organisation, the *Campesino* National Unity Front (FUNC), and the brave decision to fight [made] by the former Executive Director of the National Agrarian Institute – INA – Lieutenant Colonel Mario Maldonado Muñoz.[4] The irresponsible conduct of the Chief of State, maintaining the INA without a leader during the most critical months for the *campesinos*, is reprehensible. Today, university students along with the rest of the Honduran people remain vigilant so that the Government's promises of the immediate parcelling out of land become reality.

It is fundamentally important that the military officials understand that they may drive the State permanently into a position of arbiter between different conflictive social forces, constituted on the one hand by the vast majority of the Honduran people, made up of workers, peas-ants, students, teachers, democratic intellectuals, progressive military officials, and other social groups; and on the other hand a microscopic minority that is very loud, made up of semi-feudal landowners, inter-mediary bourgeoisie, corrupt bureaucrats, and other social parasites who are servants of imperialism. The Honduran state cannot, because of historical imperatives, become the architect of harmony and concilia-tion between this power- and wealth-hungry minority and the supreme interests of the Honduran nation. Social changes, as timid as they may be, provoke obstinate resistance from the privileged minorities, as expe-rience demonstrates in all corners of the globe.

---

[4] One of the few military proponents of moderate agrarian reform for modernisation, on the day before his resignation, Maldonado demanded the expropriation of more than 50,000 hectares of land from Tela Railroad and Standard Fruit, according to Juan Arancibia Córdova.

We are experiencing dramatic and historically exceptional moments in [our] country. The current government finds itself at a crossroads. There is ostensibly a state of balance between antagonistic social forces, which cannot last much longer. The privileged minority is no longer sufficiently powerful to crush the great masses of the people, and the Honduran *pueblo*, through stone-like unity in their social organisations, will win and build a Honduras that is economically developed, socially just, and politically independent. A country that will resist any aggression on the part of the internal and external reactionary sectors, that will know how to get along and collaborate with like-minded progressive sectors from the rest of the world.

The FEUH has repeatedly rejected the petty, selfish, and anachronistic pretensions of the leaders of oligarchic parties who struggle for the return of a constitutionality, which, as they approach it, would mean returning to a period of social retrogression, institutionalising misuse, theft, and waste of public funds. In view of the failure of the historic parties, a sector of the Honduran Council of Private Enterprise – COHEP – in recent days initiated the so-called 'great national dialogue', which has not developed beyond being a monologue by the oligarchy. A dialogue cannot be 'great' or 'national' if only the representatives of the dominant class of Honduras, especially its commercial and landholding sectors, participate.

The current leadership of the COHEP and the oligarchic parties are tributaries of the same river, which flows in one direction: old-fashioned obscurantism, support for stagnation, consolidation of backwardness, and strengthening of dependency. Will the current leadership of COHEP and the North American Embassy try to repeat the political farce and historic failure of the National Pact of (oligarchic) Unity of 7 January 1971?[5] It seems they will. They have invited the leadership of the peasant and worker organisations and are awaiting a response. The FEUH reckons that the inter-relation of forces in the worker and peasant movements is not the same [now] as in 1971. The situation has changed substantially to the advantage of progressive sectors; in other words, a democratic, anti-*latifundio* and anti-imperialist conscience has developed [among them]. In sum, we see the 'great national dialogue' as a tactical action of the creole right, conceived within their general strategy, through an elite organisation: the COHEP.

---

[5] The election results were split evenly between the National and Liberal Parties, so they signed a pact agreeing to a coalition government; the government lasted just a year before a coup by Oswaldo López Arellano.

Through truly representative organisations, the *pueblo* should search ambitiously for a popular, democratic alternative, to overcome the grave crisis that overwhelms the Republic.

We believe that the most suitable instrument to achieve this patriotic objective is through the immediate observance of a National Assembly of Popular Organisations. The objective of this would be to draw up a common platform on national issues, which would be taken into consideration by the Executive and Superior Council of the Armed Forces.

The structure of power of the military government can be characterised as essentially vertical and authoritarian, but it has tried to legitimate itself through the proclamation of some Decree-Laws of a reformist character in favour of the popular majorities. But even when the people receive marginal benefits from these changes in some cases, they are not the protagonists of them. The facts have shown that military officials are against popular mobilisation, the power of decision-making has remained virtually monopolised by the Armed Forces, and the participation of civil technocrats is modest and diminishing. The administration of justice remains dependent on decisions that they expedite and tidy up.

We university students propose that the *pueblo* should participate in the steering of the destiny of the Nation through genuinely representative channels, and for this reason we are in favour of the integration of the Advisory Council under the following conditions: That the [COHEP] Council Board transform into a Council of the State with legislative capacities indicated by the Constitution of the Republic of 1965; that it be made up of Workers, Peasants, Teachers, Businessmen, Journalists, Cooperative workers, Bosses, and Students; that the mechanisms to select the representatives be those chosen internally by the participating organisations. The term limit of this Council should be for the amount of time that elapses before the election of the National Constituent Assembly.

These solutions, alternatives, and suggestions are presented as a responsible contribution by the studious youth of Honduras, which is forged in the classrooms of the Highest House of Studies, so that they may be submitted to a serious, deep, and reflective discussion by all the sectors that make up our nation.

EVER ONWARD TO VICTORY!

Tegucigalpa, D.C., 11 January 1976

EXECUTIVE COMMITTEE OF THE
FEDERATION OF UNIVERSITY STUDENTS
OF HONDURAS

Translated by Rachel Nolan

Excerpts, Enrique Astorga Lira, 'Marginal Models of Agrarian Reform in Latin America: the Case of Honduras'

(1980)

The text below comes from the third edition of a then-new magazine called *Alcaraván*. The edition begins with a note 'To the Reader', wherein the editors explain their delay in production and fend off accusations that they demonstrated a bias against certain types of submissions. They rail against 'heretical Stalinism' and 'vulgarity', and charge that if some articles were rejected, it was because they lacked intellectual sophistication. This article by a Chilean, not Honduran, intellectual named Enrique Astorga Lira made it through a seemingly daunting review process. In it, Astorga Lira calls into question the whole of Latin American agrarian reform in the twentieth century as another mode of North American imperial meddling. He discusses at length the conference of the OAS held at Punta del Este, Uruguay, in 1961, where all twenty member nations (except Cuba) formalised their acceptance of US President John F. Kennedy's Alliance for Progress by signing the Charter of Punta del Este. Ernesto Che Guevara was Cuba's delegate at the meeting and famously delivered a speech that included a long quotation from legendary Cuban anti-imperialist José Martí denouncing the Inter-American Development Bank and the servility it demanded from debtor nations. Below, Astorga Lira provides an analysis of how internal and external factors together produced deleterious conditions for meaningful agrarian reform in Honduras by outlining the impact of the Alliance for Progress in the hemisphere more than a decade later.

Seventeen years have passed since the OAS conference in Punta del Este, Uruguay, at the beginning of the 1960s. During this period, some countries have made certain reforms to the structure of landownership, and others have not even touched the old structures of *latifundios* in spite of their formal promulgation of laws of agrarian reform.

The countries that most profoundly changed the structure of landholding did so before Kennedy's policies at Punta del Este, as in the cases of Mexico, Bolivia, and Cuba. In retrospect, the Chilean experience of the Popular Unity [government] managed to dramatically influence the agrarian scene [that was] dominated by great unproductive properties.

The government of General [Juan] Velasco Alvarado in Peru also made significant advances in the appropriation of lands to be given to cooperatives or other peasant associations. The counter-reformist offensive unleashed after September 1973 in Chile[6] and the virtual paralysis of agrarian politics in Peru after the fall of General Velasco Alvarado marked the historical twilight of certain agrarian experiments conceived of as means of transitioning to socialism or intending to establish a more open and participatory agrarian society.

The model of agrarian reform sponsored by the United States at Punta del Este is characterised by being selective and partial, without peasant participation, oriented toward forming private property on the basis of a family economy, and of course maintaining the elusiveness of basic needs in rural society.

The result of this focus is that fewer than five per cent of low-income peasant families have received land. A similar model propagated by the North American delegation did not fit the scheme proposed by the Popular Unity [government] in Chile nor reformist Peruvian politics.

The experience of the Honduran case from 1973 onwards is that of a country that came late to the brief phase of reforms that many civilian politicians (in Chile) and military members (in Peru) saw as linked to a broad class alliance. Honduras came to the reformist or revolutionary opening when the counter-offensive against agrarian reforms was already prepared, coming as it did out of the model of the OAS. It is clear that the counter-reform was not generated exclusively [in reaction to] the agrarian policies of the reformist or revolutionary governments; it was also the product of the deep reach of social forces into the traditional structures of economy and society. It seemed that the more important the sector in terms of productivity, social importance, or political importance, or foreign investment, the larger the mobilisation of the counter-reform.

Honduras is a predominantly agricultural country, with an export economy of raw goods, subject to the norms of the international division of labour, with strong investments of foreign capital and nascent

---

[6] Refers to the 11 September 1973 coup against Salvador Allende and the rise of Augusto Pinochet.

industry and industrialisation. In this context, the agrarian reform introduced by the military government during the period of 1973–76 ended up being an action of marginal significance to the *latifundio* and to foreign capital in agriculture. It is notable that in spite of the fact that the military coup in 1972 against the civilian conservative government of [Ramón Ernesto] Cruz had support from peasant masses, workers, and students, it did not have nor did it gain sufficient power to carry through a measure of progressive change to traditional agrarian structures in this small Central American country.

Neither could the civilian government of President [Salvador] Allende, established by a extensive cast of worker and peasant forces, along with political parties with an extensive and militant past, summon the political power to complete the programme of transitioning to socialism. Therefore the essential power for agrarian transformations as part of national transformation does definitely not reside in military governments even if they have support from the masses, nor does it [reside] in civilian governments, supported by parties and [social] classes. Irrevocably power has been in the hands of the local bourgeois classes allied with the foreign hegemonic centre. As long as the question of power remained unresolved, the dominant groups did not accept even the marginal agrarian reforms that tended to give more fluidity to the old structure of the [agricultural] sector. Officials paid a high and fearsome price for browbeating landowners, whether they are civilians or military men.

When reformist or revolutionary programmes harmed the interests of the dominant classes or the investments of transnationals, whether sponsored by civilians or the military, with more or less support [from the people], they were harshly attacked, with the greatest variety of techniques of resistance and counter-offensive. In Honduras, the freezing of agrarian programmes [and] in Chile, the counter-reform in its most direct and crushing form, in order to hand over the economy to foreign capital.

In Honduras, the army played, on one hand, the role of promoting progressive measures and, on the other, incubating the seed of resistance planted by dominant creole groups together with foreign capital. The absence of unity of action and transformative consciousness, owing to the shared government–military plan, permitted the formation or reinforcement of channels by which bourgeois and foreign capital could easily move between different classes and military tiers, instrumentalising resistance and paralysing progressive measures.

The Honduran experience is that of a country whose government aspired to a historic advancement through a package of reforms, the first of which being tied to the agrarian sector [and] unleashing, as a result, a siege of alliances of resistance, acting as a nerve centre for the banana enclaves and foreign investment in banks, industry, and commerce.

It is interesting to point out that in Latin America it is less and less common to speak of agrarian reform and increasingly common to propose agricultural modernisation plans without touching the *latifundio*; very marginal agrarian reform tends to terrify the landowner into modernising, but he, upon seeing the weakness of governments, will not accept progressive measures, and if he is terrified, he is terrified into demonstrating his strength, paralysing governmental agrarian programmes.

Translated by Rachel Nolan

Excerpts, Editorial, *El tornillo sin fin: The Virile Organ of the University Students of Honduras*

(1981)

This editorial comes from a student paper whose title may be translated as 'The Endless Screw'. The title vividly captures a common feeling among many Honduran students by 1981. The editorial tells a national history that makes Honduras seem destined for plunder, first as a marginal colony and, more recently, as a banana enclave. Here the topic under discussion is Suazo's election after the end of the Paz presidency in 1981. President Jimmy Carter had celebrated the Paz administration for its purportedly democratic transition and commitment to democracy in the region. In exchange for safeguarding democracy, Paz's government received economic and defence aid. But robust corruption, drug trafficking, and paramilitary repression undergirded the façade of democracy. Below, an anonymous student or students outline(s) their complete distrust of the electoral process and denounce(s) the new government as simply another pawn of the US in the hemisphere where 'every puppet is playing their role.'

It is a fact that the global capitalist system suffers from a deep crisis, and that the effects of this crisis are felt more heavily and with more excruciating expressions in backward countries.

The Third World finds itself sunk in, perhaps, the deepest crisis of its history, paradoxically in the moments in which the scientific–technical revolution has put in the hands of man the most sophisticated tools, capable of making the forces of nature submit to serve the highest interests and objectives of humanity.

This crisis suffered by the backward part of the world – which optimists call underdeveloped – affect Honduran society with the most alarming features, for two principal reasons: one, because of the terrible cancer of corruption that has penetrated the whole organism of society; and two, because of the high levels of incapacity and mediocrity exhibited by State leaders and the institutions representing the dominant classes.

Because, in effect, corruption is not the exclusive province of civil servants and the high command of the Army, corruption proliferates with the repugnant quality of a worm, in private companies, in administrative councils, in the comfortable meetings of executive boards of banks and utility companies.

If bureaucrats, officials, and dishonest public employees construct magnificent residences, if they live in the most offensive extravagance and fatten like pigs at the cost of the power and the money of the people [. . .] they were confident they controlled the fundamental decisions on political economy through traditional parties and were able to promote a process that would fully respond to their anti-democratic and anti-national interests.

In this way, in 1980, the Honduran people were led to an electoral process designed to dress the already-governing military–*Zúñiguista* government[7] in constitutional clothing, [a government] that had already put into effect corrupt, repressive governance that was accommodating to foreign monopolist capital, primarily that of North Americans.

The elections were surrounded by an intense radio, press, and television campaign intended to convince the people that the elections would bring us to new economic, social, and political experiences, while the National Party prepared itself to take over all of the positions of government and elect a Constitutional President in the Constituent [Assembly]. Against all predictions, the Liberal Party won. Allegations of fraud required the military government to break all its commitments to *Zúñiguismo*. But since the process was fraudulent and excluded the *pueblo* at every turn, the margin of victory was small enough to make it easy to bring about the most disastrous of negotiations, such that politi-

---

[7] Ricardo Zúñiga Agustinus, leader of the National Party and former Vice-president, who exercised power behind the scenes from the early 1960s to the early 1980s.

cal power was placed in the hands of those against whom the Honduran people had voted on 20 April 1980.[8]

We must be clear: the majority of the people did not vote for the return of the Liberal Party, as its leaders like to believe; the great masses of workers, peasants, teachers, and organised students voted AGAINST the military government headed by general Paz García ... [...] . The liberal leaders have been and remain part of the oligarchic–imperial game, and as such are responsible for the surrender of our Fatherland.

Behind a non-existent third position was hidden the hand of imperialism and the objective of opposing the democratic and revolutionary sectors' struggle for an authentic process of national liberation. Of course some people and groups that now appear as representatives of the 'third position' could be part of a scheme to move Honduras towards democratic policies.

The Honduran Patriotic Front, as first step of their profound political project, could be the pivot around which a broad revolutionary movement of the masses is structured to confront the grave crisis experienced by Honduras. But for that, it would have to overcome its serious internal limitations and challenges due to a lack of experience [among] a left-wing Honduran unified conscience, [as] some leaders continue with factional, sectarian practices that demonstrate their incomprehension of the new circumstances in which Honduras and Central America live.

This is, in broad strokes, the state of affairs of the political forces that participate in the present electoral process that will culminate on 29 November.

The electoral route has been and will continue to be the principal tendency within national politics [and] even though it cannot fully undo the *coup d'état* (preparation is now under way for after elections, based on 'incinerating' the future constitutional government), [it] could still advance, and that would be convenient for the imperialists' counter-revolutionary plans in Central America. Until now, the government of the United States, as is widely known, has been pressuring the military junta to go through with the elections ...

[...]

The North American government is convinced that it is not possible to defeat the guerrillas given the current inter-relation of forces, which will become more favourable to the guerrillas in the future, enabling the

---

[8] According to Dunkerley, when elections for a Constituent Assembly were held in 1980, Zúñiga's party suffered a defeat in the elections, winning 42.2% of the seats as compared to their opponents, the Liberals, with 49.4%.

destruction of the puppet army of El Salvador, which would completely unbalance North American domination in the region, and thus, the Yankee diplomats will try to avoid this at all costs.

Under these circumstances it is easy to understand who has been pulling the strings of the puppets: [Fernando Romeo] Lucas, [José Napoleón] Duarte, and Abdul Gutiérrez [Avendaño] in their diplomatic manœuvres near the Government of Tegucigalpa headed by General Paz García. Everything foretells that there is a plan of great magnitude afoot, of which the invitation of Paz García by the government of Venezuela forms part, which is Washington's principal instrument to put [its] plan into effect in Central America and particularly in El Salvador. The arrival on the scene of the unfortunately *célèbre* 'Baby Doc' the Haitian dictator, and his declarations of support for the government of Honduras in the 'fight against communism', even though he is indeed marginal and minor, confirms once again that this is effectively a complete plan of North Americans faced with their failures in El Salvador, and every puppet is playing their role.

At the same time as this diplomatic 'run-around', they speak of a possible postponement of the elections in Honduras so that, according to what Paz García said before the parliament of Venezuela, the Honduran political officials can faithfully fulfil the function that the Army has permitted them, to organise elections that pave the way for a 'democratic regime of popular expression', an appearance that the United States needs to drape over Honduras so that it can present this as an example of 'democratic' responsibility in the region and have better chances of executing the mission that it has been assigned. Backstage they also talk about extraordinary events for the second fortnight of September, that very well could be some important changes at the heart of the Honduran Armed forces, which point in the same direction, which is, to wash the face of the high command for imperial schemes . . .

Translated by Rachel Nolan

GUATEMALA

Excerpts, 'Bulletin No. 2 of the Huelga de Dolores'

(1980)

The Huelga de Dolores bulletins usually trafficked in the same fun word play that characterised the *No Nos Tientes* (featured in Chapter 4). In 1980, however, the bulletin began with a more sombre tone. While the first section is readily understood, the rest of the text presents a real challenge to the reader, as it is filled with contemporary political, social, and cultural references, some very obscure, and written in the playful student argot of the era. This text is hard to read unless you imagine it in the style of a formal declaration, which is precisely the type of text that the bulletin is mocking. Unlike the *No Nos Tientes*, the bulletins were usually read aloud to inaugurate the event, often at Central Park or on campus. The erratic punctuation of the original is maintained in the translation below. After the introduction, the first three paragraphs outline the interests and identity of the group who is writing; the fourth, which ends with '*pueblo* of Guatemala', identifies and describes the audience the authors seek to address. The remainder of the document follows the format of a declaration by beginning 'let it be known', then enumerating a list of denunciations of individuals for violations of sovereignty, foreign incursion, and, ultimately, violence toward the *pueblo*. The brief interruption of the structure of decrees ('let it be known') by 'did you know . . .' almost succeeds in turning horrific realisations into playful anecdotes. Two weeks after this bulletin was issued, three students who met to distribute the other important Huelga de Dolores text, the *No Nos Tientes* newspaper, were kidnapped, tortured, and killed. The government no longer tolerated even the students' traditional sardonic critiques.

TERROR AND DEATH IN GUATEMALA

People of Guatemala: Once again all of us workers, peasants, residents, and students have endured the criminal onslaught that the current fascist military cadre has initiated in order to decapitate and annihilate our Guatemalan democratic movement. The most shameless representatives of the national bourgeoisie and North American imperialism, personified by [President] Romeo Lucas Garcia, [Interior Minister] Donaldo Alvarez Ruiz, [National Police Director] German Chupina Barahona, and [Chief of Judicial Police] Manuel de Jesus Valiente Tellez have orchestrated a whole terrorist plot that is accelerating the assassinations, in the most diverse of manners, of the best-known leaders of the Guatemalan popular movement.

Shamelessly and openly, over the last few days they have assassinated representatives of different democratic sectors, they have civilly and militarily invaded every zone where popular demands are presented. This honourable committee [of the Huelga de Dolores], injured by the loss of brave sons of the *pueblo*, but assuming an energetic, popular and democratic position, denounces the most recent assassinations by the military fascist cadre full of mad and corrupt minds.

[The] assassination of university professor at the Western branch [of USAC], Jorge Everardo Jiménez Cajas, member of the United Revolutionary Front [FUR], the assassination of student of the *Facultad* of Law and ex-leader of the secondary school students, Julio César Cabrera y Cabrera, the kidnapping of the student of the *Facultad* of Odontology, ex-member of the Association of University Students and current director of the FUR Youth, César Romero; the invasion of two sugar plantations by members of the army where agricultural workers demanded a salary increase; the assassination of twenty peasants in the region of Nebaj, Quiché, by the army and all of the assassinations that have remained anonymous.

René Alejandro Cotí López, President of the Association of Students of Engineering, 1977, Member of the University High Council 1977–79, candidate for Secretary General of the AEU, 1978, was kidnapped the day of Wednesday, 5 March in the area of 18th Street in Zone 1 by twelve men who were heavily armed and whose vehicles had licence plates from the series 78,000 and 79,000 (of known origin).

By making the present denunciation, this Honourable Committee, as have all of the student and popular associations, holds the government of the Republic solely and exclusively responsible for this brutal attack on the student and popular movement and calls on all popular and student organisations through popular and revolutionary Democratic Unity to end this wave of terror and death that thrashes our people. The *Pueblo* has demonstrated that, in practice, these attacks make our power grow and that the alternative, more painful if you will, would be one that would give us complete freedom, as our *compañeros* in Costa Sur and Quiché demonstrated that the enemy trembles when the struggle is unified and militant. We call on the Guatemalan *pueblo* to join in the popular struggle and accelerate their actions for defence and self-defence because the decline of the beasts is near.

BULLETIN NO. 2

[FROM] THE VERY LOYAL, HONOURABLE, NEVER VERY THOUGHTFUL somewhat Spaniardified but for reasons not of his own will . . . To the odious PIGS but [also] to the beloved girlfriends; to the excommunicated priests, but to the blessed *Pueblo*; to the threatened rich, but to the protected poor; to the ESA,[9] cornered, to the rescued worker; to the hunted DEATH SQUAD but [also] to the hidden peasant;

---

[9] The Secret Anti-communist Army.

to the kidnapped DONALDO[10] but to the liberated EGP; to the massacred CHUPINA, but to the avenged ORPA[11]; to the defamed MANUEL DE JESUS COWARD TELLEZ,[12] but to the vindicated PGT;[13] to the amputated COMMAND 6,[14] but to the grafted FAR; tortured by the MOBILE MILITARY POLICE, but cured by the Colegio BELGA; with tongue removed by the KAIBALES, but thanks to the sweethearts of the IGA, . . . Bilingual![15] Struggling in the mountains of IXCAN. Fighting with the indigenous side by side in the whole transversal.[16] Fighting with a machete along the whole Costa Sur. Fighting with kicks in SAN MATEO IXTATAN. Fighting with clubs in NENTON and in USPANTAN. [. . .] Bringing down aeroplanes with stones in POPTUN. Bringing down helicopters with a slingshot in SANTA CRUZ DEL QUICHE. Repelling flamethrowers with our spit in SEBOL. Repelling airborne bombs with trampolines in PANZOS.[17] Sowing thorns along the way. Sowing pavements in Chichicastenango. Sowing traps in the mountains. Sowing barbs and misdirection. Sowing the courage in peasants to immediately annihilate the asinine army and, thus, sowing the orange blossoms of destiny. Shaking up their petit bourgeois customs.

[. . .]

Sitting on a powder keg. Smelling gunpowder on birthdays, smelling gunpowder in marches, smelling gunpowder in the Corpus [Christi]; smelling gunpowder at weddings; smelling gunpowder at baptisms; smelling

---

[10] Donaldo Alvardo Ruiz; see above.

[11] The Guerrilla Army of the Poor (EGP) and the Revolutionary Organisation of the People in Arms (ORPA) were two of the most prominent guerrilla groups at the time.

[12] Then Chief of Judicial Police.

[13] The Guatemalan Communist Party, or Guatemalan Workers' Party.

[14] A counter-insurgency unit of the National Police; Command 6 led the attack on the Spanish Embassy, described below, and seems to have received some training from the US; Command 6 and the Pelotón Modelo were the most dogged pursuers of leftist university students. This is documented at length in Archivo Histórico de la Policía Nacional (2011), *Del silencio a la memoria*, Guatemala: AHPN.

[15] The Colegio Belga was an elite private all-girls' school in operation in Guatemala City since 1933. The Kaibiles were a fearsome special operations force of the Guatemalan military, known for their cruelty. The Instituto Guatemalteco Americano (IGA) was founded in 1945 and expanded in the 1970s as a bilingual English and Spanish school that trained young women to be bilingual secretaries; see Velvet Franco, '70 años al servicio de Guatemala'.

[16] The Franja Transversal del Norte; see Chapter 3 of this volume.

[17] This is a fairly comprehensive list of places where the government sought to combat the strongholds of the guerrilla with a system of combined military action and natural resource extraction, and development.

gunpowder on holidays; smelling gunpowder in embassies; smelling gunpowder even in the powder compacts and in dust; and having sex with the smell of gunpowder.[18] Wasting gunpowder on magpies, wasting a [salary] rise with friends; wasting tyres on the Periférico.[19] Wearing out tired jokes. Wasting money with RUTH CHICAS[20] in Jutiapa, giving tractors as gifts. Wasting saliva in the rallies. Wasting shoe soles at marches. Wasting sperm in the sperm banks of the Gringo Super-Babies. Wasting the last lumps of *panela* to supplement the hidden sugar.[21] Wasting the last tears at lunchtime to salt cod. Wasting the last cartridges before dressing ourselves as *cucuruchos*[22] [for the Huelga], which this year will be sparse because ... 'Mutts don't eat mutts, and when they do they don't eat much.' With cookouts in January, with carnival in February (but carnival of punches). In March, with the permission of Engineer URRUTIA, a wave of cool air. Remembering don MINGO BETANCOURT,[23] who also stretched the quill well ... Before they took away the RAILWAY TO THE HIGHLANDS.[24] Yearning for sovereignty. Defending autonomy. Celebrating strikes day and night. To mix things up, being a pain and talking too much and always remember-

---

[18] This long section draws together the social occasions on which fireworks are usually detonated – birthdays, Corpus Christi, weddings – with occasions of revolutionary violence, like the recent Spanish Embassy fire. The sex joke, built around a slang phrase for having sex, '*echar un polvo*', makes sense in Spanish because *polvo* means powder or gunpowder.

[19] Also called the Anillo Periférico, this is the traffic-congested ring road around the western side of Guatemala City.

[20] Ruth Chicas Rendón de Sosa was a key figure on the advisory council of the anti-communist National Liberation Movement (MLN) party and the wife of MLN politician, General Luis Ernesto Sosa Avila, who ran for president in 1990.

[21] *Panela* is dark, unprocessed sugar that is used widely in Guatemala while more refined sugar is reserved for export.

[22] *Cucuruchos* are people who wear long purple robes with elaborate pointed and hooded headpieces to denote their penitence for sin during Holy Week. Sometimes these penitents are barefoot and wear chains on their legs.

[23] Most likely referring to Claudio Urrutia, an engineer who surveyed the border with Mexico in the 1880s, and Domingo Bethancourt, famous composer and marimba player from the highlands city of Quetzaltenango. Marimba is Guatemala's national instrument and Bethancourt is a source of pride.

[24] Most of Guatemala's railroads were built in the 1880s and 1890s with loans from British banks; after the Guatemalan economy plummeted, then-president Estrada Cabrera contracted construction with US companies and, in 1904, the International Railways of Central America (owned by UFCO) bought out the railways and effectively owned all of the rail lines in Guatemala and El Salvador by the 1920s. But the Railway to the Highlands (Ferrocarril de los Altos) remained outside of IRCA control and was built between 1930 and 1933; it was destroyed by a hurricane and never rebuilt.

ing to get yours and not mine . . . COMMITTEE OF THE HUELGA DE DOLORES OF 1980.

ALWAYS:

Salted and sugared, foul-mouthed, tasteless. With low blood pressure and high pressure, from the POLICE. Bloodless, hopeless, fired, stuck, plundered; with minimum wage raised 186 per cent and the living costs up 500 per cent. With the discounted menu. Cut back; almost always unemployed; well-mannered – but in the sense of manning the skirts – .[25] Hot, but on a cool wave, with deep feeling. Listening to RADIO HAVANA on short wave, the TGW[26] on long wave and the girlfriend on medium wave. [. . .] Believing themselves to be revolutionary, because when it runs the ANTI-RIOT POLICE is at 5,000 revolutions per second. Believing themselves well armed, because they ate 'Revolver' in San Felipe. Believing themselves well served by the MUNICIPALITY because it is going to give them water. Believing themselves always prepared – like a Boy Scout – because they wear trousers sold at the 'TURKISH' CASTAÑEDA[27] in Antigua that fall apart on the first washing. Believing in SEMPER FIDELIS because of believing in FIDELIS CASTRUS. Believing themselves to be *COBANERO* because they like to mess with the referees.[28] Believing themselves to be *universitarios* because of having a three-century-long hunger and living in '*La Carolingia*'.[29] Believing themselves a MAGNIFICENT [USAC] RECTOR because of going around in a bundle of rags covered in shit. Believing themselves chosen by the gods because they are alive by pure miracle. Believing themselves to be *SANDINISTA* because their girlfriend uses 'Sandino' hairpins. [. . .] Believing themselves to be the mayor of the city because they have a dumb face and cannot deal. Believing themselves to be SALVADORAN because they laugh at

---

[25] Word play that refers to paying attention to young women.

[26] Radio Havana is the official government-run radio of communist Cuba; TGW is the official radio station of Guatemala, established around early 1931.

[27] This was the students' nickname for a police officer, according to Carlos Guzmán-Böckler's essay, 'La Huelga de Dolores que viví con mi generación, 1947–1977'.

[28] The professional football team of Cobán came close to winning the national championships in 1979, finishing in third place; this must be a reference to their style of game play.

[29] 'Carolingia' was part of the colonial university's motto (referring to the lover of education, Charlemagne) and has been a sort of ultra-formal nickname for the university since. There is also a neighbourhood called 'La Carolingia'. The reference to the hunger of three hundred years points to how long the university had been seeking knowledge.

any dumb shit. Believing themselves to be HONDURAN because they never do anything and continue to get paid. Believing themselves to be COSTA RICAN because they travel on Tica Bus.[30] Believing themselves PANAMANIAN because they defend with total patriotic pride the zone of the canal ... the anal canal. Believing themselves GRINGO because, anyway, they will not win at the Olympics. Believing themselves RUSSIAN, because they drink VODKA BALALAIKA. Believing themselves JOSIP BROZ TITO, for the long agony in which they live. Believing themselves BULGARIAN because of their vulgarity. Believing themselves ARABS because from rubber they sweat oil. Believing themselves to be JEWISH because they did not miss a moment of 'Holocaust'. Believing themselves believers and very gullible because they are always discredited, dispossessed, decried, unkempt, grubby, unenthusiastic, slow, but always *GUANFIRO*,[31] PEOPLE OF GUATEMALA.

LET IT BE KNOWN:

FIRST: In accordance with technical reports received directly from NASA, via the ESA and courtesy of ESSO,[32] if the dynamite prepared with such love for CHUPINA had exploded in the precise moment in which he was passing, this asshole would still be in orbit, lost in space, making laps around the star near to Centaur, which, according to precise calculations by the Cybernetic department of these Honourables, will be found five light years from earth – including an adjustment for purchased energy – very near to Ursa Major and Ursa Minor, the constellation of Orion, and just a 'leap' away from DORIO, near the mass of velocity of light squared. Holy shit, we know our astronomy!

SECOND: That this Honourable committee, in view of the fact that the government of the president'ass LUCAS does not want to pay even a miserable cent for the rescue of our Ambassador to Colombia, AQUILES ZURRO RALO, we have decided to take the following emergency measures to guarantee a 'Tender, Juicy, and Crunchy' death for the so-called '*Churrasco*' in Brine'[33]:

---

[30] Costa Ricans are affectionately called 'Ticas' and Tica Bus was a popular bus company with routes throughout Central America.

[31] The meaning of this term remains a mystery.

[32] NASA is, of course, the National Aeronautical and Space Association of the US, the ESA is the Guatemalan Secret Anti-communist Army, and ESSO is a US-owned petrol company.

[33] This whole section is a particularly grim reference to the deadly fire at the Spanish Embassy on 31 January 1980, which resulted in the deaths of thirty-seven people, most

1st. Beg the Colombian consulate not to give a visa to CHUPINA 'TAMBASTO' LANDAETA, to avoid his sneaking into the country during the occupation of the Dominican embassy, also notifying them that in Colombia, during Lent it is forbidden to grill and eat meat.

2nd. Ask Dr MARIO AGUIRRE GODOY and ex-ambassador MAXIMO CAJAL Y LOPEZ to make a short report and remit it, via [Uncle] SAM, to our ambassador in Colombia, so that he knows how to get out of the fucked-up embassy before it is set on fire.[34]

3rd. Order the souls of ADOLFO MOLINA ORANTES and El Chenco CACERES LENHOFF to abstain from making any recommendations, because any opinions that they have given are fully proved to be not worth a shit.[35]

4th. In response to our pleas, Mr MAXIMO CAJAL Y LOPEZ has taken on responsibility for bringing matches to the Dominican Embassy in Colombia, because we know that they have cigars but lack ... FUEGO.[36]

5th. We order the recently released (from where!) General Director of Fine Arts, JULIA VELA,[37] to remit to our ambassador in Colombia, a dozen candles of the famous brand 'the Great Power of God' and a seven-stringed lyre to accompany his last rites in the style of Nero when his shit has caught fire.

6th. Just in case, this Honourable Committee reserves the right to be the first to express to the distinguished family of Chiquimultenango and the

---

of whom were rural *campesinos* from Quiché who were protesting against recent military repression in their communities. The protestors and some allies from USAC student groups entered the embassy early in the morning and declared that they would not leave until the government promised to investigate their complaints. Several police and military units surrounded the embassy and, despite the ambassador's insistence that the situation could be de-escalated, raided the building. For reasons that have remained unclear to this day, the building caught fire and burned aggressively for a surprisingly long time before firefighters intervened. President Lucas purportedly ordered the raid, shouting 'Get them out by any means!' by telephone.

[34] Mario Aguirre Godoy was an expert on civil procedural law who was killed in the embassy fire.

[35] Both men were notable jurists who were, like Aguirre Godoy, killed in the embassy fire.

[36] On 27 February 1980, the M19, Colombian guerrilla forces, occupied the Dominican embassy. '*Fuego*', the Spanish word for fire, referred not only to the Spanish embassy fire, but also cleverly to FUEGO, the student group whose members also participated in the occupation.

[37] Daughter of famous journalist David Vela, Julia Vela was a student of architecture at USAC and a renowned dancer and choreographer. Other than the play on her name, '*vela*' (a word for candle or wing), it is unclear why she should send the candles.

rest of the ARANA-ITES sons of the greatest bitch! . . . our most exhilarated condolences.[38]

THIRD: Hereafter, this Honourable Committee communicates to the people of Guatemala, live and in colour, a small excerpt from the section 'Did you know?' contained in the *Encyclopaedia Britannica*, translated and adapted into Spanish from German by KARL HEINZ CHAVEZ and the Sephardic missionary JULIO CATU (the purest bullshit you are)[39] that says the following:

DID YOU KNOW? . . . that now we are close to finding a solution to the conflict between EL SALVADOR and HONDURAS, originating in the so-called 'Soccer War', but after the thrashing of 8 to 0 on Wednesday by FAS of Santa Ana against MARATHON of Honduras, the pounding began again, forcing a member of the Salvadoran government to resign?[40]

DID YOU KNOW? . . . that LUIS GALICH could not win the OTI SONG FESTIVAL because at the last minute he forgot to bring the other half of his orange?[41]

DID YOU KNOW? . . . that the index of illiteracy rose considerably in the country when the National Police began a literacy campaign?

DID YOU KNOW? . . . that the person who ran fastest when they set the Spanish embassy on fire was 'POLITO' CASTELLANOS CARRILLO but not exactly to save the victims but with the hope of ending up with a replacement leg?[42]

DID YOU KNOW? . . . that the president'ass LUCAS does not want to exploit Guatemalan oil because he says that it comes out crude and we would need a lot of firewood to process it?

DID YOU KNOW . . . that one of the Spaniards who will soon

---

[38] The presidency of Carlos Manuel Arana Osorio (1970–4) was marked by the escalation in disappearances and torture by paramilitary death squads and renewed counter-insurgency efforts supported by the US; Cáceres Lehnhoff was his Vice-president.

[39] Karl Heinz Chávez was a famous Guatemalan–German journalist born in Quetzaltenango who created radio, print, and televised media and live events. I was unable to find information about Julio Catu, but Francisco Mauricio Martínez's article in *Revista D* provides excellent information about Heinz Chávez.

[40] FAS and Marathón are, in fact, football teams in El Salvador and Honduras.

[41] Luis Galich, son of Manuel Galich, was a singer–songwriter whose best-known song was entitled, 'La mitad de mi naranja', a play on the Spanish colloquialism '*mi media naranja*' or 'my better half'.

[42] Leopoldo Castellanos Carrillo was a journalist and signatory to the infamous 'Document of the 311', which demanded that Ubico end the state of exception and reinstate the Constitution in 1954.

have to leave the country is the 'political scientist', graduate of the Marroquín [University] [ALFONSO] YURRITA CUESTA?

DID YOU KNOW ... that LEONEL SISNIEGO OTERO, one day when he was doing dissections in the amphitheatre of the ESA, cut himself with a scalpel and upon seeing his blood exclaimed in terror, 'Holy shit! Even I am a communist!'?[43]

DID YOU KNOW ... that the city bus company THE CONDOR is not working any more because the directors were actually 'Barefoot Eagles'?

DID YOU KNOW ... that among the *gringo* hostages in IRAN is Mr MAX TOTT?[44]

DID YOU KNOW ... that in Escuintla and Santa Lucia Cotzumalguapa, a dustup with a girl of medium height costs five quetzales and that the peasants only got a minimum wage increase of 3.20 quetzales, so they are asking for a decrease in minimum salary, just for the whores?

DID YOU KNOW ... that NAJERA SARAVIA wrote his column in *Prensa Libre* 'From the Mountain' because if he came down [the people] would beat him?[45]

DID YOU KNOW ... that on their trip to the moon, *gringo* astronauts not only brought 'Bayer' pills but also ... Mr Yemo's *papelitos*?[46] [...]

DID YOU KNOW ... that the most flourishing businesses in Guatemala currently are funeral parlours because – those little shits give away everything, even almanacs!?

DID YOU KNOW ... that the daughter of CARLOS 'COSTELLO'

---

[43] Leonel Sisniega Otero was a CEUA student leader at USAC in the 1950s and became a nation-level anti-communist politician as a result of his collaboration with the CIA. This line is especially funny because bloodthirsty anti-communist Sisniega Otero bleeds red and, stupidly, believes he must therefore be a communist. Little was funnier to San Carlistas in the late twentieth century than making fun of the idiocy and paranoia of anti-communists.

[44] Max Tott was the founder of Guatemala's most famous road race; since 1938, Guatemalans have competed in this race that winds through Guatemala City. Given this, it seems as if the joke here is on 'Iran', as in 'I ran'.

[45] A colloquial expression, '*dar chicharrón*', is used in the original. Antonio Najera Saravia wrote a short column entitled 'Desde la montaña' for the *Prensa Libre* on Mondays, Wednesdays, and Fridays, according to a feature in the *Toledo Blade* on 15 June 1973.

[46] 'Los papelitos de Don Yemo' are an old-fashioned remedy for diarrhoea and, thus, an object of endless amusement.

TOLEDO VIELMAN got married in Oklahoma to a *gringo*, but she had to do it because the consulate would not give her a visa?[47]

DID YOU KNOW . . . that PANCHO VILLAGRAN KRAMER is so off the chains, so off the chains that in spite of having been invited to visit the Ivory Coast he bought tickets and went instead to the Costa Brava?!

DID YOU KNOW . . . that ALVARITO 'TRAVEL-TOURS' ARZU[48] was named honorary member of AMNESTY INTERNATIONAL after reliably testifying that in Guatemala the human rights of all the living are respected . . . from the lizards on down?

DID YOU KNOW . . . that in Guatemala TOURISM consists only of a group of flea-filled *gringos* who do not shower and [who] travel on the chicken bus to find 'Vietnam Rose',[49] and that they sleep in the hostels on 4th street – and even haggle there – and that they shave their dicks and contaminate the environment on the streets of Antigua, Panajachel, Tikal and Chichicastenango, to such a degree that in Panajachel now you cannot find a sign in Spanish, and when a Guatemalan arrives they look at him as if he were a Martian, and he has to find a sign where it says 'Spanish Spoken' and even the downtrodden Indians ask 'Where are you from?'[50] (NOTE THE LINGUISTIC SKILLS OF THE HONOURABLES): and whoever does not understand English should consult the polyglot [President] LUCAS who barely mastered Kekchi, the gum 'BUBLE YUM' [*sic*] and a little bit of Spanish. And,

DID YOU KNOW . . . that in a local microbus with capacity for 15 people, 180 people can really fit, without counting the *gritón*, the spare tyre, the ticket collector, and the wife of the driver.[51]

FOURTH: This Honourable Committee, in order to combat crime, orders all of the functionaries of the [president's] cabinet and the representatives – the supposed fathers of the nation – to begin athletic

---

[47] Carlos Toledo Vielman was President Lucas García's secretary of public relations.

[48] Álvaro Arzú would become mayor of Guatemala City four times and president once, but before that, at just twenty-two years of age, he owned a travel company called 'La Castellana'.

[49] Vietnam War-era slang for sexually transmitted infections, named for the appearance of characteristic genital sores.

[50] In English in the original.

[51] The *gritón* is a person who shouts out the route and sometimes intermediate stops as buses pass crowds at bus stops. This is funny because it describes the normal 'staff' and occupancy of a so-called 'chicken bus', a full-size repurposed and repainted US school bus, used for cheap national and regional travel, not a microbus, which usually only serves local routes.

training as soon as possible and with great intensity, because as the sage Greek of Sapotitlán MIGUEL ANGEL ORDOÑEZ L., says 'ONE MORE SPORTSMAN . . . ONE LESS CRIMINAL!'[52]

FIFTH: given the announcement of President'ass LUCAS regarding the fact that the Spanish government demands payment of damages done by CHUPINA to the Spanish Embassy,[53] Guatemala will countermand Spain to pay for the 'RESCUE' of this Honourable Committee and recommend also to our loquacious President that, complementarily, he should also take the following measures:

1st. Prohibit the running of the bulls, because we already have enough of this with the *PELOTON MODELO.*[54]

2nd. Prohibit cockfighting . . . and only permit the fight between 'GALLO IN A CAN' versus 'GALLO IN A BOTTLE'.[55]

3rd. Marshal a BATTALION OF POLICEWOMEN and enlist the Spaniard Mrs CARMEN 'SCRIBE' DE LEON to exhibit herself in the reception salon of the National Palace as a NUDE REPTILE and her husband, RENE DE LEON SHEROTER [*sic*] as the HORNED REPTILE.[56]

4th. Tell PRUDEN CASTELLANOS to get rid of the 'ACCENT' and put a 'POINT' on it (and eat . . . shit).[57]

5th. Prohibit the consumption of all kinds of Spanish wine and only permit FAROLAZO because 10 metres later you feel the 'lasso' and also CHIRICUTA adds the final touch to the son of a bitch.[58]

6th. Demand that Mrs Alida ESPAÑA because of her Caribbean colour, change her name to MORATAYA . . . also because she is black up to the parting in her hair.

---

[52] Miguel Ángel Ordóñez L. was a popular radio sportscaster and this was his best-known tag line; Sapotitlán was the nineteenth-century name of parts of present-day Suchitepéquez.

[53] The Spanish government did demand reimbursement for damages and denounced the Lucas García government; relations between the nations remained strained for the remainder of his presidency.

[54] An anti-riot police unit.

[55] Gallo is the most popular beer in Guatemala and it also means cock, so is used colloquially as a term for penis.

[56] René de León Schlotter founded the Christian Democratic Party after the counter-revolution.

[57] Pruden Castellanos was an actor who enjoyed some fame in Central America. There is a joke about punctuation (commas and periods) that is utterly lost in translation.

[58] Farolazo wine and Chiricuta liquor are very cheap.

7th. Demand that Mr CHAIAS REBOLLEDO not sell 'Pa'ella' but rather 'Pa'nosotros'![59]

8th. Do away with the name of the Plaza ESPAÑA and give it another pompous one like 'PLAZA DE ORINOCO' so that all the *mariachis* come back to urinate in the square and defecate on autochthonous music for the happiness of the neighbourhood and of Mr LENCHO MONTUFAR, the 'Huge Balls of Reforma Avenue' who only sits and . . . does crossword puzzles.[60]

9th. Regarding Lenchos, demand that Mr LENCHO AUSINA TUR, who not even insults to the mother country could tear down, should at least change his last name to that of 'DELGADILLO' and abstain from walking around with RIGOBERTO BRAN AZMITIA [*sic*], because they seem to like the number '10'.[61]

10th. Change the name of the park 'ISABEL, THE CATHOLIC' which should simply be named 'CHABELA' in honour of the emblem of university students.[62]

SIXTH: For his part, the very cultured and, surely a candidate for the Nobel Prize of Literature, CLEMENTINO 'TREMENTINO' CASTILLO Y CORONADO, brand-new Minister of Education – elected by vote – ordered the following reprisals against the threat of the Spanish demands:

a) Charge the Spanish government for the death of the Head of the Transportation Department, Erick Ponce [. . .] because they could prove that he committed suicide with an 'Ebro'-brand pistol [. . .] listening to the Quetzal trio singing the song 'SPANISH EYES'.[63]

---

[59] I have not been able to locate information about the person referenced here, but the joke is in the last clause of the sentence: the authors play on the Spanish dish *paella*, which in Spanish could be a contraction of '*para ella*', or 'for her'; they call instead for this man to sell 'for all of us', or '*para nosotros*'.

[60] Lorenzo Montúfar y Rivera was a Guatemalan jurist, law professor, and Liberal politician. There is a monument to him on Reforma Avenue; as the students point out, it is an unusual statue, as Montúfar sits somewhat inexplicably hunched and stares at the ground.

[61] Lorenzo Ausina Tur was a Spaniard who managed Guatemala's national football team. Bran Azmitia was a journalist for *La Hora*, a historian, and a library director.

[62] Refers to replacing a plaque in honour of Isabella (the Catholic Queen) with one for the Chabela, the dancing skeleton mascot of the Huelga de Dolores.

[63] 'Ojos españoles' is a classic popular song.

b) Change the name of the 'CAVE OF CAPTAINS' to the 'CAVE OF COLONELS'.[64]

c) Change the name of the 'TAVERN OF DON PEDRO' to the 'TAVERN OF WALTER PETER'.

d) Change the name of the 'CAMINO REAL' to the 'TROPICAL PAVEMENT'.[65]

e) Urgently call a new National Constituent Assembly to reform the Constitution of the Republic and establish as an official language instead of SPANISH . . . Castilian.

f) Send that old guy who is behind the 'clock of flowers' to decapitate Mr BERNAL DIAZ DEL CASTILLO. BY the MLN . . .[66]

SEVENTH: Violence is not Christian! Shamelessly stealing the labour of workers and peasants is not either! Making money by the pain of others is violence! Abusing public power is violence! Haggling workers down to minimum hunger wages is violence! Disappearing, torturing, massacring, annihilating political adversaries is violence! Permitting malnutrition among children is violence!

Guatemalans, reflect! Do not let them stuff capitalist ideas into your kids so that a few can live in opulence to the detriment of the majority who live in misery. Do you want them to keep killing your bravest men and women like Fito Mijangos, 'Cuca' López Larrave, Mama Maquín, Rogelio Cruz, Oliverio Castañeda de León, Alberto Fuentes Mohr, Alejandro Cotí, and our brave brothers in Panzós, Nebaj, Rabinal, Rio Negro, among others?

Reflect and make your decision, because there is only one road! (Taken from the Episcopal Christian Conference).

[. . .]

Guatemala, of the Ransoms – in cash – Friday, 8 March 1980
THE BOYS OF THE *HONOURABLE*

---

[64] The Cave of the Captains (*La cueva de los capitanes*) was a fashionable bar, according to one popular webpage, *Hablaguate*.

[65] The Camino Real, or Royal Road, in Spanish colonial cities was the main street on which the palace and best shops were located. 'Tropical pavement' was more attuned to the reality of the present.

[66] The watch made of flowers was commissioned in 1965 by Mayor Francisco Montenegro Sierra (1963–5) near the airport. It is unclear why he should be sent by the MLN to decapitate the conquistador Bernal Díaz del Castillo.

(Courtesy of the *Empresa Eléctrica* of Guatemala, S.A. who in order to pay for this *Bulletin* will once again and for the umpteenth time adjust account balances.)

Translated by Rachel Nolan

Saúl Osorio Paz, 'Open Letter to the University High Council'

(1980)

Saúl Osorio Paz, an economist, won election to university Rector on a plat-form of social justice, university autonomy, and popular sovereignty. He vowed to increase the percentage of the national budget allocated for USAC in order to expand the role of the university in society, especially in marginal rural and urban communities. He proposed nothing less than to remake the university's relationship to students, to the *pueblo*, and to the state. Precisely for this reason, he was the sworn enemy of the Lucas García government. As Rector, Osorio Paz delivered pointed diatribes against the government and its functionaries in the all-too-frequent eulogies that he gave for martyred stu-dents and faculty colleagues. He was controversial within the university, too. In fact, many faculty and administrators resigned after his election, though he enjoyed the on-going support of FRENTE and other student organisations. In March 1980, he was forced to flee to Mexico. He resigned in July after it became clear that it would be unsafe for him to return. In this September letter, the former Rector clarifies his reasons for leaving and his hopes for the university. It was printed in a tri-fold pamphlet with a photograph of Osorio Paz on the front cover, and on the back a quote from the letter: 'Individual life is short, but the historic future will always belong to the people!'

Mexico, D.F. 10 September 1980

Honourable University High Council
Of the UNIVERSITY OF SAN CARLOS (USAC)
Guatemala, Guatemala, C.A.

University community:
Workers, students,
Professors, all *universitarios*:

Owing to the conditions that in recent months have obliged me to live outside national territory, I must communicate with you through this medium, although I would prefer to do so as I usually do, in person.

In our country, as in others in Latin America, in light of the exasperating failure of the model of development propitiated and supported by transnationals, which has entailed the erosion of salaries and inflation, unemployment and marginalisation, and amassing of income and riches, the internal reactionary sectors have opted for the silencing of growing popular discontent through the fascist repression: Vain attempt to head off history!

In a regime characterised by incivility, fraud, dispossession of the worker, and crime, [and] stripped of all legitimacy, a democratic election, like the one that brought me to head the national university, was jarring; even more so when you consider how the unambiguous triumph of the various [ideological] currents who have supported me were a reflection within the university of the ascendance of the *pueblo*'s struggles for its freedoms, rights, and basic interests. This explains, in part, the official harassment that has required us to work in very unfavourable conditions, to carry out programmatic tasks – in great measure already achieved – with the greatest of effort and defying death every day. In this way, danger grew to the extreme, [and] I had to leave the country persecuted by external terror associated with a little group of coup-plotters, which is encouraged by the government to 'pauperise' our house of studies in order to submit it to the system or at least influence it so that it is focused on technical scientific tasks and not moved by national problems.

Since the aforementioned coup, rumours have spread that some 'sacrificed themselves' to maintain the university while I made myself comfortable abroad. Several events, 'purges', and facts of the past and the present evince the opposite, and throw light on the intentions of this subtle provocation, echoed by a minister of the regime invoking the legality of the university (!). This is about destroying me physically if present [in the country] and morally if absent: a conundrum that attempts to impede the serenity and duties of the university, such that immolation or individual heroism of another kind would only free me personally, when here the dignity, autonomy, and development of the culture, which represent collective, organised, or institutional endeavours, are at stake.

But I wish to categorically declare that, as I have shown, I am committed *at any moment* to carry out *intramurally* the office to which I was democratically elected. For me, this is an unrenounceable term. Now, it would be illogical to naïvely expose one's head to the assassin's sight. This would lead to even more destabilisation of the university: it would be a scenario for the 'legal' empowerment of the reactionary forces or an internal coup, aims only desired by fascists and their allies, the enemies of humanity.

From this perspective, my stay abroad is understandable to anyone who is not an open or undercover accomplice of the regime. Justice, official aversion to the democratic roots of my election, the negation of or haggling over the civil and cultural value of the university autonomy, [and] monstrous disrespect for life and other human rights.

In pain, exacerbated by my exile, I have suffered the continuous assassinations of heroic *universitarios* who are very beloved by the community; their 'crime' was to love the *pueblo*, to fight for them to overcome misery, backwardness, and dependence, and the slavery in which large interests and their undignified conscripts wished to hold them. But at the same time, I am comforted and filled with optimism to affirm that the great majority of university workers and thinkers continue in the struggle, defying institutionalised barbarism with ideas. Individual life is short, but the historical future will always belong to the people! For this reason, the struggle for true democracy is just; we Guatemalans will not allow ourselves to be confused by propaganda that claims to defend democracy but really damages or asphyxiates it, nor by the accommodating 'apolitical' academic postures that explain away and sidestep fascist aggression, the maximum exploitation of the worker, and vilification of knowledge.

To dispel misunderstanding or ill-speaking, I should clarify the following. It is true that I called the government to dialogue seriously about social and national problems. I take full responsibility for this action, situated in its historical context. I took this opportunity, without delay, prioritising in every case the autonomy and principles of the university, cautioning that this was about honestly confronting the basic problems of the *pueblo* and likewise making clear the causes of violence. Today's travesty must be addressed. I affirm that it is unacceptable to start a dialogue behind the back of the *pueblo* or the university community, because doing this fuels insinuations or offensive or corrupt actions, covering up repression; the one who dialogues becomes an intermediary between the government and the victims, an element of a university administration that is 'acceptable' to the regime, favouring an internal strike against autonomy, which has cost so much Guatemalan blood to achieve.

With a few exceptions, *universitarios* know how to safeguard principles. Throughout the history of USAC's autonomy, they have battled for academic freedom: for plans and conscientious scientific methods and investigation that never dodges national and social problems; we *universitarios*, even under adverse conditions, should maintain our right to study and evaluate, proposing adequate solutions. It is our ethical imperative to develop the cultural reserves of the country, to ensure freedoms like life, well-being, and the dignity of the people. University humanism is patriotic, and demands the rejection of despotism, the refusal to submit ourselves to foreign interests, and above all: the effective overcoming of the misery in which a people who have been plundered for centuries live and work, when they are not discriminated against for their social condition or their ethnic identification. USAC, which since 1944 exceeds the bounds of a mere juridical institution, is the promising fruit of the Guatemalan people's struggle for freedom, and it has an irreversible social–humanist desire that, notwithstanding the complex and difficult present, we all know how to maintain and exalt!

'GO AND TEACH ALL'
Saúl Osorio Paz

'Individual life is short, but the historical future will always belong to the people!'

Translated by Rachel Nolan

EL SALVADOR

'Salvadoran Students Facing Imperialist Intervention in El Salvador'

(1981)

The anonymously authored newspaper article below lists North American and Israeli weapons and equipment donations, special training, and direct intervention as the source of the Salvadoran *pueblo*'s suffering. By this time, *Opinión Estudiantil* often featured quotations and symbols that celebrated the popular struggle. No longer focused on cultural or economic imperialism, Salvadoran students' anti-colonial writings detailed the actions of US statesmen and military, and openly denounced the government and military for so readily accepting and even courting US aid. A quotation from FMLN leader Salvador Cayetano Carpio (alias Comandante Marcial) was printed just beneath the article. It read, 'After 50 years of suffering under military tyranny, how could the *pueblo* not have the right to use all means at its disposal to fight to gain its freedom?' Together, the quotation and the article position the AGEUS and FMLN as combatants in a struggle for popular sovereignty and natural rights.

Day by day, the North American intervention in El Salvador deepens and hastens, demonstrating that:

a) The decadent North American imperialism and the warmongers led by Reagan who seek to annihilate the struggle of our people at all costs supply their puppets in the Christian Democrat Military Junta with unlimited 'aid': they have sent a large number of patrol ships, advised by Yankee marines; they have sent advisors for the bombardment of our people, advisors for the Air Force. They have sent the so-called 'Green Berets' that are Special Forces infamous around the world. The king-pins of the White House, the Pentagon, and the State Department have sent armed Huey helicopters, modern bombers of North American and Israeli manufacture, napalm, white phosphorus, and two-hundred- and five-hundred-pound bombs, and all classes of modern and sophisticated weapons of mass destruction.

b) The North American officials do not only train Salvadoran puppet officials, not only prepare and train forces specialised in combat and the extermination of the population, but they have [also] turned to more direct and head-on action: in the theatre of war, they direct opera-tives who seek the annihilation of revolutionary combatants, supervise massacres and the destruction of populations, command combat opera-tion units, [and] pilot planes and helicopters that bomb and drop shrap-nel on the population.

The genocidal junior officers of the army of the Military Junta confirm the imperialist and mercenary presence. In early June, a com-muniqué written by the FMLN reported the capture during combat, recorded in Las Vueltas (Chalatenango department), of four National Guardsmen, among them the criminal José Lázaro Guevara, who shared details about the participation of North American advisors in counter-insurgency actions. National Guardsman Guevara confirmed 'the advi-sors and many mercenaries are off-loaded through special flights at the military airport at Ilopango, clandestinely controlled by US military functionaries in El Salvador,' as well as the participation of 'advisors in the manœuvres of helicopters and planes during combat.

In El Salvador at present our *pueblo* faces an imperialistic escalation of direct intervention that every day makes more apparent the possibility of a North American invasion.

Under its plans for intervention in El Salvador, North American impe-rialism pressures the government of Guatemala to intervene directly and massively with its army against our *pueblo*, but they will not succeed in this, because the people of Guatemala and their democratic, progressive, popular, and politico-military revolutionary organisations powerfully fight the dictatorship of Romeo Lucas García, thus managing to tie the bloodied hands of the Lucas regime.

More, imperialism pressures the army of Honduras to launch a brazen invasion of Salvadoran territory.

The warmongering imperialists seek to justify their direct and massive invasion of our land by accusing Nicaragua and Cuba of intervening in El Salvador.

Also, the warmongering hysteria of the wild beasts of the Pentagon, the White House, the State Department, and the CIA has led them to concoct the disgraceful 'White Book' that they use to justify increased intervention, crime, and genocide against our *pueblo*.

But the *pueblos* of Central America and the world know that the accusations against Nicaragua and Cuba are absolute fallacies; these are *pueblos* whose fundamental task is the development and construction of a new society and a peaceful and happy future. They are nations that do not have economic and political ambitions for other *pueblos* as do the imperialists, they are *pueblos* that, conscious of their own historical experiences with the puppet tyrannies of Fulgencio Batista and Anastasio Somoza, [know] that only the people with their own strength, sacrifice, and heroism are the creators of their own history, of their unconditional freedom.

The reasons for our democratic revolutionary process, for our struggle for definitive liberation, are found in the exploitation and oppression that we have suffered for years; they lie in the tyrannical, oligarchic, and imperialistic domination to which our *pueblo* has been submitted; they lie in the fact that our economy is dependent on North American imperialism, which has for years ensured that the sweat, strength, and sacrifice of the workers, *campesinos*, small and medium businessmen are used for their insatiable imperialistic interests.

Being that these are the reasons for our struggle, it is our *pueblo* that, with its heroism and pugnacity, will overthrow North American imperialism, [and] achieve its final victory and a new dawn: unconditional freedom, [in] the realisation of a Democratic Revolutionary government.

Our *pueblo* is ever more invincible; its organisational, combat, military capacity and its consciousness grow irrepressibly. This is the result of more than eleven years of struggle. Today our *pueblo*, after the 10 January offensive,[67] has regular units, special commando forces, popular militias, and self-defence committees throughout the whole Republic.

---

[67] The date on which the guerrilla launched their so-called 'final offensive' was 10 January.

The masses are fighting tenaciously against imperialist intervention and the genocidal Christian Democratic Military Junta.

The more the imperialists illegally intervene, the more they launch thousands of phosphorus bombs, napalm, the more they massacre, they will never defeat the struggle for the liberation of our people, because they are not fighting against small, medium, large-sized groups of isolated guerrillas, but rather against the will and determination of an entire *pueblo*.

And now our *pueblo* is defeating the imperialist aggressors. One concrete example is the extermination of three North American mercenaries by FMLN forces in the department of Chalatenango in the month of June:

The first mercenary fell on 8 June at 11am when a contingent of the genocidal regiment formed by the National Guard and paramilitary groups attempted to enter the road to Zazalapa, [in the] Arcatao jurisdiction 112 kilometres north of San Salvador.

Another mercenary was killed in the town of Arcatao on 10 June when Huey helicopters tried to land reinforcements and supplies for the troops of the Christian Democratic military. Opening fire, they managed to lower one squadron and the FMLN combatants responded. In addition to the mercenary, four other genocidal agents were killed. Meanwhile another FMLN military unit killed three guards that protected the airfield.

The third mercenary fell on 19 June in Las Vueltas.

Our *pueblo* has endured fifty years of military tyranny, fifty years of exploitation, misery, and oppression; fifty years of repression, jail, torture, and death. For this reason we Salvadorans fight with gun in hand.

Today our hard-working, honest, humble, and simple *pueblo* fights because it wants to live in peace, because it wants to enjoy freedom and progress. Our *pueblo* fights to achieve self-determination, the right to be sovereign and to decide its own destiny independent of the ambitions and impudence of North American imperialism that is accustomed to seeing people in terms of their income, as an appendage to their economy, the economy of the North American multinationals.

Because the fight of our *pueblo* is just, it enjoys the wide and broad support of the people of the United States, of the people of Latin America, Europe, and other regions of the world.

Repulsion for the North American warmongering and interventionist politics has reached such a degree that the people of the United States have turned against the imperialist warmongers.

The *pueblo* and the students of El Salvador appreciate this gesture of solidarity and fraternity that the people of the United States and other people of the world are making in support of our struggle and to stop imperialistic intervention in El Salvador and Central America, intervention that could generate a world war.

It is therefore necessary to stop the interventionist actions of North American imperialism in El Salvador and Central America. And in order to achieve this, there are two fundamental considerations in which the people play an important role. These considerations are:

'First, it is the free will of the Salvadoran people to achieve their freedom at any cost.'

'Second, it is the worldwide public opinion, the massive militant desire of all of the people of the world, to help our *pueblo* achieve its liberation.'

Thus, we the students of El Salvador make a fraternal plea to all of the people of the world: to the people of the United States, to the Canadian, to the Mexican, to the Latin American, to the European, and to all people in general to maintain this generous and active solidarity with our heroic *pueblo*, that with its determined struggle and ample and global support will achieve its final victory and will overthrow the imperialistic aggressors.

In the spirit of brotherhood, we ask and we call on all people and the students of the world to organise the following activities:
- Massive mobilisations in front of embassies and consulates of the United States and El Salvador, repudiating the imperialist intervention and genocide in El Salvador
- Politico-cultural events
- Meetings
- Mass rallies
- Statements of solidarity
- Round tables
- Conferences
- Events by democratic, progressive, humanitarian, and Christian individuals, organisations, institutions, or groups to denounce and condemn

All of these actions are aimed at stemming imperialistic intervention in El Salvador and stopping genocide [and] at slowing and defeating the warmongering policies of Reagan, the Pentagon, the White House, the CIA, and the State Department that threaten to ignite Central America at the cost of the sacrifice and blood of the *pueblos* of the region.

Translated by Heather Vrana

AGEUS, 'Agustín Farabundo Martí, Example of Anti-imperialist Struggle and of the Popular War for Liberation'

(1982)

Alongside current events, *Opinión Estudiantil* published historical analyses and tributes to revolutionary leaders. The text below is a brief history of Agustín Farabundo Martí that highlights Martí's relationship to the university and the AGEUS. Recast as a *universitario*, Martí is meant to inspire young students to join the FMLN and to fight in the war for the liberation of the Salvadoran people. The figure of a curious middle-class youth reaching out to workers or farmers, recurrent in leftist writings of the period throughout Central America, is in this case Martí. The implication is that the guerrillas' struggle in 1982 is analogous to Martí's in 1932 and that there is little difference between Martí – a law student until called upon to lead – and the average UES student.

On the first of February of 1932, soldiers and police opened fire on the body of Agustín Farabundo Martí who fell, bloodily on to the earth, the outpouring of his blood uniting the thousands of *campesinos* and students who were in those moments being assassinated by the military Dictatorship of Maximiliano Hernández Martínez, for the simple reason that the people were rising up against misery and oppression.

Agustín Farabundo Martí was born in El Salvador in 1893, his first friends were the children of tenant farmers that worked his father's *hacienda*, [and] the crude exploitation and repression through low wages, working days without hourly limits, the enormous unemployment, the deplorable health conditions in which our people lived, were the frame in which Martí felt, like any human would feel, the desire to fight against its source, the structure of misery and oppression.

In this way he begins to seek out friendship with workers, to fuse with the ideals of the Salvadoran people, every day drawing nearer to the exploited classes until converting himself into an honest and constant leader of the interests of those sectors.

He enrols in the National University to study Law and Social Science, [and] as student leader of AGEUS in this centre of studies, demonstrates his dynamism and revolutionary, rebellious, and defiant perspective, raging against government despotism, and for these reasons he is taken to prison by the repressive forces. In jail, he makes his first displays of solidarity and strength by refusing to be freed alone since he considered himself equally responsible as the rest of the prisoners. This solid position that he held along with his classmate, José Barrientos, causes his violent exile to Guatemala in 1920, the reason he abandons his studies. Being in that country he participates in the Guatemalan Revolutionary Movement and he connects in his own flesh with the workers living in exploitation, working to make ends meet as an agricultural day labourer.

Following his entering the Revolutionary Red Battalion[68] in Mexico, in which he achieved the rank of Sergeant due to his abilities, the internationalist pages of Martí's life culminate with his delivering support to the liberation struggle of the Nicaraguan people, enlisting in the army of General César Augusto Sandino. Through his revolutionary energy and intellectual capacity he is given the rank of Colonel and is added to the general staff and designated Private Secretary to Sandino.

When, on the occasion on which an intense bombardment was carried out by the air forces of North American imperialism, Martí would abandon his desk, and firmly gripping his rifle and from the heart of Las Segovias would exclaim: 'when history cannot be written with the pen, it will be written with the rifle!'

Despite this, his great love for the Salvadoran people would make him return to El Salvador in 1930 with the intent to contribute his accumulated revolutionary experience to the construction of a new homeland by eliminating the roots of social injustice.

Farabundo Martí understood that difficult but glorious times had come, now that social injustice, the world economic crisis that had fallen on the backs of workers, persecution, hunger, and misery, had gathered into an enormous insurrectional potential, which he saw hastened by the massacre of the general strike initiated in Ahuachapán. The electoral fraud that arose to which the tyrant Hernández Martínez refused to find a just solution, makes it so the date of insurrection becomes fixed in Martí's mind.

Nevertheless, on 19 January 1932, four days before the insurrection, Martí is captured along with Mario Zapata and Alfonso Luna; and after a false trial is condemned to capital punishment by a war tribunal.

His blood, like those of the thousands of Salvadorans who have fallen to date, enriches the present anti-imperialist struggle and strengthens the roots of the tree of the new society that will be born.

Agustín Farabundo Martí has played a historical role in the advancement of the student movement, planting in it a seed that has grown in the

---

[68] The Revolutionary Red Battalions were anarcho-syndicalist workers' brigades that fought in the Mexican Revolution, but were dissolved after 1916. It is, therefore, unlikely that Martí actually joined them.

subsequent generations that inherit his tradition of struggle, his love for the revolutionary cause, and [following] his example, we must combat the enemy relentlessly and decisively and without fear of losing our lives.

Because of this, now more than ever, the children of Farabundo Martí stand willing to vanquish and erase from the Salvadoran map the injustices and ambitions of US imperialism. The power of the *Farabundista* forces grows meteorically, while we are engaging the decisive battles for the victory of the Democratic Revolutionary Government (DRG) that represents the interests of our people.

Study and Struggle
AGEUS

Translated by Jorge Cuéllar and Heather Vrana

NICARAGUA

Daisy Zamora, 'Commander Two', 'Report of the Demonstration in Front of the US Embassy Protesting the Pino Grande Manœuvres', and 'Song of Hope' from *Clean Slate*

(1993)

Poet Daisy Zamora is one of many Nicaraguans who fought *Somocismo* with pen and arms. Zamora, who joined the FSLN in 1973, was a key figure behind Radio Sandino, which delivered important news and heartening messages to Sandinistas in combat and around the world as the guerrilla closed in on victory. Her commitment to the struggle is evident in the poems below, where single words or sparse phrases belie the complexities of loss. 'Commander Two' celebrates Dora María Téllez, an UNAN medical student-turned-combatant who commanded the occupation of the National Palace in August 1978, a turning point for the Sandinistas who were able to negotiate for millions of dollars and a prisoner release. The next poem, 'Report of the Demonstration in Front of the US Embassy Protesting the Pino Grande Manœuvres', calls forth two important moments in Sandinista history: the final stand of martyr Leonel Rugama and protests at the US Embassy in Managua against the so-called 'Pino Grande manœuvres'. Rugama died in a heroic one-man and hours-long stand-off with the National Guard, purportedly charging out of his barricade, shouting, *'Que se rinde tu madre,'* translated here as 'Up yours!', when the National Guardsmen urged him to surrender. This phrase is famous among Sandinistas. The Pino Grande manœuvres were joint US/Honduras military manœuvres conducted near the Nicaraguan border between 1983 and 1985. Finally, 'Song of Hope' imagines a bountiful future for a Nicaragua nourished by the blood of its martyrs.

Commander Two
Dora María Téllez
               twenty-two years old
slight and pale
in her boots, her black beret
her enemy uniform
               a size too large.

Through the banister rails
I watched as she talked to the boys
the nape of her neck
               white beneath the beret
and her freshly cut hair.
(before they left, we embraced)

Dora María
young warrior woman
who caused the tyrant's heart
to tremble in rage.

Translated by Margaret Randall and Elinor Randall

Report of the Demonstration in Front of the US Embassy Protesting the Pino Grande Manœuvres
WHAT DID LEONEL RUGAMA SAY?
               UP YOURS!
WHY?
               BECAUSE A PEOPLE'S SOVEREIGNTY
               IS NON-NEGOTIABLE.

     WE DEFEND IT WITH GUNS IN OUR HANDS.

Across from the statue of Montoya,
arriving through all of Managua's streets,
the afternoon sun strikes our faces
as we advance
               advance
               A PEOPLE UNITED
               towards the embassy.

Along the highway edged with *Chilamates*,
thousands and thousands of comrades ahead of us,

thousands and thousands more behind,
and bobbing alongside their heads,
hundreds of placards, like waves.

Translated by Margaret Randall and Elinor Randall

Song of Hope
One day the fields will be forever green
the earth black, sweet and wet.
Our children will grow tall upon that earth
and our children's children . . .

And they will be free like mountain trees
and birds.

Each morning they will wake happy to be alive
and know the earth was claimed again for them.

One day . . .

Today we plough dry fields
though every furrow is soaked in blood.

Translated by Margaret Randall and Elinor Randall

Jaime Wheelock, 'The University for Economic Independence: The Militant University'

(1983)

While some students had responded to Fonseca's call to join the FSLN as combatants, the revolutionary state required something different from students after the war. It needed students and professionals who would see themselves as allied with the workers and *campesinos* in the construction of a new society. Wheelock was a model of precisely this kind of student: educated at UNAN, the University of Chile, and later, Harvard, he was also the author of a celebrated master's thesis-turned-monograph entitled *Imperialism and Dictatorship (Imperialismo y dictadura)*. Below, Wheelock begins with the premise that the military triumph of the revolution was just the beginning of the revolutionary process. In order to continue, maintain, and even develop this triumph, Nicaragua needed to forge a new relationship with trade, agriculture, and industry. For one, the university must play a decisive role in the development of new industrial techniques. To illustrate his point, Wheelock discusses the deficiencies in his own education at UNAN before the revolution, where he failed to learn about cotton production despite studying in a cotton-growing zone. Wheelock emphatically urges students and faculty to pursue development by expanding the curriculum and even participating in exchange programmes with workers and campesinos. Wheelock's militant university 'for economic independence' sought to produce new generations of engineers, architects, agronomists, and veterinarians who were connected to the proletariat.

The guns of the Revolution have begun the *pueblo*'s tasks. On 19 July, for the first time, the opportunity for full development and national independence opened up.

We have shed *Somocismo*, we have recovered the will to do, to create, and even to rediscover ourselves in our wildest dreams. We have recovered our sovereignty, but we have an inheritance of backwardness, of underdevelopment, and of dependency that we cannot change through a mere act of sheer will.

You know that today we have challenges. Challenges also rooted in the international crisis that manifests in the contraction of foreign exchange. [For example,] we have to import a great quantity of medicines; if I ask you, here, all of you, 'Who can make penicillin?' would there be anyone who could do it? I am in the National University, which is to say, the highest House of Study. Yes, and now we know that there is no one. This is one problem of national independence.

What is the challenge of the Revolution? To change the relations of property and to develop the nation, not only in the realm of internal changes, but also in [the realm of] the external relations that require us to continue the Revolution, to defend it in order to open an independent and prosperous international economic space with a clear direction. You will agree with me that this is a historic demand for Nicaragua; to stop being a source of consumption without production; to stop being the producing nation of the desserts of capitalism, but to come to be a nation that creates industry from its natural resources, its riches, is this clear? This is the path toward the economic independence of Nicaragua. This is the first great challenge in terms of independent development.

We turn to examples: we should not sell our cotton in fibre, but rather we must industrialise it and sell it in fabric. We should not sell our metals as raw materials, but instead impart to them the value of production with our labour and technique. We should not sell our wood as round wood, but rather we must sell it in furniture, moulding, wood pulp, in pulp and paper. Our resources from the sea, we have to industrialise them. We do not want to industrialise or refine the natural resources of the United States or the natural resources of any other nation.

We want to manufacture our own natural resources! We want to create industry for THE FIRST TIME IN NICARAGUA. Additionally, we want to have the opportunity to make spare parts; to manufacture tyres with Nicaraguan rubber. If we have rubber, we do not want to have an artisanal industry of jackets, which appears in national statistics under the boastful category of 'Rubber and by-products', but rather to make tyres; because we have the rubber for it and superb conditions [in which] to make them.

In the 1940s, Nicaragua was one of the principal producers of natural rubber and why can we not again be, but this time as producers of tyres for local needs and the needs of friendly nations.

We have a splendid natural agricultural and livestock base. We can industrialise our agricultural and livestock products with great competitiveness and be an agribusiness producer, an agro-exporter of foodstuffs, at the same time as we solve our growing nutritional needs. We have excellent land, perhaps the best in the world; enviable hydrological resources, conditions that are ultimately splendid. There is our natural wealth, our future, our most genuine opportunities to break with the previous *Somocista* model and advance in the construction of a new one!

This is precisely about making national decisions and breaking with the nexus of dependency that always told us to make and to produce outside of our interests and in the favour of the interests of imperialism. For these interests, we sow coffee, sugar cane, cotton, and for them too we pawn our chances for development and remain immersed in material poverty and technological frailty. The present moment is about beginning to use the sovereignty that the *pueblos'* victorious struggle has given us and to take an independent and prosperous course. We will decide what to produce and how and for whom. We will change our role in the international division of labour and climb the scale: from producers of inexpensive raw materials to the producers of industrialised natural resources that we will sell through fraternal and mutually beneficial relations. This is the solution.

We will jump up the rungs and begin to ascend by way of technology. The path is not easy, rather it is difficult, but ultimately, [we are] on our way, righteously. Climb in order to hold the keys to development and economic stability in our own hands.

[. . .]

We seek to extract from our natural resources, from the air to the sea, all of the wealth, all of the potential for the transformation of our nation. That is when we will hold science in our hands and use science as an opportunity to transform nature. Until then we can say that we are beginning to move toward ECONOMIC INDEPENDENCE. And we are far away, as I just said, with a certain air of bitterness, [for] we were a nation of field labourers; that it is not gratuitous that almost all of our community is illiterate and it is also not gratuitous that our University has inherited the conditions of this qualitative impossibility bestowed by underdevelopment, backwardness, dependency, of being unable to apply scientific knowledge to the concrete problems that demand production, industry, and finally, development from us. But here we are, with challenges in our hands and this is in itself a great advancement. To recognise the challenges. Now that we are going to grow, we will need cadres in great numbers, the University, you all, must revolutionise, shake things up!

And I want to tell you, after many things that seem to have derailed us, the Revolution feels so satisfied that now the University is steadfastly taking the lead down the path that we want to follow after the triumph of the Revolution.

In the term of 1980, 34,000 students in total registered [for classes]; in the term of 1983, 34,200 students registered. But while in 1980, 685 graduated in Law, in 1983 only 500 graduated; in Industrial Engineering in 1980, 113 graduated, but in 1983, 600 graduated; in Electrical Engineering where there were only 46 in 1980, now there are 494; in Medicine where there were only 1,000, now there are 2,290; in Agricultural Engineering where there were 350, today 846 are registered; in Agronomy where there were 190 there are now 1,270 students. This is your triumph! The nation's triumph! A triumph of independence! And a historical triumph of the Revolution!

We need Electrical and Industrial Engineers, Designers, Architectural Draftsmen, Industrial Draftsmen. We need many Agronomists; we need many Veterinarians and we do not even have a Veterinary Faculty. We still have the Animal Husbandry students taking night school.

University comrades, I want to tell you that we face a tremendous challenge. We, as Nicaraguans, have to break this chain in the international division of labour, to go from being less than farmers to being industrialists. Go from being cane-cutters to being technicians. Go from being stenographers and servants to being scientists. And who can do this? **Man can do this**; man making a very noble and extraordinary effort, because we must show them we did not inherit our resources from capitalism, imperialism, or *Somocismo*, which left us a plundered and impoverished nation.

Doctor [Joaquín] Solís Piura[69] told us that we would not have the opportunity to improve classrooms for very long, and here we are faced with a tremendous desire, in these same classrooms fifteen years later. They [continue to] lack laboratories, resources. Despite the fact that now there are more than a thousand professors, more than 850 full-time professors, ten times more than there were fifteen years ago and we have thirty-some thousand university students, we [still] do not have many resources.

Our first priority is the material base. We are creating a material base. Note that while in Central America there is an economic depression, a crisis, while the transnational companies complain that in Central America they do not even sell a nail, Nicaragua is making great investments: a sugar factory in the order of $250 million; a Dairy Project that is worth $100 million; and we have more than twenty development projects in action, among them two great plantations of African Palm [and] a Cocoa Plantation; we are going to develop in the Jalapa Valley; [open] an agribusiness project in the Sébaco Valley to process vegetables and fruits; a large Tobacco plantation, and of course all of the projects of infrastructure and health services, education, etc.

Thus, we need to create a foundation so that this **raw material** base can demand resources from the University and it [can, in turn] fulfil educative, technological, staffing, etc. needs. We still have old bosses in the areas of production who do not know how to read. There are Rice-Producing Businesses who are among the largest in Central America who do not have even one technician trained in Rice. We suddenly feel as if we are making a false start, outpacing the necessary technological foundation and presently there is a [development] gap.

Sugar Factories like the Factory of Benjamín Zeledón only has two engineers. We also have a Minister of Agriculture who is half-lawyer. We cannot improvise. This demands that the youth of Nicaragua step up to the challenges of the Revolution, and above all, that they make their greatest effort to excel, in the midst of the great challenges and the poverty and the limitations that we will have.

Today at noon, we spoke with Commanders Humberto Ortega and Bayardo Arce. Quite nervous about the task to speak with you all today with which they had entrusted me, I asked them very anxiously which topics should be addressed. 'Tell them again,' Bayardo Arce said to me, 'once and then ten more times what I have been saying and what

---

[69] Solís Piura was a student leader at UNAN in the 1950s and CUUN president in 1959 when the 23 July massacre against students occurred.

everyone has been telling them: they have to make a great effort to study and to improve themselves, even as they receive classes while sitting on the floor, without a room, and in the rain.' And I follow him by repeating this, because Nicaragua has to rise out of this misery, of the ashes, of underdevelopment, for the love of the Revolution, although the skies rain fire; we have to move forward, drawing strength from our weakness. **Because when the raw materials are not those of a poor society, man must do something.**

When the inherited material base is backward and weak and obstructs revolutionary transformations, this hinders the accelerated advance toward socialism **[and men] with their revolutionary consciousness** are the ones who must act and rise above, over the limitations, over the obstacles that are placed on us by an underdeveloped and backward and unequal society to ensure that this desired development occurs, no matter what.

Thus, it is man who in the midst of this crisis must draw on all of his strengths. And it is certain what Humberto and Luis said today: we have to tell you yet again that we are going to experience serious difficulties. The year 1983 is going to be the year with the most difficult challenges yet, not just for the University, but for the entire society as a whole: less foreign capital, less capacity to import.

None the less, based on confidence in the *pueblo*, in you all, in the Revolution, we anticipate that there will be economic development, we expect to produce more cotton, more coffee, more sugar, than in 1982. [Even then,] given everything and the economic crisis and foreign exchange we produced more cotton than in 1981; we produced more coffee; we produced more sugar. We have had three record harvests. Why? Because there has been an answer from the people, from the *campesino*, from the worker, from the technician, from the business manager, from the students, who with a gun in their hand have fired back against the counter-revolutionary bands, while here, in the University, they study, there, they harvest coffee; here in the factory, they manufacture and there in the trenches, they defend our gains. With the sacrifice of their sweat and their arms, the *pueblo* is cultivating the roots of happiness and the future.

But there is more, [and] it is true that we have difficulties. But we have to figure out precisely how to work these difficulties to our advantage.

I am going to tell you all a story to conclude. When Standard Fruit left Nicaragua, you all know that they technologically dominated the process of banana production and we all went there, to Chinandega, and we saw the faces of uncertainty on all of the workers and their families that depend on banana cultivation; more than four thousand families dependent upon this cultivation [were suddenly] without a market, without a future. We said to those comrades: we will work, we are going to get back into the United States market by our own means. But we were stuck with the problem of technology, because producing bananas is complex; it requires a series of very complex agronomical and technical methods that we did not really master.

Among these problems there was one relative to the control of a plague that only transnational businesses had been able – by means of the application of a specific pesticide – to kill. And, 'From where are we going to acquire this specific insecticide called Bravo 500?' I asked. 'We have no idea what this thing is,' they responded to me. We asked, 'The chemical formula – what is it? Is it a base of chlorine or what is it? Is it methyl? Is it carbolic acid?' 'We do not know, we do not know for sure what the answer to this question is,' they responded. 'We only know that it is a specific substance against the Black sigatoka.' So I headed home, preoccupied with this idea that we carry deep within us, of the role of the University in the future of the nation and of national independence, and [because we were] passing through León, we went to UNAN; directly from a banana plantation, having requested a meeting with Dr Rector Mariano Fiallos Oyanguren.[70]

Also, I want to confess to you that when I studied in León, imagine this, absolutely in the middle of a cotton zone, which gave me the opportunity to learn something about its cultivation, the very separation of the University, of the student and production made it such that, nevertheless, when they entrusted in me the responsibility of Minister of Agriculture, I want to confess to you, I did not know when or how to sow cotton. Do you think that I knew that there were schedules for planting? Well, I knew absolutely nothing about this and nor did I know that there was such a thing as the Scientific Centre, which is the Cotton Experimental Centre [CEA], where they have produced thousands of genetic varieties of cotton, from where we get the seed of our principal crop. *Somocismo*'s disconnected National University, which aptly reflected the schema of capitalist development that prevailed in Nicaragua, neglected this [centre] such that there were also biologists whom the CEA, much less the private plantations of Standard Fruit Co., had never even sought out.

So I said: I am going to go to the University to talk to Doctor Fiallos

---

[70] Son of famous UNAN lawyer, academic, and administrator, Mariano Fiallos Gil.

and then I am going to go to Managua to speak with comrades Ernesto Castillo [and] Joaquín Solís to pose these serious questions. We are going to have challenges and because now we have a high concentration of scientists and there is a strong movement of innovative students, we have to create a link between production and the problems of foreign exchange, blockades, and imperialist asphyxiation that we are experiencing, so that the University can begin to solve these problems.

The connected University and resolving the problems of production. Presently, the *Facultades* of Biology and Chemistry, instead of producing a professional who only sells over-the-counter drugs, are beginning to investigate whether they can replace some [foreign] products. If the students research, do their thesis, [they can] tackle concrete problems that we have in production. The students can go to the producers and there do some practice, connect to the units of production, improving them, and [in turn, the university will] welcome students from the units of production; receiving in their training a curriculum that is educational and highly pedagogical. Thus we are improving our strengths, refining them, focusing them, around urgent problems. The University begins again, alive, militant, active, and production receives an influx of forces that it does not have today.

Today we are signing an agreement between MIDINRA [the Ministry of Agricultural Development and Agrarian Reform] and UNAN to receive support so that it can carry out research into areas of interest for development, with a special budget, [and] special programmes. Production, financially supporting scientific and technological investigation; [the university] in turn, helping production solve its specific problems. Students stepping out of the classroom to find real, pulsating life in the laboratories; going to the laboratories that are Sugar Factories, Banana Plantations, Cotton Plantations, Mines, the Sea, and Industry: these are the real opportunities for splendid laboratories that you have at your disposal. Which is to say, the Laboratory of the Revolution is open for all and for your creative revolutionary spirit.

I want to tell you that the Revolution, by nationalising a good part of agriculture and industry, has given the University and its students probably the best laboratories that one could find in Central America.

Finally, this means, brother professors, students, that we also have to prepare for a different connection to the national economy and the work of the Revolution. To you all today corresponds the difficult task of being students, producers, and combatants at the same time. This requires tremendous resolve, selflessness, and sacrifice. Daily improvement is your moral obligation. The economic independence of this country is the patriotic responsibility of you all today more than ever. We are conscious that we cannot do this without the University and without the students and without the cadres. Neither Bayardo [Arce], nor Humberto [Ortega], nor Tomás [Borge], nor Daniel [Ortega], nor anyone is going to raise up this nation without the support of the *pueblo* and without your support.

Not only this, but we are never going to rise up without the strength of the cadres of the future, which is you. There are great tasks, and they are greater, I think, than Bocay, Pancasán, 19 July;[71] and better academic performance, which is still insufficient for the needs of the great task that has fallen on the shoulders of this entire generation, is necessary. Onward. We are conscious of the difficult and monstrous weight of the work of the youth, which has to defend the nation, to boost production, and on top of all of this, also has to take charge of the economic independence and future of the Nation.

FOR FREEDOM THROUGH REVOLUTION
FOR FREEDOM AND NATIONAL INDEPENDENCE THROUGH
THE UNIVERSITY
A FREE FATHERLAND OR DEATH

Translated by Heather Vrana

Works Cited

Arancibia Córdova, Juan (2001), *Honduras: un estado nacional?*, Tegucigalpa: Editorial Guaymuras.

Archivo Histórico de la Policía Nacional (2011), *Del silencio a la memoria*, Guatemala: AHPN.

'Bares de hace 30 años', *Hablaguate*, 27 April 2010, <http://hablaguate.com/articles/2405–bares-de-hace-30–anos>. Accessed online 19 February 2016.

Barillas, Byron Renato, Carlos Alberto Enríquez, and Luis Pedro Taracena (2000), *3 décadas, 2 generaciones*, Guatemala: Heveltas.

Dunkerley, James (1988), *Power in the Isthmus*, London: Verso.

Franco, Velvet, '70 años al servicio de Guatemala', *IGA's Voice*, <http://www.igas-voice.net/70–anos-al-servicio-de-guatemala/>. Accessed online 19 February 2016.

Guzmán-Böckler, Carlos (1998), 'La Huelga de Dolores que viví con mi generación, 1947–1977', Guatemala: USAC Facultad de Derecho, <http://derecho.usac.edu.gt/La_Huelga_de_Dolores.pdf>. Accessed online 28 February 2016.

Kobrak, Paul (1999), *Organizing and Repression in the University of San Carlos,*

---

71 Three decisive battles: the Ríos Coco y Bocay offensive in 1963, which was a deadly failure; Pancasán, a decisive defeat in 1967 that called the FSLN's strategy into question; and 19 July, the battle – ultimately victorious – for Managua.

1944–1996, Washington, DC: American Association for the Advancement of Science.

Maddocks, Melvin, 'Columnists Seldom Trade Ideas', *Toledo Blade*, 15 June 1973.

Martínez, Francisco Mauricio, 'Karl Heinz Chávez, la voz del bingo', *Revista D*, 20 November 2011.

Way, J. T. (2012), *The Mayan in the Mall: Globalization, Development, and the Making of Modern Guatemala*, Durham, NC: Duke University Press.

Contemporary Resistance

Four years after the Sandinistas' victory in 1979, in 'The University for Economic Independence: The Militant University', Jaime Wheelock seemed optimistic about the future: 'we have recovered the will to do, to create, and even to rediscover ourselves in our wildest dreams. We have recovered our sovereignty, but we have an inheritance of backwardness, of underdevelopment, and of dependency that we cannot change through a mere act of sheer will.' Indeed, Nicaragua, like Guatemala, El Salvador, and Honduras, would face even more demanding challenges in the years to come. Difficult questions about justice and reconciliation, as well as economic obstacles, new forms of foreign investment and incursion, on-going political instability, and the historical memory of revolutionary pasts confronted Central Americans, whether their side had won or lost the struggle. And across the region, the meaning of youth and of the student, or *universitario*, had shifted.

The civil war in El Salvador ended on 2 January 1992 with the signing of a peace agreement between the government and the FMLN in Mexico City. Over the next year, an international commission appointed by the United Nations conducted investigations into human rights abuses committed during the war. But the report failed to bring about any meaningful reconciliation or reparation; the civilian government and army rejected the commission's findings, the legislature passed a general amnesty law, and only minor judicial reform was carried out. According to the United States Institute of Peace, no plan for reparations was made or carried out. In Guatemala, representatives of the Guatemalan guerrilla and the army met in 1996 to sign a number of peace accords that formally ended the thirty-six-year-long civil war. As in El Salvador, these peace accords demanded an investigation into wartime human rights violations, but the commission was unable to prosecute or take judicial action and was again paired with a partial amnesty accord. Whether truth commission reports or criminal prosecutions will present opportunities for reconciliation among the *pueblo* remains unclear, though they have resulted in the formation of robust networks of international human rights lawyers and non-governmental organisations (NGOs).

While the Salvadoran and Guatemalan Truth and Reconciliation Commissions (TRCs) sought justice by making known the abuses of the government (and, to a lesser degree, the guerrilla), some individuals and NGOs began to gather information for criminal prosecutions at the national and international levels. But only recently have cases against high-level government leaders like former Guatemalan president Efraín Ríos Montt and Salvadoran colonel Orlando Montano been brought to trial. At the same time, youth groups like the Sons and Daughters of the Disappeared for Identity and Justice against Forgetting and Silence (HIJOS), inspired by their sister groups in Chile and Argentina, took a broader view of the question of justice. The group promotes historical memory and in many respects fights against the drive for reconciliation that would have the community forget or forgive, and move on. Guatemala's branch of HIJOS was founded in 1999 and has organised marches, public cultural events, and graffiti and *escrache* campaigns for nearly two decades. Used widely by HIJOS activists worldwide, *escraches* are demonstrations wherein protestors go to the home or workplace of an individual or group implicated in a human rights abuse in order to humiliate them and pressure the community or government to intervene. These demonstrations often involve graffiti and performance art, and mark the homes and businesses permanently or semi-permanently.

More recently, Honduras released its own TRC in 2012 in an effort to clarify the human rights violations that occurred following a *coup d'état* against President Manuel Zelaya on 28 June 2009. The coup is demonstrative of the general political disquiet that endures in the region. In May 2015, Hondurans took to Facebook and the streets to organise protests against the embezzlement of 200 million dollars of social security funds by the President's National Party. Raising Honduran flags and burning torches, the protestors – many of them students – demanded government transparency and accountability. In Nicaragua, the FSLN – no longer insurgent but now the 'official party' – has struggled to maintain political unity. After losing presidential elections in 1990 to opposition party candidate Violeta Chamorro, Daniel Ortega consolidated his control over the FSLN; some members left the party to found the Sandinista Renovation Movement (MRS) in 1995. Ortega regained the presidency in 2006 and has served since. In 2015, he signed an agreement with Chinese billionaire Wang Jing to build the Interoceanic Grand Canal, a project long dreamed of by foreign speculators since the seventeenth century. For Sandinistas who remembered the anti-colonial nationalist arguments of the revolution, this agreement amounted to nothing less than proof that Ortega had abandoned the revolution. In January 2014, the FSLN-dominated National Assembly abolished constitutional term limits; though general elections are scheduled for November 2016, many Nicaraguans are sceptical.

And yet amidst this complicated panorama of civil society, the ranks of Central American university students are growing more rapidly than ever before. With the construction of more secondary schools and the expansion of course offerings in night-school and weekend programmes, it is now easier to meet the prerequisites for university attendance. Many people, too, have the experience of taking a few classes at university but never finishing their degrees. There are more programmes, more campuses, more private universities, and as a result, more university-educated professionals. This also means that there is more unemployment and underemployment in this sector. Overall, this has led to an atomisation of the public and private universities and of the once-cohesive social class of *universitarios*. This is similar to the privatisation that is happening in universities across the UK, US, and Europe. Increasingly, university education is seen as a means to an ever-narrowing and ever more elusive end: a professional job for which one has been specifically trained. A corollary to this is the suspicion among some students that the highest positions of student governance – the AEU General Secretaries who were celebrated in the 1970s and 1980s – are little more than opportunities for graft and self-enrichment. Ultimately, the meaning of the university has changed. Students may still be constitutionally bound to lead their *pueblos*, but the *pueblo* itself seems less interested in what they have to say.

Maybe this is why a common lament among adults of the revolutionary generations, both in Central America and abroad, among combatants and solidarity movement comrades alike, is that today's youth are apathetic about the gains of the revolution or even about social justice. Ageing revolutionaries have charged that young people care only for fashion, sports teams, films, smartphones, YouTube videos, and rap lyrics. Of course, the generation gap has long been politicised – remember when R. Morua wrote about how the youth must critique the world they inherited and when the anonymous Costa Rican student who participated in the protest against ALCOA at the Legislative Assembly in April 1970 decried the passivity of earlier generations. Or even more plainly, in the words of the anonymous author of 'Cuba y

Latinoamérica, Sí! Yankis, No!' in the September 1960 edition of *El Universitario*: 'Simply put, previous generations do not want to understand that [it is] the Youth and only the Youth [that] is wholly responsible for the future, just as it is equally true that the Youth is called upon to resolve our immediate problems. It has been traditionally believed – and is it false to believe [this] – that the Youth, in the most pedestrian and vulgar sense of the term, is 'idealistic'. No sirs, among the youth there are truths that history and experience teach us.' In recent years, young Central Americans have been using films, smartphones, YouTube videos, and rap lyrics to frame their demands for social justice and desires for the future in their own mass media argot.

This was very clear among the students at the forefront of the protests that swept Guatemala for most of 2015. Almost every single weekend, groups of protestors gathered in front of the National Palace demanding the impeachment of President Otto Pérez Molina, a former military commander. Pérez Molina and his Vice-president, Roxanna Baldetti, were implicated in a customs fraud scheme under investigation by the government and a UN body, the International Commission Against Impunity in Guatemala (CICIG). By late August, USAC and other universities closed so that students, faculty, and administrators could participate in the protests. As a result of this public pressure, Pérez Molina, the face of a military establishment that seemed above the law even twenty years after the end of the war, resigned on 2 September. Yet much of this political fervour was tempered by the disappointing results of the September and October presidential elections. The Guatemalan citizenry had poor options: two candidates represented the corrupt political establishment and the other was a comedian renowned for playing a poor indigenous character in brown face (complete with fake rotten teeth, a straw hat, and a shirt made of traditional Mayan fabric). Some young people launched a 'Null Vote' (*voto nulo*) campaign on social media in protest against the elections, posting photographs of ballots with creative responses that included deliberate disqualifying marks, words like 'No', 'corrupt', or rabbit ears drawn on the images of the candidates. The comedian, Jimmy Morales, won the election.

Across the region, impatience or disgust with the present political system has also given rise to a sort of vigilante justice where community militia groups circumvent the courts altogether and mete out punishment in accordance with local customs and loyalties. This points to the failure of post-civil war reconciliation and to the illegitimacy of the governments that profess to rule. Violence, in general, has been one of the major features of life in Central America since the end of the civil wars: gangs, the drug trade, deportation, and migration have further destabilised communities. Central American cities like San Pedro Sula, Tegucigalpa, San Salvador, and Guatemala City are routinely ranked among the most dangerous in the world. Nicaragua and Honduras often report the lowest gross domestic product per capita in Latin America, with Guatemala and El Salvador not far behind. Income inequality has remained high. This endemic poverty and violence has pushed millions of Central Americans out of the region. The large diasporic communities of Central Americans in Los Angeles, New York City, Chicago, Washington, DC, Miami, and Houston are still another outcome of the anti-colonial struggles of the twentieth century.

Many of the most exciting youth movements today are not linked to universities at all, but rather to community or neighbourhood groups. For instance, while multinational mining projects continue in El Salvador and Guatemala, so does anti-colonial resistance to them. Since 2012 in La Puya, Guatemala, community members of all ages have maintained a twenty-four-hour blockade against a mine proposed by Kappes, Cassiday & Associates, a firm based in Reno, Nevada. In May 2014, the protestors were violently evicted, but returned and continued to occupy land near the mining site. They also sent a number of petitions to the government, and in July 2015, a Guatemalan court ruled that the company must suspend activities until a community meeting was held. Despite the ruling – and unsuccessful appeals – the company has continued to move equipment around the mining site. As recently as February 2016, though, the Guatemalan Supreme Court ruled to provisionally suspend the company's mining licence. What will become of this remains to be seen. But throughout the struggle in La Puya, young people from the community and leftist students from Guatemala City have been steadfast. Clearly, the anti-colonial struggle among Central America's youth remains unfinished.

Works Cited

'Cuba y Latinoamérica sí! Yankis no!', *El Universitario*, September 1960. Instituto de Historia de Nicaragua y Centroamérica (IHNCA).

United States Institute of Peace, 'Truth Commission: El Salvador', <http://www.usip.org/publications/truth-commission-el-salvador>. Accessed online 28 February 2016.

Wheelock Román, Jaime (1983), 'La universidad por la independencia económica: la universidad beligerante', in *Hacia la independencia nacional por la revolución: la universidad beligerante*, Managua: UNAN. Instituto de Historia de Nicaragua y Centroamérica (IHNCA).

Index

Page numbers followed by the letter 'n' indicate footnotes.